SPARKS

My childhood memories which may help sweep away
the cobwebs hidden within the crevices of your mind
to set a "SPARK" and recall your own memories.
(A book to let the younger generation know
why we call it the "good old days!")

By Pauline E. Petsel

JCP

Jan-Carol
Publishing, Inc

"every story needs a book"

Sparks
Pauline E. Petsel

Published June 2016
Express Editions
Imprint of Jan-Carol Publishing, Inc
Copyright © Pauline E. Petsel

ISBN: 978-1-939289-96-4
Library of Congress Control Number: 2016944298

You may contact the publisher at:
Jan-Carol Publishing, Inc
PO Box 701
Johnson City, TN 37605
publisher@jancarolpublishing.com
jancarolpublishing.com

Author's Note

The stories within this book are not in any order as to when they took place. It's funny with "memories." They have no rhyme or reason as to when they bubble up or float forth from the recesses of the mind. Yesterday's event may be buried at the bottom of the stack beneath a five-year-old memory becomes more important for now. Our experiences are apparently filed within the storehouse of our minds under various senses categories. A sound, sight, smell or aroma, taste or visual encounter may find the mind reaching down into our file cabinet of memories to recall some kind of a connecting tie. It's as if we are making vegetable soup and a variety of ingredients is added but with no special timeline, yet it comes out with great flavor to share at the end. Only the master "wizard" within knows why memories recalled as they are and their enjoyment found with every turn of the wheel. I hope you enjoy "my world of memories" and may they cause a spark for you to spin your combination wheel to open your "vault" and sweep away the cobwebs of the mind to find your treasure stored within.

A storyteller reads or tells a story.
Poets verbally recite works so others hear.
A speaker stands before a class in lecture.
Each with a message they want to steer.

A silent movie shown on television or movie screen,
The message displayed merely with a view.
Each story left for the watcher to decide,
Exactly what wordless message they ensue

Sitting with a radio or CD player,
We hear music, stories, words, or news.
Nothing is there to be seen or watched.
It's up to us to inwardly picture a view.

Sometimes fragrances, smells, and aromas—
Can bring memories, thoughts, and stories to mind.
Apple blossoms, salty air, lemonade, or fresh bread baking—
Each, bring pictures for our inner mind to find.

At times, tangibles, feelings, or mere thoughts felt.
Words or memories spill forth with a picture to view.
The touch of a tiny soft kitten or impish pup—
Anything in life, can spark a memory for us to ensue.

Sometimes television, a play, or movie on a screen
Have visuals and sounds for an emotional touch.
Other times, a smell, aroma, touch or sound,
Might trigger a memory for which we regain much.

Looking at pictures or reading a magazine or a book.
Listening to words of others, or those within a song,
Watching life going on around you each day.
Can bring back memories forgotten for so long.

We all have memories within the theater of our minds.
Some are funny, happy, hurtful, scary, fearful, or sad.
The one thing with memories is they are just ours to keep.
We can recall those we want to and release forever, the bad.

Bad memories are over, gone, and done with.
They can't hurt or harm you anymore.
Yet the happy memories are still alive within you.
There, they are kept safe within the minds store.

Those memories are yours forever, never to be erased.
Stories of the past rise upward, from very deep within.
They live once more to share with others,
Bringing happiness, laughter, a smile or a grin.

To all my friends and relatives, neighborhood friends, classmates, strangers, entertainers, comedians, singers, movie and TV stars, inventors, researchers, and products/advertisers for all the great memories I gained from each of you. Because of you, my life has been worth living and each memory that has carried on through the years is a treasure to behold. I learned the lesson of what is important in life. I see just how good our days were when I see how bad things are in the current times in comparison. I thank God for allowing me to live and experience the "good ol' days" era.

I hope that in some small way this book may bring back memories with a smile for those who were lucky enough to have lived it as I did and give a history of how things were and actually could be again in some ways to those who missed it. To any leftover people perhaps if the days were not as happy as mentioned here, think back for memories of your own for any good times mixed among the not so good, and look for uplifting things of today to start better ones.

To my children, grandchildren, and great-grandchildren—may you find the lifestyle of our time interesting and one to treasure from its information from where you eventually stemmed from. To my husband and friend Londa Vining, who waded through these pages looking for language and spelling mistakes and trying to figure out the ones I misspelled on purpose and the language, I murdered for the same purpose.

...And to you the reader who may have memories come flooding back of your own experiences, which you can share with your friends, loved ones and family. What you will find is when you bring up a memory you will find it also sparks a memory of also the person you are speaking with and a time of happy sharing comes alive in your own life. The younger generation might read something that makes you ask your parents or grandparents if they encountered such a thing and will find some of your own family history emerging.

I have left a couple blank pages in the back of the book for you to jot a memory that catches a spark and is rekindled. Share them with your friends and family.

ENJOY!

Sincerely,
Pauline E. Petsel

Chapter 1

When I was little, I liked to have books read to me. It was easier to get people to read to you back then because there was no television, computers, or cell phones to make people have something better to do for themselves. (Wow! Am I old?!) Eventually, we did get television, but it was black and white pictures at first with only three channels to choose from which were often very 'snowy' from interference. When we did get television, we mainly watched it in the evenings, so afternoons were a perfect time to con someone into reading to you. I had a favorite book, *Peter Rabbit!* I may have had other books, which could have become a favorite, but first, we had to finish this one, and that looked very unlikely to happen. Whenever someone would read to me, they wanted to start at the beginning, apparently so they could get into the story themselves. The problem is, each of them got tired of reading at about the same place in the book so put the book down. One day my mother said she would read to me, and she too began reading, as I looked at the book while she read. I chimed in saying the same words she was saying. She was astonished! Did she have an unusual child who could actually read at such a young age? No, I had those same first pages read so many times I had just memorized it. To this day, I have no idea what the rest of the book was about. (Hmm, maybe I need to put that on my "to-do" list before I die!)

So this book is here to allow you to step back through time to experience a memory when there were no televisions, iPods, or iPads, computers, washer and dryers, color televisions, microwaves, cell or smartphones, fancy cars or fancy foods. It may help you see why people back in time call it the "good ol' days" even without all those modern advances. We did not have much, yet we had more. As you read these stories, picture in your mind how different life was back then in comparison to what it is like today. Then realize how much better it was...for it was! We lived lives that were caring, patriotic, religious, and had respect for laws and the police.

If we were bad, we were spanked. If we got into trouble at school, it was not anything compared to what we would get when we got home. We were all part of the family. No one was without doing something to be part of the household. Taking out the garbage, setting or clearing the table, washing or drying the dishes (by hand; there were no dishwashers) or putting the dishes away. We pulled weeds, mowed grass, and more.

We also had a variety of ways to earn some spending money, because our parents didn't have much money for that. I mowed other people's lawns or shoveled the snow off their sidewalks in the winter. It's funny how many lessons we can learn from life, no matter what our age, if we merely pay attention. I charged fifty cents for shoveling walks, and that was a lot in those days especially for a nine-year-old. I was excited when someone actually told me to go ahead and clear his or her walk. As I shoveled, I added up in my head the money that I was making that day. Well, I not only learned that by doing hard work achieved a goal towards being able to get things I wanted and otherwise couldn't have, but I also learned you have to pay attention to each situation you are planning to do. As I proudly finished shoveling one front sidewalk of this one house, I was excited I was finished. Then, I discovered something. The house was a corner lot...meaning I had just begun! No wonder the people were so excited when I agreed to shovel two sides for that amount of money! I still had another whole side to do.

I went door to door selling both Christmas cards and all occasion cards. My mother also made things for me to sell and I got a few cents for each one. She made orchid chenille flowers of many different colors or mixture of colors for a woman to wear on their coats. At Christmas, she made chenille Santa Clause coat pins and Bunnies at Easter time. Later she made rickrack earrings and eventually even made stuffed monkeys out of Rockford socks. There were probably, even more, things she made which I cannot recall right now. Whatever there was, I would take and sell them door to door. With my parents by then being divorced, it helped with our family's income and gave me some spending money too.

I got money for myself with each thing I sold. I got five cents for the rabbits and Santa Clauses, which were about fifteen cents and fifteen cents for each more expensive fifty to seventy-five cent flowers. The problem was I was also responsible for the things I sold. Should I have lost one, I not only did not get my cut but also had to pay for it from my other money. One day I lost one of the fifty-cent flowers somewhere along the way. I was devastated because I was out fifteen cents. I retraced my steps back through the snow to everywhere I had been. Finally, there lying in the snow in the middle of someone's front yard was that stupid purple and yellow flower! I can still see that spot and could show it to you even today. Maybe the quote from the Bible about "Idle hands are the work of the devil" was why we were so happy in those days. We were too busy being productive, which caused us to earn self-esteem leading us towards our happiness. I learned at a very young age that even though we might get something given to us from time to time, for some reason there was something very special when you earned money so were able to buy something for yourself. When we could actually use our own money to buy something for someone else and seeing the happy look on his or her face, gave us more than our money's worth. We felt important at the power we had to be able to bring happiness to others. Working and earning money has a reward but making others happy has one all its own, with nothing you can put your finger on, but something which happens from deep inside you.

That is why I get upset with our government handouts to people. Some of them are in need, but others are fit and could be working. The government thinks they are doing such a good thing for people by giving them welfare but in reality, they are doing a great disservice to these people. The government is robbing people from being able to feel those inner treasures they have, and being able to see the accomplishments their own talents could do if they were brought out for the world to have and share. They would have money they themselves earned plus the feeling of prestige that comes with it.

Free stuff has an opposite side. The saying "Give a man a fish and he eats for a day but teach a man to fish he eats for a lifetime" is a wise saying, and I have felt that experience firsthand. Instead of giving able-bodied persons a handout, give them a hand up by teaching them a skill to earn money with, or to develop the skills and talents they already have.

Even with our home chores and earning money, there was plenty of time to just be kids and have fun experiencing life and forming memories for a lifetime. We were free to roam the neighborhoods and allowed to go places within the neighborhood as kids. Our one rule was to be home before it got dark or at suppertime. Until then we went everywhere to explore and do things with our friends. We did all kinds of things. We played baseball in the street, made hopscotch patterns to play on with chalk on the sidewalk. We then would throw a rock into various squares, one at a time, then jump on the other squares, missing the one with the rock.

We jumped rope, both with our own single rope or a long one held by two people twirling it for one, or two people who had to coordinate their jumping at the same time. We also sat on the sidewalk with a ball and jacks having contests with others as to who could win by bouncing the ball and picking up a number of jacks then catching the ball before it bounced again. You started by picking up just one jack which was pretty easy, but then you had to pick up two at a time and on and on until having to pick up seven or eight, and finally all of them catching the ball before it bounced again. Sometimes when the jacks were thrown, they fell in such a way that we had several jacks spread way out making you having to quickly sweep your hand around the area to get them before the ball hit the ground again.

We played tag, hide and go seek, and Cowboys and Indians as favorite outdoor games of the time. Taking turns, we would swing each other around in the air by their wrists and then set them down to watch them stagger as they dizzily walked about. Our bikes were ridden down the middle of the street while we tried doing tricks like going no handed or putting out feet on the handle bars. That led to the real outlandish trick of going no hands and putting both feet on the handle bars. One time while using my sister's bike, I ran it up a telephone pole trying to do that. I left the bike at the bottom of the pole and limped home with cuts and scrapes. It wasn't my bike! My sister walked right past me, even though I was cut and bruised. She wasn't hurt, and it was her bike.

Hula hoops, yo-yos, squirt guns, Slinkys, magnets, and a toy called Jacobs Ladder, cards games like crazy eights, old maid, authors, rummy and go fish, table games like chess, checkers, India, *Parcheesi*, *Monopoly* and Tic-Tac-Toe were all things we did to keep busy with our friends.

We held marble contests trying to win the other kids marbles. We climbed trees, and roller skated on the sidewalks. The roller skates clipped onto our shoes, and the darn things were always coming off and ended up hanging from our ankles making us limp and jump trying to gain our balance. We had to carry a skate key with us so to lock the skates more tightly when they came off.

We played badminton, volleyball, basketball, and croquet. We laid on the grass gazing up at the sky to make pictures out of the clouds as they floated by. Dandelions were placed beneath a friends chin to see the reflection with some stupid thing about if we saw the reflection the boy we liked also liked us. We also ate the yellow dandelions plus purple clover. White daisies with all the petals were another "fortune telling" image for us to use to see if our boyfriend liked us, or to some other question you wanted to ask. "He loves me, he loves me not" or "true, not true," was recited as each petal was plucked. If the answer did not come out the way we wanted we just plucked another flower and did it again. Searching the grasses to try finding green four clovers was a real treasure hunt for four leaf clovers are hard to find and if found are considered to be good luck! We picked wild flowers to make bouquets for a glass mason jar of water, looked for bugs and chased butterflies across the empty lots.

Whenever someone got married anywhere in the area, the word seemed to get sent out over the silent airwaves which was mysteriously picked up by every kid for blocks around. We would all gather together at a designated time with kids coming from all over the neighborhoods bringing noise makers like pan lids as cymbals or a stick and a pan, and we'd meet in front of the newlywed's house. We'd make the loudest racket you ever heard and would keep making it until they came out and gave us each a candy bar to get rid of us. That was called a shivaree!

We went to the movies downtown, sometimes alone, sometimes just two or three, yet other times as a group. Even though we were only seven or so, we took the bus, or sometimes if the bus hadn't come to our bus stop yet, we'd walk to the one where it would be coming to us from. If we got there and it still hadn't come, we'd go to the next one. If we walked to that next bus stop and the bus hadn't come yet, we figured we'd walked so far and were now so close to town we might as well just walk on to town and save the money for the bus ride to buy candy with at the movies.

We had several theaters, but two stood out in my mind. The one was called the Iowa Theater and had a huge lit up a sign in the shape of an ear of corn. (After all, that is what Iowa was known for... "Where the tall corn grows.") My favorite theater, however, was the Paramount. It was like a castle. Our hearts almost did a flip when we'd went into the lobby. When you walked in, there was huge floor to ceiling mirrors covering both sidewalls. The red carpeting led to a huge staircase with a gold metal railing. (Maybe the staircase wasn't as big as it seemed to us as kids but was very impressive to us then.) As you'd climbed the stairs, you found yourself in a very quiet, darkened hallway with red walls trimmed in green, framed pictures in gold trim on the walls. It was quiet like you would imagine a castle to be. The halls led you to the balcony seats, but it was the halls themselves which seemed to call to me. No matter how poor you were you felt like royalty in that theater. I was amazed that recently I've read or seen that there are several of those Paramount theaters being refurbished back to their original state. The one in my hometown of Cedar Rapids had been, but I think got a lot of damage during the 2008 flood. I believe there are three others being restored and, believe it or not, one is about an hour from where we live now. Oh, how exciting to be able to relive such a fond memory from my youth.

We rode bicycles everywhere. We even went to parks with a playground which was probably as far away as twelve to fifteen blocks from our house. The park had a merry go round, swings, chin up bars and slides. We even rode from our southwest part of town to the northwest part of town because they had the swimming pool.

The city orchestra went to a different park each weekend of the month to play a free concert for the people. We could always visit the others when it was their turn if we wanted but most people just waited for their own parks turn. The family would take chairs, or blankets to spread out on the ground, to listen to the free concert. While they played their music for the adults, we kids played on the park's jungle gyms, merry go rounds, swings, etc. but we also heard that music and it was special. A lot of times we would sit on the park equipment and simply watch the musicians playing their instruments. When it began to get dark, the musicians packed up their instruments and made space for the truck with the movie screen on the flatbed to pull in. They started off with 'sing a long' movies on the screen where a bouncing ball leaped up and down from word to word in the rhythm of the song, so everyone could sing the word it was showing us to sing and when. That was fun and drew the families together as one. When that was over, they would show cartoons. *Popeye, Casper, Woody Woodpecker, Mr. McGoo,* or *Donald Duck* were some favorites. It was a great family time. Sometimes they then had an actual movie. There was always something for everyone during those nights.

We were patriotic people and did things with, and for, our military. We had parades and memorial services as well as collections of material needed for the war effort. We bought savings bonds to help the war too, and even kids had a way to earn money to be able to get bonds. We went to ceremonies for remembering our vets as wreaths of flowers were thrown off the downtown bridge in remembrance and in their honor.

There was respect for our laws and policemen. If we got in trouble at school, we were in for even worse at home. We were reprimanded and yes, even spanked. When you got spanked, you thought twice before you did something again. If you did do something again, you were reminded why you had thought you shouldn't.

There were skeleton keys for our house. We were told to be sure to lock the house when we left and even at that age I could never figure out why. Everyone had the same darn key! If we lost or forgot our key, we simply went to a neighbor to borrow theirs. So, again why did we lock the door to begin with? Apparently somewhere the keys could be a bit different, but there were only maybe three different ones, but our whole neighborhood had the same! When I asked that very question as to why we even had to bother to lock the door when everyone could get in with their own key anyway, I was told that when the gypsies or circus came into town, it would help keep them out of our homes if they came near our neighborhoods. That didn't make sense either. They were skeleton keys! They were all the same! They probably had one from wherever they came from!

In the fall, we would rake the leaves and pile them in huge heaps in the street next to the curb. At night, we set it on fire and with the golden flames shooting upward carrying the wonderful smell of a bond fire through the air, the neighborhood kids grabbed sticks and brought marshmallows or sometimes even hot dogs (called wieners back then) to toast them over the fire. What a taste!

Another thing of those times was the ice man. Even though we had refrigerators by then, we still had our icebox in the basement and kept things there too. So did a lot of others. The ice truck would pull up with blocks of ice under a canvas, and the man would take his ice tongs and spread them on the block of ice and carry it into the house where he placed it in the one part of the Icebox. While he was inside a house, we kids ran to the truck to reach up the best we could to get ice chips that were laying there. We really thought we were doing something. I still have some of those kinds of tongs.

We ran around barefooted most the time. The paved streets were very hot, and we would run across them as fast as we could, to reach the coolness of the grass on the other side of the street. During one of my barefoot days, I went up the steps to our houses old weather-beaten front porch. I'd been up and down and over that porch forever but this one night the roughness from the sun and rain-weathered wood took its toll. As I went onto the porch a sliver (actually more like a log of wood) went into one side of my foot and out the other side. That darn thing must have been six inches long. I ended up going to the hospital to have it removed, along with hundreds of tiny sliver pieces which came from the main one. The hospital was a stark old dark building with dim lighting. The operating room I was in had painted walls, which reminded me of our church ceiling that had fallen in one time. There was a single light bulb with a shield around it hanging from a chain coming from the ceiling in the center of the room. There was one sort of tall, medium wide wooden case with wire over the doors like a pie safe, standing in the middle of one wall. That was it, except for the hard gurney I was laying on. They tried to give me an anesthetic which was a mask with ether coming through. I fought it by violently moving my head back and forth trying to get away from it and even though everyone was trying to hold me down they gave up and set to taking out hundreds of tiny slivers that broke off from the main huge piece. I've visited hospitals many, many times since then, but I can still see that one as if it were yesterday. I might add that hospitals have sure changed over these years. The only thing the ether did was make me sick the next morning just as we got to church. We usually walked to church but because of my foot we got to take a car. I got sick just as I was getting out, luckily missing the inside of the car. We also missed church.

Church was a big part of our life. We had ice cream socials, which was where people would donate cakes to sell pieces or even whole cakes, to make money for the church. We got the ice cream from the creamery and sold ice cream social tickets around the neighborhoods to get people to come. The salesman in me did my job to sell as many as I could. I always seemed to be the one who sold the most. With those tickets along with my cards and my mother's things, I think people must have hated seeing me come.

At our ice cream socials, we also had activities to get the family together to do things. We had contests for a chance for the people to win prizes. They were homemade things in those days. People might be given a variety pieces of cloth, wooden round head clothespin, sticks of chenille or pipe cleaners, pieces of crepe paper, etc. and each person had to make a clothespin doll from it. They could get as fancy as they could with what they had and use their own ingenuity. It would then be voted on by the entire group. We also did things like giving everyone three saltine crackers to be eaten dry as fast as they could and then be the first to whistle. The first one who could eat them and whistle won a prize! Have you ever tried to whistle after eating a dry saltine? It ended up being pretty funny! We played many games and among them were games like musical chairs, cotton ball game and drop the clothespins. All of these are games; we have carried onward from that time to playing with the generations. I taught them to youth groups in later years and when I got married and had birthday parties for my own children those games were still there as entertainment. You would be surprised that all ages love to play these even today. For those who don't know about them, I will stop my memory stories to give you instructions, so if you would like to try playing them yourself, you can. You will find a "spark" to start memories to carry forward in your life. (You'll need ten round wooden clothespins, a gallon milk jug and a straight back chair. Round-headed clothespins aren't as easy to find, but they are still available. If you can't find them, wooden pincher type of clothespin's will work but aren't as good.)

THE CLOTHESPIN GAME

Take ten clothespins to play with. Put a straight back chair so you will kneel on the seat and place your hand on or level with the top back. Sit a gallon milk jug below the back of the chair on the floor (In our day we had glass milk bottles that we used). You try to get as many of your clothespins to drop into the bottle in the ten tries. The person with the most at the end is the winner. The thing to watch for is that people don't try stretching their arm down closer past the top of the back of the chair.

COTTON BALL GAME

You need a large tablespoon, a blindfold, a large bowl, and a package of large cotton balls. The cotton balls are spread out on a table in front of the blindfolded contestant. The person is given a bowl in one hand and the spoon in the other. They have three tries to get as many cotton balls into the bowl that they can. They can slide the spoon along the table to gather the balls without feeling for where they are. When they think they have cotton balls on the spoon they can lift up the spoon and dump them into the bowl. They cannot slide the spoon up the sides of the bowl. They have to lift the spoon. They get three turns before removing their blindfold. You cannot feel any weight of cotton balls, so it is hilarious to watch as the person might have a whole spoonful of the cotton balls but doesn't think they have anything so turns the spoon over to try filling it again.

This time, they might not have anything at all but think they do so carefully take the spoon toward the bowl so they won't spill what isn't there! The viewers have a lot of laughs watching the procedure. The winner is the one who gets the most cotton balls. You'll love it!

We had family nights throughout the year. All of them were different but a time to bring the entire family together as one, along with other families too. One night we had a Halloween party with all the kids dressed up in costumes. One girl was walking with my sister and me when all of a sudden the grass from her Hawaiian skirt swished outward as we passed a heater. The grass skirt caught fire in seconds, and my sister ran but the girl latched on to me, and I fought to get away from the flames were engulfing her entire body. My mother reacted quickly and threw a heavy winter coat around her to put the flames out. The ambulance came to take her to the hospital and although she lived she never grew after that. She graduated from school many years later, the same size she was that night.

Church was a place of activities for the kids. Our minister was a female which in itself was unusual, especially in those days. Her husband had been a minister and was killed in a tornado years before she came to Cedar Rapids. Her sister's husband also was killed, so the two lived together, and Rev. Husband took over her husband's place as a minister. We kids had taffy pulls which were ingredients put together in a sweet candy type mixture but was gooey and we had to mix manually and pull, stretch and keep pulling it until it got a consistency to harden. We did skits, and we played games like "Three Blind Mice," "Farmer in the Dell," "Button, Button, Who Has the Button," and "Drop the Handkerchief."

Needless to say, with the church having a woman for a minister everyone sort of helped out with different things. I even had a job, which to pull the rope to ring the church bell on Sunday morning. You had to pull the rope just right, so you got a single clear ring at a time. If you 'tolled' the bell with double rings, each time indicated someone of the church had passed away and their age. I was only, like maybe seven or eight at the time; the heavy bells rope got the better of me more than once causing me to go up with the rope and having to have someone pull me back down. I also got to help choose the songs we'd sing for the day and announced the page numbers to the congregation.

My sister played the piano for the younger kids Sunday school opening singing session before they went on to their individual classes for Bible stories and activities. There were little wooden chairs each in different colors sitting in rows behind the piano. We kids would race in to get our favorite color chair before someone else got it. The church was old and had faded painted walls and ceiling. One Sunday as we were singing our songs, I was sitting directly behind my sister. All of a sudden there was a huge loud sound and immediately the ceiling between my sister and me came crashing down and landed on the floor between us. Everyone scattered but I stood up yelling at my sister. "I told you played the piano too loud!" (This was the reference to the hospital room I used.)

That wasn't the only thing that pointed to the church being old and in need of repairs. In the basement we had restrooms. If you flushed the girl's toilet at the same time someone flushed the ones in the boy's side, they overflowed. Now they didn't just overflow like you might be thinking of at your home toilet. They really overflowed. The entire basement flooded! When we went down the stairs to the basement for the Sunday school classes, we had to open the door first to look and make sure there wasn't water. A lot of times there was, and we ended up having to have classes outside on the grass, or during rain or in the winter had to go in the sanctuary and share part of the space where the Adult classes were. That issue with the basement flooding wasn't just a once in a while occurrence. We even had it happen on family nights making everyone rush to grab tables and get them up three steps to a slightly higher basement area. However, then we still couldn't get ourselves to the door which we came to the basement through. Instead, we had to go through a different door which was not usually used. That church sure had a lot of memories.

We had someone who brought a young blind boy to church with them while he was visiting their family. He was my age, and I took it upon myself to sit with him to make him feel welcomed, and we become friends. Even though it was a short-lived friendship, it was close enough for him to write me a letter from his school for the blind. It came written in braille as he wrote it, and then the school also sent a paper as to what it said. That was very special to me and to this day I have it somewhere in a box. It's funny what memory sticks to you, and gets embedded so deeply you never forget them. They can also take up room in your house when you keep the things that caused those special memories over the years. A lot of them set an example for life or a lesson that build self-esteem. They also have one other thing which can never be taken away from you. As the eyes grow dim with age, and vision becomes a memory of the past, the pictures of the movie screen of the mind still show those repeats of treasures of long ago as treasures to be able to hold dear.

We were ice cream lovers and winter found us eating as much as in the summers. We had two new things come into being at our age. The Dairy Queen was the first to introduce coating the ice cream cones with the chocolate which hardened into a protective coating. With my mother working at a grocery store whenever a new product came on the market we saw it right away there. One day I was at the store when a new ice cream came in which was the creme sickle or another name was dream sickle, but I got to buy the very first one at that store.

Chapter 2

There seems to be "levels" to memories we recall from life's past experiences. They come with happy memories, but there are also some that are sad, funny, depressed or even scary. Like everything in life, there is good and bad, pro and con, right and wrong, happy and sad, wet and dry, hot and cold, north and south, east, and west, positive and negative. The list goes on.

The one thing about the sad memories is that somehow even though the hurts are not felt anymore, the memories can still be recalled, and it's up to the person if they allow themselves to wallow in the sadness or move beyond it knowing it is over and can't be changed. If they can look for things that are happy events now, which are positives in their life, they may be able to change their outlook on life. They then keep the old memory of, "what was, but not, is." A loved one's death or parent's divorce, loss of a beloved pet, a job loss, having to move and leave friends behind, betrayal of someone close, or even name calling or not being popular in school are but a few in this category.

The frightening, physical, and harmful memories, are harder to let go of. They may hold a distrust, build in fear or at times carry scars that may have been set deeply. The only way one can keep those memories from continually harming them is to keep telling themselves those days are over, and they are not being harmed now. It is easier said than done. However continually saying, "I'm okay, this isn't my experience anymore. It can't cause me harm now. It is over. I move now to a better place looking forward to positive experiences." Trust me. Try it. Keep trying it. The mind cannot think of two things at once. It is possible to put new grooves into the record of time by changing the message. You can't change what happened, but you can change it from harming you anymore. (As an adult I became a hypnotherapist, and I've given this advice to many, and it has helped them greatly) These then need to look for and really think about how many things are better now and try to build up positives from there. A person doesn't always have a choice as to what experiences or situations they have to go through in life, but they do have a choice as to whether to allow those things of the past hold them back from enjoying and making new happier life experiences to enjoy now and for the future. The problem with these people is a sound, smell, taste, or visual scene can cause instant reactions years later, long after the incident is over. Servicemen and women go through this a lot as well as people who've been in life threatening situations like accidents, kidnappings, rape, fires, or horrible abuse.

A person can live in an "oh poor me, look what I had to go through" atmosphere or, the mindset of "this happened to me and because of it everyone around me needs to make up for it" or, "I will never forgive the person(s) involved, and I will never be able to get over it" but if they do they will always be unhappy and will have to live a life of negative, depressing and frustrating situations. There is a Bible quote that sort of reveals the answer. "By the changing of your mind, so too are you changed." By living in the emotions of what someone did to you, you are allowing that or those persons who did it, to still have power over you. They will be happy to see their power! If you want to make them unhappy, you need to be happy and move on. When they see you gain a better happier life, they will be the ones unhappy! You can move beyond old roadblocks. Many times situations may be taken a certain way at the time it happened yet later is looked back with a different perspective.

Situations, causing actual body scars or injuries is a different situation to deal with. These are visual things that ones have to live with rather than the hidden emotions ones can try to hide. It's easy for me to say, as I have not had to deal with something like this, but I will say these people still have talents, skills, knowledge and inner beauty to share with others. A missing limb or a deep scar is not whom the people are. They are what is hidden within. Their talents skills and abilities just have an added challenge. They have other people's inappropriate attitudes for issues in life, to contend with, but never give up. These people may have a mission to teach and change the world in some way. Again a Bible verse comes to mind about being careful how you treat strangers for they might be Angels unaware. One thing for sure. If these persons shrink back and give up, they are giving up on themselves as well as keeping the world from enjoying their talents and reaping happiness they so deserve. There are many stories out in the world of successes like this. The maimed or disabled war veterans and the blade runners are a few examples.

Life isn't over.

We didn't have much when we were growing up, but we were happy. We found happiness where we were but did things to try to make our situations even better. We used our ingenuity to get more money for more things we wanted to have yet couldn't afford. We knew sitting back and doing nothing would get us nowhere. Another Bible verse says that if a person doesn't work, then he shall also not eat. We took that thought a little further. If we just wanted something we couldn't afford, we sure wouldn't get it by just wishing. We had to do something.

As I dip down into the pot of alphabet soup, where letters get mixed to spell out a story, I stir the flavor, and I skim the top to take a taste of the memories gone by. Even though dipping down deeper might get to the meat of life, I accept the memories that bubble up from the depths just as they come.

My parents had a restaurant, called the Hollywood, which was located by the approach to the Wilsons packing plant in Cedar Rapids. My dad worked there as my mother had at one time. They opened the restaurant right at the approach to the plant, so a lot of the workers who poured out at noon for lunchtime came to the restaurant. When the loud siren sounded indicating it was lunch time, everyone started pouring from the plant, and my sister and I would run to see which of us could spot my dad first. Then while they were busy inside the restaurant with all the customers, we would play outside on the sidewalk right next to the busy street where trucks were bringing in cattle to the plant. We had a dog and one day the dog stepped out into the path of one of the trucks and was killed. I remember standing there watching it die. It was funny, but at that age (around three or four) I guess there wasn't any real emotion concerning death. It just "was." I don't even think it gave me a lesson in any traumatic way that that could also have been me, as we'd already been taught not to go into the street or we could get run over, so we didn't. Apparently the dog had missed that lesson. However, maybe that was why my parents sold that restaurant and opened another one closer to home and not on so busy a street with the atmosphere of big trucks and smelly men's clothes from the plant.

The new restaurant had new types of customers. The Red Dot was at the bottom of the hill leading to the high school, so teenagers were there all the time. This restaurant also had a big jukebox with all kinds of music where the kids would come to play it and dance. There were two songs that were choices which I always wanted people to play: "Mule Train" and "Cool Water." Why I liked those then, or why they still stand out in my memory now I haven't a clue, but as memories go, they just are. I did like it when the teens were dancing to the music they chose though, for as they jumped around, and sometimes money would spill out of their pockets, with eagle-eyed me watching closely for it. The second I spotted a coin dropping or rolling across the floor I'd make a beeline, ducking low under their tall twisting bodies like going through a moving tunnel to retrieve my prize.

I had a girlfriend who would come to the restaurant from time to time with a nickel to spend. She was small like me but wasn't with her parents. They dropped her off as they went next door. (In those days we did things like that.) One time she was sitting on the stool at the counter trying to decide what candy she wanted from the shelves of candy on the other side. She kept putting her nickel in and out of her mouth as she was trying to decide but one time as it went in, she swallowed. The nickel went down. I yelled, "She swallowed the nickel; she swallowed the nickel!" Actually, I was more worried about the nickel, than her. She was going to share whatever treat she bought, with me and now it was gone! A policeman was sitting on another stool at the counter so quickly picked her up and turned her upside down as he carried her toward the door to his cruiser to take her to get help. As she was upside down, I walked next to her bending over to see her face. All of a sudden the nickel rolled out! I was thrilled! Again, because she now had her nickel to spend! I yelled my discovery, "It came out; it came out" and I chased after it as it rolled across the floor, then gave it to her! She was put down to go back to the counter stool where she had been, and as if nothing had happened continued deciding what she wanted. By this time, I didn't care what she chose...just don't swallow that nickel. I even told her not to put the money in her mouth again. I wasn't concerned about her, but I was just afraid if she did it again it might get stuck for good, and she might not have it to spend. Then naturally I wouldn't get some too. Luck was with us. She bought her treat which we shared. Boy, was I happy!

With all that candy on the shelf, I could never understand why I just couldn't have whatever I wanted when I wanted it anyway. It didn't make any sense to me. They tried explaining to me they had to pay for those things. So then, "If they paid for it, it was already there so all the more why I should be able to have it. I have to say it, but sometimes adults make no sense.

One morning I was actually going to get one of the candies of my choice but...it came with one of those 'conditions' parents like to use. "If you eat all of your breakfast, then you can have candy." I sat at that counter with all that supposedly "good for you" foods placed before me. I didn't want that food. I wanted candy. My grandpa (on my dad's side) was there and very willing to help me out. He threw it away. When my mother came downstairs and walked by the counter, she was so surprised and pleased to see I had finished all my breakfast. Why she couldn't have just left it at that, I don't know. No, she had to say those words, "Pauline, did you eat all your food?" Couldn't she just be satisfied to see it was no longer there? I was taught not to lie...so I didn't. I said, "No, grandpa frew it in the garbige!" Well, here was another person, this time, my grandpa who had an incident which was never forgotten until the day he died. (I seem to be a magnet for those things.) I did get the candy, but it wasn't for eating my food, but for telling the truth. Heck, I've told the truth a lot. Why did I only get something that day? That added to the list of people who shared things I seemed to become famous for, and never let me live down.

The incident I never lived down concerning my dad, whom also carried it to the day he died was when the kids at church were taken on an outing to a park. After being there for a while, we heard the music and bell of the Good Humor truck approaching, offering a variety of treats to buy. With my mother being the Sunday school superintendent, the church funds were going to be used to treat each child to the one treat of their choice. I actually wasn't old enough for this outing but with my mother having to go I got to go too. We could get ice cream, a candy bar or other choice of candy, gum, or pop. When it became my turn to tell them what I wanted, I said, "I'll have a beer!" My astonished mother quickly corrected me and said, "You mean you want a root beer." (Did I say root beer? Can't she hear?) I immediately corrected her. "No, I want a beer!" Here my superintendent mother said, "Pauline, you've never had a beer!" How many times am I going to have to set her straight? I quickly corrected her, again! "Yes, I have. Daddy gives me a zip once in a while." Well, I didn't get a beer and had to choose something else, but I think my dad got something he didn't want either when we got home! (Thanks to me!)

Oh, it doesn't stop! This brings to mind another such episode that left a permanent imprint for memory recall. I was maybe three or four when we visited my parent's friend's tavern. Because of my sister and I being so young, we were not legally allowed in the tavern itself, so we had to stay in the back living area. One time when we were there, the tavern was empty, so they allowed us to go into the tavern area to sit in a booth to eat. We ordered a hamburger (what else. Kids love hamburgers) and then another group of people came in but were only there to eat, not drink, so we could still get to stay in the tavern area. The room had a different smell to it as you could catch the aroma of beer in the air. All of a sudden I looked up and exclaimed in my not so quiet voice. "Look, mom, there's a cockroach!" "My mother very quietly and quickly leaned over to inform me "that's not a cockroach." Here I go again having to educate an adult while in my usual informative loud voice "It may not look like a cockroach to you, but it sure looks like a cockroach to me" With that, we had to grab our food and return to the back room. Geez...ya can't even let people know what ya see! We were told not to lie, and I wasn't lying! Adults! Just try to figure them out!

While being in the Red Dot restaurant, my sister was already in school, but I wasn't old enough. Being left to entertain myself most the time while my parents ran the restaurant, I did a lot of "pretending." There was a gumball machine on the street between our place and the store next to us. I discovered that some small pieces of round silver stuff the size of the money needed for the machine worked in the machine. These things were all over the place just lying around, left from some type of construction job. They were called slugs but to me, they were "pennies from heaven" but actually were shiny silver pieces. I found we could get gum or candy free with them just by placing them into the money slot. My sister and I searched all over for them and then picked them up to put into the machine. When my mom found me with candy all the time she asked me where I was getting it. Questions, questions, why do they always have to ask those stupid questions. When I showed her the neat discovery my sister and I had found, she was once again a spoiled sport and bearer of bad news. She said that was illegal and just like stealing! What do ya mean, stealing? I put something into the money slot to get it. I didn't steal a thing. She told me that it was against the law, and I could go to jail for it. She swept up any left-over slugs and kept track, so there were never any more. What a spoiled sport!

With that fun gone, I went back to pretending again. Unless that was going to have something wrong with it too, but my mom played along with me, so I guessed that was still okay. One day I told my mother, "By, I'm going to school now." My mother came back with what she was also thinking was playing and said, "Okay, be careful crossing the streets. Look both ways." What? My mother actually just told me I could go to school! I was only playing, but my mother actually told me I could go and to be careful crossing the streets. So, I did! I was four! I walked seven blocks, crossing about five streets which weren't busy and crossed the Avenue which was! I did exactly as she said and I looked both ways before crossing. When I got to school I tried to open the large double doors but, boy, were those doors heavy! Luckily there was a woman walking by at the top of the stairs inside and she saw me, so came down to open the door for me. She knew who I was and also knew my mother. I told her my mother said I could come to school to be with my sister, but apparently she wasn't sure my mother had actually said that so went to call her but before she got to me, my mother appeared at the door. When mom couldn't find me,

17

she thought back to the last thing we talked about and figured out I may have really gone to school. What was there to figure out? She told me to go! Geez, make up your mind! No one ever lets you have fun!

Well, I found out that might have been a mistake. They decided if I wanted to go to school so bad they put me into a kindergarten class the next fall. I thought it was great, at first, but by lunchtime I learned what the word 'mistake' means! Before lunch, we were lined up to go to a table where there were little cups of orange juice all lined up in a row. I liked orange juice. The thing was, not one of us looked the whole scene over and missed what happened before you got to the orange juice. We may have been little, but we knew how to push and shove each other to get to be first in line to get that juice. Well, first there was a bottle of something which the teacher poured from onto a spoon and slipped it into each kid's mouth before they could get the believed prized juice. That juice was no prize. It was to try to wash down that awful cod liver oil taste they had just given you. There were a lot of cases of the 'rickets' in a society which was deforming of the bones caused by lacking certain needed things. Unfortunately, cod liver oil had those things in it. So each kid got a spoonful every day. Do you have any idea what cod liver oil tastes like? The smell is even horrible. It didn't take more than once for us to see we didn't want to be first in line anymore. Instead of pushing and shoving to get up to the head of the line, we tried pushing others in front of us so they could go ahead. I did get my first boyfriend shortly after that, so that made school a whole lot better.

The memories of school were many. During recess, we went outdoors to climb on jungle gyms, play tag, keep away, dodge ball, or chase each other in games of cowboys and Indians or cops and robbers. We could take chalk out to make hopscotch designs on the sidewalks to play on. Winter time had us in snowball fights, making snow angels in the snow or make outlines in the snow to play the game of goose, goose, who can catch the goose. We had a small embankment going from the playground to a sidewalk below, so we would slide down it over and over. The more we did it slipperier it got. In fact, it would get so slick we often had trouble getting up it again. When we went inside, we put our boots on the floor by the floor steam heater and laid our gloves full of snow with our hats on top. You could hear the spit and spattering noise coming from the melting snow mixing with the heat.

In kindergarten, we had cubby holes to keep our own personal things in. Even though it was only a long section of wood with square openings, with each square a different color, it was special to us. No one was allowed to do anything with another person's things. They could not put anything of theirs in, nor take any of our things out of it. We had play sinks, stoves, cupboards, and a refrigerator to play with plus had blocks, wooden trucks and more, with each thing teaching us to share and play well with each other. It also stimulated everyone's personal imagination.

By first grade, I have a wonderful memory of having our own desk to sit at, and the top opened up to put supplies inside. We had our own books and tablets to learn to write in. The book we learned to read with was *Dick and Jane* and, believe it or not, you can still find those books. The notebook of paper was red and had an Indian head on the front. I can remember how exciting it was to read those first books. It was a feeling of importance and power. Yes, those were the days.

Our school had assemblies where all the classes in the school met together in the main hall standing along the wall. The kids from upstairs sat on the steps coming down. At Easter, we had a contest as to who could make the best bonnet to wear in our Easter Parade. As each person who made hats walked out in a parade style to show off their hats, the music "In your Easter Bonnet" was played. At Christmas time, we gathered there for a Christmas program and to all sing Christmas songs together.

On May first, we had a maypole dance with long pieces of colored crepe paper hanging down from the top of the outdoor flag pole where we took turns in groups holding one of the strands and dancing around the pole to music. That day was also celebrated in our neighborhoods, with kids taking small sprays of wildflowers in homemade paper baskets and sneaking to someone's house, placing the basket on the doorstep, then stomped their foot on the porch or knocked on the door and ran before the person could answer and see who it was from.

The "yo-yo" man came to the grade school usually once a year. He would show kids all the neat things he could do with a yo-yo and was amazing. He'd even sell yo-yos to the kids. Soon everywhere you looked were kids spending their recess time trying to do all these wonderful tricks he had shown us but, for the most part, it was a positive if we could just catch the darn thing when it came back up again. For a lot, it didn't even come back up but instead tangled the string. Many an hour in those days was spent untangling string.

Marbles was also a favorite recess activity of the older grade school kids. We would make a circle in the sandy area of the playground, and everyone put a marble into the center. Then one by one we would shoot with our biggest marble or a special steel one if you had it, called a steely, and try to shoot the marbles in the center and hit them out. Any marbles that were shot out of the circle by you, you got to keep. I was pretty good at it and won a lot of marbles.

When you think of it, that was like gambling, but we just looked at it as learning how to get better at something. Anyone could be a winner or, at least, get more marbles than what they had put in if they practiced a lot.

We played softball in school, and the gym teacher also taught us how to leg wrestle. You laid next to your opponent on the floor with heads at opposite ends and locked your inside arm next to the others body with theirs. You then brought up your inside leg by them, counting one, then dropped it down again. Then the count of two raised the leg again, and back down. On three, you hooked your leg around the opponents and tried to throw the other person over. I was good at that and after being the winner of the class, I challenged the gym teacher himself. He declined but after the pleading of all the kids, he agreed to do it. I think with me being just a grade school kid he didn't try real hard so to give me a chance but when I threw him he redid the match and forgot about me being a fourth grader. He was red faced when I, a fourth grader, threw him that time too.

One of the memories that really stuck from grade school and was probably retained because it was something like swearing, which would usually have our mouth washed out with soap, was something my sister taught me on the playground at school. She was older, and it was her last year in grade school with me, and I thought I was so special to be taught this by her. However, when she first told it to me I said, "Ooooh, I'm going to tell mom!" That's when she explained it to me and said I couldn't get in trouble because it wasn't really swearing. I really think secretly she was hoping I would get in trouble anyway knowing I'd be the one to tell it to mom. After her explanation as to how I couldn't get into trouble for it, I thought it was the greatest piece of literature around. The saying I learned was… "I went to the dam to get some dam water. The dam man told me I could not have any dam water, so I told the damn man to keep his damn water." I was even brave enough to tell it to my mother like my sister figured I would and even though mom was not happy, I quickly informed her I didn't say anything bad so she couldn't punish me. She didn't punish me, but I was told not to say stuff like that anyway, and my sister didn't get in trouble for what it said, but she was reprimanded for teaching it to me!

I wasn't in the most popular group of girls in school. I had braids and lost my front teeth and wore glasses. (Now isn't that a picture to behold!) There were two girls that were even farther from the popular group than I. One was fat and the other short and skinny and poor or straggly looking. I latched on to them as friends because they looked up to me. I did mention I lost my front teeth, had braids and wore glasses, right? You'd think they wouldn't want to be friends with me if looks had anything to do with it! These 'two' were actually nice, and we had a lot of fun together. I learned a lesson in those friendships. At first, for me, it was to make me feel superior because they liked and looked up to me, but I then realized that no matter what a person looks like they have something good to give and make very good friends. In later years, I seemed to carry that same pattern onward to places to live. When I got married, I was more than satisfied to have a home in a mediocre neighborhood, and when it just happened that our house was looked upon as being the best one on the street even though I didn't think it was, it made me feel on top again just as those friendships from school had. I didn't feel or act superior to any others in my neighborhood, but somehow there was still a feeling inside that I learned from the years of not being in the 'in group' in grade school. Not negative, just a remembrance.

I was always picked on at grade school because I wore glasses. I had that famous "four eyes" title. I could have shrunk back and let it bother me which again, could have continued forward through life with feelings of being picked on and took up the 'poor me syndrome." I, however, started pushing back. I would have someone hold my glasses, and I'd take on the boys when they taunted me. I won the fights and I soon became a challenge because the boy's egos were being threatened as one by one was found to have been beaten up by a girl. One day one kid tried to push me down into the snow, so I went after him. I gave him a shove, and he slid in the snow and headed toward the street where a city bus was approaching. He fell out into the street right in its path. With the roads also icy I wasn't sure it could stop in time. I said the fastest prayer to God that he probably ever got. I said, "Please God, don't let him get hit and I'll change my ways. I won't fight anymore." He didn't get hit, and I kept my promise from that day on. The boys started admiring me because I had never been beaten and now refused to fight any of them, so they gave up trying too. (Maybe they were just glad they didn't have to try anymore and end up losing face for being beaten up by a girl.) Even girls started becoming nicer to me but that I don't know why. They even included me more with some of the 'in' girls or at least started to include me in some things, but I never did give up my other two friends. I found how special they were and to this day think of them often. They will be thought of fondly forever. Because of them, I learned the greatest lesson in life. Never judge a book by its cover. Sometimes the least thought of, is the best and have the most to offer for life. The most popular may just end up being superficial. Look at the person as a person, no matter their popularity. There are winners in both groups. I learned to be a friend and kind to everyone because of this lesson. I also found where the value lies in life. Money and prestige aren't where real life and happiness are found.

Popular kids are fine but so are the not so popular. The characteristics of a person are what counts. Being kind, friendly, helpful, caring and sharing of our gifts and talents with others no matter who or where they are in life and how they treat others is what life is all about. (Even in high school with being accepted in the mainstream group I never forgot my grade school lesson)

I had one girlfriend with whom I was friends with from little up and in fact still am to this day. We were both cowboy enthusiasts, and we collected comic books of our favorite one. In my mind mine, Roy Rogers, was better than hers, Gene Autry, even though I liked him too. We decided to buy the comic books of our favorite one and then exchange them for the other to read. That way we got the best of both worlds. We had comics of our own favorite one but saved money by being able to read the other one too. We had an adult neighbor who was a Tarzan fan. He and his wife were friends of my mom and also of my girlfriend's family. They had no children so enjoyed having us kids around. Because he bought Tarzan comics, it gave us another one to read without having to buy it when he joined in our threesome exchange.

We had a telephone that was so old that when people asked to use our phone they didn't see it even when they were standing right where it was. When they did see it, they then wondered how to use it. I was proud of that phone as it looked just like the ones used in cowboy movies. One day we had trouble with our telephone, and the telephone company came to fix it. He couldn't see the phone either. How dumb can you be? When he finally did see it, he asked my mom if we would like a modern phone. I couldn't believe it; she said yes! Oh no! How disappointing! I lost my cowboy phone, and part of me was lost that day! I have missed it ever since. What a bummer.

My girlfriend also used that phone, and she was fond of it too. As adults, Toni found a phone like it at an antique store and bought it for me. It now proudly sits in my family room, but we got a laugh over it. The one she bought was even older and better than the one we had. Ours did have a rotary dial on it but the one she got you would have had to pick up and connect with an operator to give them the number you wanted. So actually, I like this one better. It was even more of a cowboy model than what we had! I called her to tell her about it, and she hadn't realized the difference. They look the very same except for that. She went to check the one she bought for herself and discovered hers didn't have a dial either. We laughed about it, and she said, "I'll yell into the air, and then you can pick up your phone, and we can talk!"

When we were growing up, Toni and I also used to send away to get free pictures of movie stars, and naturally cowboys too. I still have a picture of

Roy Rogers and his wife Dale Evans with their then two girls and young boy Dusty, which I got back then. You can tell how old the picture is as they ended up adopting kids so had eight or nine. I guess you can never take the cowboy influence out of a person once it is embedded. Next to that picture hanging on my wall is another picture, taken only a few years ago. It's of me with that same boy, Dusty, but now who is a married adult. On a trip back to Iowa we happen to see that he was going to be in a small town not far from where we were. He was going to dedicate a museum a farmer was opening of Roy Rogers things he'd collected over the years. So now the two pictures hang together on my wall.

When I was around six or seven, my mother worked as a secretary in the Czech village for Culligan soft water service. It wasn't that far from our house. I spent all my time in the Czech village while she worked and when I wasn't in school. There were two bakeries in the village, and the smell of fresh bakery floated through the air, and through the streets. What a wonderful aroma. There was a barber shop by the one bakery, and the smell of shaving crème came out their door as you stood watching the red, white and blue barbershop sign twisting the colors around inside the tall pole. There was a dime store to browse through things we could only wish we could have and even inside that store it too had its own smell, but I can't quite describe it. Maybe just an old type of place. There was a drug store where you could get ice cream, floats or scrumptious milkshakes. It too had its own aroma, but it might have been a cleaning substance used on the floor, like Germtrol.

There were also two meat markets in town which each had their own same likeness aroma coming out their doors. Fresh cut meats. Carcasses were hanging from hooks from the ceiling while a variety of meats were also displayed inside a glass case. They had a huge wide roll of brown paper meat wrap on the counter along with a spindle of string which once the meat was wrapped; the package was tied with string.

A small one room library stood among the stores where they had children come around three o'clock, and they would read stories to us. Halfway through the stories, we got a break, and they gave out cookies and milk. We sat on small wooden chairs with the reader sitting in front of us on a chair where she could turn the book around to show us the pictures of the book as she read. I looked forward to those times, and when we were done, I'd go next door to my favorite place, the leather shop.

That saddle and leather shop had a huge window and in that window was a beautiful gray horse statue the size of a real horse. (In fact it might have really been a taxidermy one, but in any case, to me, that was my horse. Other

23

kids did not stand there every day visiting it! The wonderful smell of leather came from 'that' shop.) The entire village was a land of smells with wonderful aromas that tied memories galore which lasted throughout time. They are still as alive in me of that village today as they were back then! I can almost bring back the aromas and smells just by thinking of the stores they came from.

What's funny is that that same leather store was still there with that same horse in the window when we went back to visit after my own kids were grown and left home. In fact, that window is where we saw the advertisement for Roy Rogers's son Dusty who was going to be in the area to dedicate a farmers Museum of Roy Rogers things he collected over the years. Here I was, married with grown and married kids, and I was reliving a childhood memory still there. Also, there was still one of the two bakeries as well as one of the two meat markets, plus the barbershop. However later, in 2008, a massive flood happened in Cedar Rapids and the Czech village was under water with massive damage and sadly the one remaining meat market plus the saddle shop either left the area or went out of business. My horse was gone, but I don't know if he survived and was moved to the business or was done in by the flood. That was so hard to see. The entire area was flooded, and homes were damaged to the point of having to be demolished. Businesses gave up after all these years, but luckily the memories couldn't be washed away and are safely tucked inside the movie theater of our mind where replays of the movies are still available. The one bakery didn't give up, though, but they did lose their antique ovens so even though they are there, it's not the same.

It was from this village that I took a bus at the age of seven and went downtown by myself to go to a store to find something for my mother's birthday. I remember getting her different colored inks in small fancy glass bottles that you had to dip a pen into to write. I really thought it was a neat gift, and she seemed to be happy with it. However I really never ever saw her use them, and years later I began to wonder if she really liked them but satisfied myself with perhaps she liked them so well she was saving them for a special time. I guess she never got that special time as they were still in a stand in a drawer of her things after she died. Now I have them. I haven't used them either...of course, I think the ink has probably dried up by now, and we have ball point pens now that are much easier to use than dipping a pen! Those bottles are antiques, as apparently am I.

It was this village too that had a bank with a cowboy saving account for kids. The more you saved, the higher rank of cowboy status you reached and got a badge. ("Wrangler," "Trail Boss," etc.) I saved my money there just to get the next badge. Then, after saving diligently for so long, my mother informed me that I had enough money to buy myself a new winter coat. I sure could have found something I wanted more but, life isn't always fair no matter what age.

Chapter 3

Like mentioned before, why memories crop up as they do is a mystery. Why a memory from ten years old is topped by one of three years old and then jumps to teenage years or adulthood doesn't make sense, without rhyme nor reason to it all. Yet hidden in the puzzle of life seems to be "targets". A word, a smell, a sound, or incident, that rings a bell and opens the door to the "prize" for the day...a recollection of years gone by bringing a smile or two along the way.

Memories seem to be like a jigsaw puzzle pieces all poured out on the table in a heap and piece by piece they are moved into an easier to view layout, yet with no pieces grouped together with their linking friends. Then like in Bingo, one piece is brought forward after another until you have a winning combination. So like in the movie of *Forrest Gump*, stating, "Life is like a box of chocolates, and you never know what you are going to get," so as it applies to your memories recalled of reviewing your life. It's a mystery until it pops in! You reach in that pile of puzzle pieces or box of chocolates and retrieve one piece without knowing what you will come up with.

I can have a mystery guest pop in for a moment but at times, other guests are pushing at the door to be the next to come in and not very patiently waiting because they want to be known. Who gets in seems to be just the 'luck of the draw'. As I mentally dip down into the pile of puzzle pieces to retrieve or withdraw just one link from the memory bank, I await the prize to be revealed. Sometimes pieces do seem to link from one to the other and flood in like an open cattle gate with one after another coming through. Other times it's as if a guard is at a gate stopping all but one, and allowing only that one to pass through.

One such grouping of memories actually covered different periods of time yet were tied together because of the people involved. They contained incidences with my best friend and her family from little up. My parents were divorced, and somehow her parents became the second set for me. Their daughter was an only child, but I melted into their family as a close second.

When I got my glasses at the age of seven, I had to go to a special office which was an optician's office where my girlfriend's father was one of two or three who worked there. Boy did I feel special when the other man called my number to go up to be fitted for glasses, but Mr. Grey stated that HE would take me and for the man to call the next number. Then, when it was my turn, my girlfriend's dad called me up by name! Boy did I feel like a celebrity...no one else was called up by their name! They were called only by the number they drew when they came in. On top of that, the President of the Amana refrigeration plant in the Amanas came to Mr. Grey and liked him so much he gave a gift of one of the first televisions when they came out. I was right there on top billing! I even had a better place, as I actually went to his house! Of course, when I went to his house I also saw some weird stuff. You hear about people taking their work home with them. He really did! It was a little weird to see a tray of glass eyes sitting on the desk looking back at you at the end of the table or on a desk.

With them having one of the first televisions in town it goes to say I spent a lot of time there. We couldn't afford to get one for about three years. They had a cocker spaniel dog that was almost human. When Mr. Grey came home from work, he would sit in his chair and take his shoes off. The dog picked them up as a pair and carried them to the back room. She then returned with a more comfortable pair of shoes for him to wear around the house. Every once in a while Mr. Grey wanted a different pair from what the dog brought and told the dog so, also saying which ones he wanted. The dog took them back and returned with the correctly indicated pair even though there were several others to choose from. That always amazed me!

Toni played the piano and a lot of time the two of us sat together and sang while she played. I might add the piano was in one key, and we both were in a different one, even from each other, with probably neither of us in the right one. The dog sat below us and added her voice, howling at the top of her lungs. Although I'd liked to think she was singing with us, I have a feeling she was really a retaliating critic.

One New Year's Eve I spent the night at Toni's, and we had hats and noise makers for all of us. The dog even had a hat. We blew up balloons and rubbed them on the wool carpet which made them have static so we could stick them to the front door. Mr. Grey got out his BB gun and shot at the balloons, but they didn't just pop the balloons. They also went further to the door itself, leaving dents that remain to this day, unless the door got replaced. With all our noise of balloons popping, yelling and noise makers at midnight Toni's grandmother who had been sleeping upstairs apparently felt she had overslept and came downstairs all washed, dressed, and hair neatly combed! She only spoke Czechoslovakian and didn't really understand a lot of what was going on. They had to tell her what was going on, and it wasn't time to get up yet, so she returned upstairs to go back to bed!

While we were younger, Mrs. Grey took Toni and I out to eat every Saturday and then to a movie. We took the bus to town and when we got to the restaurant we had to stand outside while Mrs. Grey poured Isopropyl alcohol on our hands to get rid of germs. In the colder weather the stuff steamed up in our hands. I can still detect that smell if it is anywhere in the area! She was like another mother to me and in later years, she just adored my small son. He was like a grandchild she never got to see. She died before Toni had any children.

(As a side note here, but like other memories that just 'pop in', this one slid in to be added here.) Shortly after she died and we had moved to Florida, I went with my, maybe three-year-old, son to visit the neighbor on the other side of our chain link fence. On the way back home Brian stopped dead in his tracks, right by the fence, and looked up into the sky! I heard him say. "Hi"... "Ya"... "eh huh"..."okay". I said, "Brian... what are you doing? ... Come on!" He got sort of disgusted with me and said, "I'm talkin' to Aunt Juju!" (His name for Mrs. Grey!) That freaked me out!

While growing up, Mr. Grey would take us out for a Sunday drive. When younger I had to go to my dad's on Sunday but then it got to going there only here and there, so Sundays became a routine. Toni came to my house for dinner and then we went to her house for the rest of the day. We enjoyed the rides, and Mr. Grey used to make sounds like a siren. The thing is it was so real that one day when he did it we were too close to the car in front of us and with the windows open, the car pulled over! Boy did he get a red face! He also didn't do that anymore if another car was anywhere close around!

As we got older, Toni was learning to drive. On our Sunday drives, we would get on a country road, and Mr. Grey would pull over and have Toni get behind the wheel where she proceeded to practice driving. I watched and listened to his instructions and the pointers he gave her because some day I would be taking Drivers Ed. at school too. One day he pulled over and told me to get behind the wheel! I thought he was kidding, but he wasn't. He left Toni on the front passenger seat and climbed into the back seat. He thought he was being funny as he picked up some chains laying on the floor wrapping up in them and saying "I'm ready to die"! (He didn't know just how close that could have been!)I had no idea what to do except watching Toni's lessons. I started the car several times but killed the motor as trying to coordinate the clutch and gas pedals. Did I mention we were at the top of a hill, so we were making progress...but only because we were going down the hill. After bumps and jerks, I finally mastered the shifting of gears, but it was with the help of Toni sitting next to me making the movement in the air of how the formation of the floor gear shift should go. Mr. Grey would all of a sudden say "stop", and I was to stop right then. I had to think first of what to do so not kill the motor. Well, he was trying to get me to stop quickly in case of an emergency, but all I did was kill the motor. He changed seats with Toni so he could give me closer instruction. At least, Toni had been there long enough I learned the direction the floor gear shift was to go. After driving the country road for a while, he decided to take me to Hawkeye downs fairgrounds, but we had to go across a very busy road. Luckily he said he would drive across, and then I could return to the wheel. We drove there for a while and then he got behind the wheel to return home. As we were driving down the road, he said, "Pauline you did a pretty good job today. How many weeks have you been in Drivers Ed?" Toni and I looked at him and almost in unison said, "I/she isn't in Driver's Ed yet! I/she can't take it for another six months!" His eyes bugged out, and he swung his head around as his foot hit the brake! "What! What do you mean you're not taking drivers Ed yet? Toni Is!" I said "Ya, but I'm younger than Toni, so I have six more months to go until next semester!" He about had a heart attack! Here he had been sitting in the back seat with chains wrapped around him! He joined with other members of my family and friends who had things that happened that they'd never forget until the day they died, which all was because of me!

Chapter 4

I had three brothers and a sister. However, my sister was my half-sister and my brothers were my half-brothers. That made my sister, my brothers step sister and my brothers her step brothers. Then to top that all off...I was an only child! Confused yet? In those days that made quite a story but in this day and age it is not only normal, but there can be even more twists and turns to be able to come up with. My mother had been married before and had my sister. My dad had been married before and had three boys. They both got divorced and married each other, bringing their children to the union and then I was born. It was much easier to say I had three brothers and one sister. (In my adult years some guy showed up, and my dad told people he was his son. He was near my age but spoke French and had the nickname, 'Frenchy.' I have no idea to this day of who he was or how he fit into the picture but while I kept my ears peeled to possibly hear a clue I never did. I couldn't bring myself to ask. Why I don't know, but no one ever offered free answers either!)

My brothers were about seven, eight and nine years older than me and my sister was five years older, so it made me the baby of the family. I don't ever remember that being an advantage, but rather was one to be picked on or see what they could do to me. One time we had the ironing board out and my brothers dared me to touch the hot iron. I was small but not 'that' dumb...well until they did it themselves to show it didn't hurt. As I started to touch the iron, my sister came to the rescue to stop me. She revealed the boys had wet their fingers first and barely touched it. When our parents weren't home, the boys brought their bikes into the house to ride. I told on them. They weren't with us all of the time as they split their time with their real mother too.

Kenny was with us the most, and so memories of him are more than the others. He had epileptic seizures, and we had to watch so if he went into one he wouldn't hit his head on something that might harm him, and we had to watch that he didn't swallow his tongue to close off his airway. He had a stamp collection and one day while he had them spread out on the table to put into books, a fly kept flying around bugging him. Well, he had this habit of keeping his mouth open when he was concentrating. I was little and leaning on the edge of the table watching him work on the stamps when all of a sudden I saw that fly heading right toward his open mouth. It must have looked like a cave to a small fly but figured it would turn away at the last minute. It didn't. It entered into his mouth just as he swallowed! "GROSS!" I yelled. "You just swallowed a fly!" With that, I went to find something better to do.

One time he was putting up storm windows on the second floor of the house when a sudden breeze caught the window, pushing him backward off the ladder. He went to the ground landing on his back but still holding the window in front of him...and it didn't even break.

When he got older, he started working at Quaker Oats Company. Their flour came in flowered cloth sacks and people used them to make clothes from. He brought home extras from time to time, and all my dresses were made from them. They had the very same design but were in different colors. The yellow, pink, and sometimes blue were the most common ones but if we got a green or purple one, which was special and rare. Those were our clothes until we got hand me downs when we got a little older, from cousins whose family had more money than us. The only thing was, my sister was closer to their age so she got the clothes first and then I got them. So, I actually got hand me downs of hand me downs.

One time Kenny got a bad case of hives. They were so bad that he couldn't put his arms down because they were under his arm pits and he also had to walk with his legs apart. They were also on the bottom of his feet and between his fingers and toes. The medications for them back then (and I might add, good even today) was to cook oatmeal and place it into very warm bath water to sit and soak in. I was little so when my brother passed by on his way to take his bath I picked up on the procedure, telling my dolls, "We have to take a bath now, but we will use Cheerios because I like them better."

A few years later when I was maybe six or seven, or maybe eight, I had a strange thing happen. It was a hot summer evening, and my sister, and I slept downstairs on the floor in front of the door leading to the screened front porch. My parents were sleeping on the porch itself. I heard a weird creaking noise and opened up my eyes in the darkened room to see a thin male figure standing over me silhouetted against the outside sky. I laid very still, peeking through slit open eyelids. When he disappeared, I ran to the porch to tell my parents. They insisted no one could have gotten passed them but checked the house for my satisfaction. They then told me it was probably my brother coming home and had gone up the steps. Wait a minute....they had just said if anyone came passed them they would have known, and now they were saying my brother might have come home? That made a lot of sense. I was still insistent it was not him, so they called him downstairs. He sleepily staggered down the stairs to see what they wanted only to say he'd not just come home but had actually been home for hours. He was sleeping. The mystery was never solved, and I can still see that figure to this day!

My brothers eventually were old enough to go into the service. Kenny went into the Army, Duane in the Air Force and Marvin went into the Navy! With Kenny's room now empty and I had always wanted that tiny downstairs bedroom, I got my wish. There was only room for a small single cot or rollaway type of bed and a small desk. Above the bed were shelves to put my things like toys, or books. I wasn't the neatest of kids and after my shelves got crammed full of my unorganized 'junk' I let it spill over to the nooks and cranny on the floor and under the bed. Soon it was so full it tried making its way toward the door. It did pretty well at doing that as I had to shove my hand or foot in first when I opened it to keep everything from spilling out. I had to climb over it all once inside just to get to the bed.

My grandmother had this really neat desk lamp of a horse that looked like Roy Rogers horse, Trigger! Knowing I was a cowboy everything kid, she asked me if I'd like to have it. Boy did I! Then my mother lowered the boom! I couldn't have the lamp unless I cleaned my room! What a bummer! Did I want really want the lamp that bad? Well, the 'cowboy in me really did! I had a lot of doubts and arguing with myself during those 'weeks' of hoeing out the stuff and almost said it wasn't worth it. Then I wondered who would get it if I didn't and if it was one of my cousins how many years would I have to look at it in someone else's house knowing it could have been mine? I continued on until finally I had to admit the room did look better being so cleaned up and organized. To top that, that horse lamp was really a special prize and still treasured to this day. In fact, that horse lamp sits in my dining area, where every time I look at it I recall that bedroom and all the work I had to do to get it.

My sister had a party one night, and some girl had to make a phone call. It was so noisy she opened my bedroom door to step in to block out the noise. She didn't realize it was a bedroom until she saw me and jumped back out, exclaiming, "There's a body in there!" I wonder what would have happened if that party would have been before I cleaned my room and when she opened the door all the stuff came tumbling out! She was lucky it was only a body in there!

When I had had a bedroom upstairs, I did a lot of sleepwalking. One time I was walking down the steps and my mother asked me where I was going. I was quite surprised she'd even ask. She should have known. "I'm going to get you a drink of water"! When I heard my own voice I woke up. Of course, I was always a "wise guy" awake or asleep! For so long I was a cry baby. No matter what happened, I felt belittled and not good enough for some reason. One day I decided I wasn't going to do that anymore and changed myself to being a "goof-off" or "comic." I may have been hiding behind it at first, and it did the trick, but soon I wasn't just hiding behind it but found a new way to live, by helping others to be happy. One day my mother asked me to go upstairs and draw her a bathtub of water. So, I did! I got a paper and pencil and drew a bathtub with water in it!

I did a lot of what I call impish stuff that got me into trouble a lot. I'm not sure that term is what my mother would use. However, I also had a compassionate side. I felt sorry for birds I'd see around the neighborhood who were hurt, so I spent hours using my bicycle's basket as the carrier for injured birds I went looking for. I'd bring them home and give them water and food and if I could, tried to fix a wing or wound. I did my best to help them, but if they died, I gave them a nice burial. Of course, those good deeds got shot down when my mother informed me that bird's like that carry disease, so my rescue days ended.

A spinster school teacher lived down the street. In those days when she first became a teacher they were not allowed to be married or even date. By the time we were growing up it had been changed but she was already older. She treated us girls in the neighborhood like her girls and from time to time she had a tea party for us in her front yard. We had to dress up in our mother's dresses and wear their shoes and hats or even gloves and purses. Yak! I did it because we really liked her a lot but with me being a tomboy who preferred cowboys and guns, I was really pushing the act of liking it as the others seemed to. It took a lot for me to don those old woman's dress and sit at a child's table set with tea cups. It did leave memories however which now bubble forth, of those days gone by.

My real character was doing things like swinging out on tree vines over the pond at my aunt and uncles cabin or climbing up into their tree house in the woods. From time to time we'd make our way once more to go back to swing out over the water in the pond. One time my cousin swung out but never came

33

back. The vine broke and plopped him down into the water. That was pretty funny to see, but luckily the water ended up being fairly shallow because at that time he didn't know how to swim. They also had a boat which us kids could take out and go down the creek. One time we were with the adults and went down the creek further than usual. As we passed by a fallen tree lying half in the water, a nest of snakes was among the branches. Now these weren't just snakes...they were water moccasins which were both poisonous and aggressive. We hadn't seen them at first because their nest was hidden so well and we got too close. A water moccasin started swimming out into the water toward the boat. My uncle put the speed of the motor into high gear, but even at that, the snake was gaining on us with its body barely below the water's surface and its head sticking up out of the water looking at us with a defiant look. My uncle hit it with a paddle which was also in the boat, and we got safely back to the cabin. However even though we were safe, those snakes sure weren't going to be. My uncle went back with his gun to shoot the nest full of them. You don't need that many snakes around and especially when they are water moccasins.

My sister and I got to go with this same aunt, uncle, and cousins for a week or so trip, to Clear Lake, Iowa. They rented a House of Scouts from where we spent some very enjoyable times and came back with memories which we relived often back then and are enjoying recalling them again now. While we were at that summer lake house for the two weeks, we spent a lot of fun times both indoors and out. We splashed and played in the water a good part of the day. We swam and had water fights or just floated around in inner tubes. Of course, one time my sister pounced on me while I was stretched out over the inner tube and it pushed me down further into the tube which flipped over as I tried to get out. I was then face down under the water and still stuck. I managed to get loose after struggling for a minute or so. Those famous words came out "Are you trying to kill me?!" (I remembered a previous incident not so many years ago when she was pounding the piano at church, and the ceiling fell in just missing me. I was beginning to wonder if that really was an accident! Ha!)

We kids fished or sat on the screened porch to read comic books or used the silly putty stuff to transfer the images from the comics to the putty. Then we'd wad the putty again and made it into a type of ball that would bounce before flattening it again and transferring more from the comics. Another simple toy out at the time were little Scotty dog magnets, which to this day bring back happy memories of that trip because I see them still for sale in magazines. Two weeks out of life, yet it never ends, because movies still play reruns within the movie theater of the mind, bringing back those days as if we were still there.

They had rented a boat, and again my cousin who was good at driving took us kids out in it a lot. Even though he was my age, with our sisters five years older, he was the one to drive it. There was an amusement park across the lake where you could see the roller coaster even from a fairly long distance as the wooden coaster came out over the water. That really made us want to get a closer look so after telling his parents where we were going we took off to go to the other side. After going there a few times, we talked my aunt and uncle to drive around the lake and take us there. We actually got to go on the rides except for the wooden rollercoaster. It had issues with the structure so was condemned. Darn! That was the thing that drew us to wanting to go there.

Those days were days when kids were free to explore and learn to figure things out on their own and enjoy life. We were free range, happy and very constructive. If the same kids from back then were in today's society with all the now restrictions and laws, they would have never been able to do the things we did. In fact, in a lot of today's areas, parents would be slapped with a child abuse charge if they tried.

The parents now lose their choice of bringing up their children the way they feel fit and the kids lose their freedom to establish their character through trial and error by using their own talent and skills and sharing life with others. The things free range kids had which are lost today are learning to get along with others and share time, space, and thoughts, or ideas by taking turns with the ideas of others. One of the biggest things kids got with our way of living was that we build self-esteem. So many kids lack this today.

While this book is to bring back memories, there may be times I will also add a statement or some kind of information which defends our "good ol' days" from some reader who tries to find fault with our ways because of their own today's beliefs. (This includes psychologists and psychiatrists who never experienced the days but tries labeling it from today's views.) Here is one of those times for information. People jump to the thoughts and fears of today's children being abducted so feel it is their duty to turn the parents into authorities, causing the parents to be charged falsely with child abuse. The actual culprits are the people trying to rule other people's lives from their own views as if the other people's views don't count. The news media also gives a false statistical view with the way they report. I feel it needs to be cleared up here.

In 1999, they had the most recent national study of missing children. Approximately 800,000 children under 18 were reported missing with 200,000 of them taken by family members, and 58,000 by nonfamily members. Ninety percent of the abductions returned home within 24 hours with the vast majority being runaways. One hundred and fifteen were the snatched by an actual stranger. Fifty were killed. One thousand three hundred children between the ages of two and fourteen were killed in car accidents. Murders of children are less than one-half of 1% of all murders in America. Of all the children under five murdered "between" 1976–2005:

31% were killed by fathers,
29% by mothers,
23% by male acquaintances,
7% by other relatives,
3% by strangers.
The information ended with:
"Your safest bet is to leave your child with a stranger."

(The source is http://bjs.oip.usdoj.gov/content/homicide/children.cfm)

Remember, we were kids out doing things together. The connections we had been with each other, and we weren't involved with adults. We were taught about strangers and that if we were ever approached by someone, to run to the nearest house for help. That was the extent of warnings. There were always plenty of houses around. In my whole life, one man stopped once at a bus stop and asked me if he could give me a ride. He said he knew my mother. I was clear on the other side of town where the rich people lived, and I knew there was no way he knew my mother. I merely told him no and started walking across the street to my piano teacher's house. He left, and I turned around and went back to the bus stop. It wasn't a big deal, and I wasn't afraid because I'd been told what to do. None of my friends ever had it happen.

Now, since 1990, sexual exploitation of children has grown. In 2006, the U.S. handled 82.8 more child pornography than in 1994. Between 2004 and 2008, state and local law enforcement agencies reported 230 percent increase for online enticement of children. Reported 1,000 percent increase in child sex trafficking from 2004 to 2008. 139 million child pornography images have been reviewed since 2002. One in six endangered runaways was likely sex trafficking victims. Sixty-eight percent was in the care of social services or foster care when they ran. 93 percent of teenagers 12–17 go online. Children five years old and younger or 80 percent use the internet at least once a week. One in 25 children 10–17 received online sexual solicitation with someone trying to make offline contact. 4 percent of teens 12–17 have sent sexually suggestive nude or semi-nude messages via text. 15 percent have said they received the same images from others they know.

So, compare the world we grew up in, free and free to be. We were out doing things and not sitting in a chair at home living through an electronic device. We were with people, exchanging ideas, skills, talents, and emotions.

The people we were with, we physically talked to and did things with. Today's youth, even if a group sitting together in the same room, will text the person even if right next to them, rather than talk. The parents go out to eat with friends or family and are on their devices too. No one communicates with each other anymore.

So even today, the "free-range" kids are not the safety issue. In fact, kids with their freedom would be a refreshing scene. The culprit is the 'stay at home' kid who spends their time on computers and other devices. The family life has eroded, and not necessarily all the parents fault. The kids are listless and doing nothing that builds self-esteem! "Idle hands is the devils playground."

So then, as you read about the things we kids did in the "good ol' days," compared to what is done today, and how the kids lived their lives before, which is better? Which made a better society? The computer has caused more criminal threats and safety issues for our youth and enticements to go out to strangers, led through words to lure them in. In our day, that could have only come face to face, and we were too busy in groups of kids doing things together. Rather than worrying about kids being Free-range, maybe computers need to be limited. Kids in our days didn't have access to the sexual or criminal abilities as a click of a key can bring to every age today.

Keep all this information in mind then, as you read the rest of memories of a time when those of us lived the "good ol' days."

We did a lot of things with my cousins even though they lived on the other side of town. My grandparents also lived there and, in fact, lived next door to my aunt and uncle. Well, actually that was a funny situation in itself. For some reason, my grandma wanted to move all the time. She would be in a house only a couple years before she wanted to move to another one. The funniest part, though, came when she wanted my aunt and uncle's house...right next door..., and, they actually moved...to each other's house! Before long they were moving back again!

There was a park straight across the street from them. In the winter, we would take sleds over there and slide down the long hill. It was much more fun sliding down and steering our sleds away from the trees than then having to pull the sleds back up the hill. It also wasn't near as fast getting to the top as it was going down.

Summertime was another time to have fun in that park. There were slides, swings, and a merry-go-round, but there was also a wading pool filled with water. The middle of the pool got deep enough to float in, but it was mainly just to wade and splash around. The only thing is, there wasn't a fence around it, so dogs also enjoyed going in the water to cool off. At first, there was a fence, but it kept falling down, so they gave up. For most people, no fence was not a problem. Naturally, for me it was! Every time I went into that pool I got impetigo. Now impetigo was sores that broke out big time on my face and the only medicine for it was gentian violet which was shiny bright purple. I got it so often people thought it that that was my normal skin coloring! One time my mother took us to grandmas and left instructions that I was not to go to the pool. It got really hot, and my sister and cousins wanted to go into the water. My sister borrowed a swimsuit, and the three of them went across to the pool, and they were having so much fun. I had to sit across the street just watching. My grandmother felt sorry for me and told me to go ahead and go. We just wouldn't tell my mom. Two days later the jig was up, and I once again donned that lovely purple painted face!

Grandma's house was sort of fun. They had a garden with yummy things to pick to eat. They would send us to get peas, beans, strawberries or other berries and we ate more than we brought in. Grandma had a huge long mangled iron that was big enough to even iron sheets folded over. I used to like to watch her use it. She always looked for things to have us do while we were there and once she carved out boats made from Ivory soap and put stick sails on them. We then floated them in the bathtub.

One night we had a storm right at supper time, and the lights went out. Grandpa got a flashlight that had the light part turned outward from the main stem. He stuck it in his shirt collar and its light lit up the entire table. That was pretty funny but what was funnier is he just sat there with this sheepish grin... and ate the whole supper as if it were normal.

Grandpa liked to ride a bike around town to look for pictures to take with his camera. He never had a car in his entire life, so he got plenty of exercise. However, he eventually had a heart attack anyway...while pumping up his bicycle tire. From then he walked everywhere, and I mean even across the town. He was a good photographer and won many prizes and ribbons with his pictures. He even had one travel around the United States and Canada winning prizes and sweepstakes. He would enter pictures in the fair competitions and seemed to always be the one to get the first place every year. I rode my bicycle with him one day, and that's how I got my love for photography. However, it was also the one and only time I rode with him. We loved the time together, but he was very particular with just what pictures he would take. There was a house up on a hill that he wanted to take, but the clouds weren't in the right place. He wanted them to be over the house but were sitting off to the left. We sat and talked while waiting for the clouds to drift the way he wanted them. We waited two hours, and the clouds passed alright, but they went too fast, and he wasn't able to take the picture. In the entire time that we were gone, he took only one or two shots. I would have taken twenty rolls by then! He took black and white pictures, but when I got into photography, I took color. I liked it better, but in later years, I did begin to see the beauty of black and white.

My uncle built a soap box car out of an orange crate for us kids to go down the hill in. We started in front of grandma's house and sped down the hill. My uncle put a steering wheel on the cart making it, even more, challenging. It was really fun, but like the sleds during the winter in the park, the downhill was a whole lot more fun than pulling it back up the hill again.

Those orange crates were used for everything. They used it for the soap box car, but my dressing table at home was also made from them. It was made from two orange crates standing up on end with a large space between them and a board connecting them on top. It made a perfect desk/dressing table. The crates had two sections to them on each side, so there were four sections altogether. Mom made a cloth draped over a spring type rod to cover each opening.

At the bottom of my grandparent's hill where we were with the soap box car, there was a house whose Christmas yard ornament burned an impression into my mind at a very young age. The small house which was set back a ways off the street had a yard decoration that lit up saying, "Merry Xmas" I couldn't figure out why it said that as everyone knew the word was Christmas! What the heck was Xmas? I was told it was a shortcut to the word Christmas. That always bothered me no matter how old I got. Then years later I realized why it was that it bothered me. They had taken Christ out of Christmas...How can you do that? It is because of him we have the day. No wonder the meaning has gotten lost allowing Santa to take completely over by some. No wonder the materialistic, money spending and expensive gifts have overtaken to a point that for some, the holiday is depressing because they can't keep up or afford to get things for their family like others do. We looked for Santa too, but were happy with simple things, and we also kept alive the true meaning of Christmas.

Our church always had a little box of candy they gave out to each kid at Christmas. It had ribbon candy, peanut brittle, round red candy filled with jelly, and brown chocolate candy drops with white centers. The boxes were special to us when we were really young because we didn't have that much candy or any way of earning money to get it. I think of those chocolate candy drops a lot as those were the main ones we looked forward to. I was thrilled when I found they are still being made to this day, and you can buy them by themselves. I bought a bag of them not too long ago, but after they sat around for three weeks, I finally threw them away. For some reason, they sure don't taste the same way as the mind remembers them. I guess not all memories remain exactly as remembered. That candy sure wasn't.

One Sunday school lesson that never lost its message but has always stayed within my mind was one I got in the third grade. Again, why things like this make such an impression to be kept over years is beyond me, but a simple story about a football team putting football size emblems on the side of their jersey is one that I'll never forget. The team kept winning all the games because no one could tell who had the ball? They all put their hands in the position by the emblem on their shirt, and the other team had no idea where the ball was. They were cheating, but no one could do anything about it. Then another team decided to do the same thing and put footballs on their uniforms too. Needless to say, everyone was so confused because no one knew where the football was. The results ended up being that the original team lost points too when the other team had the ball, and they ended up finally losing a game. This resulted in both teams removing the emblems and stayed with just playing and using the ability they had to play and compete honestly. That formed a lesson for me to follow in life. Honesty and using ones one talent and ability to win things in life.

Chapter 5

Cedar Rapids, Iowa had a unique set up which resembled Paris, in that the municipal buildings all rest on an Island with a bridge connecting both sides of town. On the one side of town were the residential areas of the more average or poorer class of people, as well as Czech village. The southwest and northwest sides had two schools which had been the senior high until later when one central Senior high school was built to combine all the students from both areas into one building. That left both of the previous school's as being junior highs.

The island itself held the courthouse, chamber of commerce, coliseum, and jail. Across the bridge on the other southeast and northeast side were all the stores, two hospitals, and a variety of residences with also the more affluent people.

When I went to the courthouse each month for the child support check, I would cross the bridge to stop on the other side where there was a furniture type store that had a big statue of the RCA dog. That dog was an advertisement and the dog had its head cocked to one side as if listening to sounds or music... I loved that dog and wished it was mine. The people saw me so much they knew me and nicknamed me little Smulekoff, the name of the store. I loved dogs so much so when the real dog, RinTinTin (famous TV. dog) came to Quaker Oats Company we went to see him. First, the people had to go through the plant. We stood in line forever. After going through the whole plant which may have been interesting for the adults, but I just wanted to see RinTinTin we were finally almost there! I could hardly wait. I could almost see where he was. Then...an announcement came. It was time for RinTinTin to not only take a break but leave altogether! What? What

41

do you mean to leave? Did I walk all over the plant for nothing? Here it was again! It just added to my now growing list of other disappointments. The fake *Let's Pretend* and *It's Howdy Doody Time* radio show where they put up signs for you to follow when they wanted people to clap, whistle, scream, or yell, and there was nothing actually going on. We went to see Aunt Jemima, who was the negro lady on the pancake syrup bottle. She was a heavy set lady with a colorful outfit and the biggest smile and twinkle in her eyes. We could hardly wait to see her too, and we did actually get to where she supposedly was. However, there was some thin skinny woman that didn't look anything like Aunt Jemima. What a disappointment. Then there was also seeing Roy Rogers in person at a distance, with all his makeup making him look like a clown. Life sure was beginning not to look like it was all cracked up to be!

At least, there was a live animal which never disappointed me, and I knew I would see it anytime we went to the park across town. Of course, I again had to wait until the people I was with went through all the other bird and animal areas they wanted to see. My favorite was a three-legged bear, and I loved going to that park just to see that bear, even though there were also a couple others. You could look down into the pit from above or follow a sidewalk around to the bottom and see the bears on an even level. Apparently the bear had gotten into a fight with another bear at some time and had its leg chewed off. I don't know if the attraction for me was it was funny to see or that I felt sorry for it, but either way, it was special to me. Even that taught me a lesson. Even with a leg gone, he overcame his disability and life continued on, and he was not being held back.

Horses were also a draw of attention for me. We visited my aunt and uncle who at that time lived in a little town where a small type of carnival came one day. One of the few things they had to see and do were five ponies stationed in a circle with spoked poles reaching out toward each fastened horse. We waited in lines until we finally got our turn. We were really going to get to ride a horse. So exciting! We no sooner got on them and hadn't even made a complete circle when my cousin's pony started acting up, trying to get loose. That ended the rides for the night and another disappointment in life. The connecting factor with everything seems to be; you first have to wait in those confounded lines which then only end up only leading to disappointment.

I had better luck using my bike like a horse. I tied a rope from the framework up front, and back to under the seat filling in the area as being my horse's body. Had I had a boy's bike that would have already been done. I put ropes on each side of the handlebars to use as reigns. It was great because

I could go as fast as I wanted and pretended I was on a horse. The drawback was you couldn't steer that way so although it was okay when going straight, if you needed to straighten out or turn, you still had to grab the handlebars.

Playing cowboys and Indians or mimicking any visual story on television peaks the imagination of the people watching. Toni and I played like we were movie stars and used cut off onion tops out of the garden for our cigarettes, to pretend we were smoking like them. There were candy cigarettes, but we didn't always have them. Older boys played out their own version of the movies by playing chicken against each other with their cars. That was a heck of a lot more dangerous than onion tops for cigarettes. In fact, I think that may be where I learned to like onions. Because of movies stars like James Dean, the boys put cigarettes rolled up in their t-shirt sleeves like their star heroes. People always seem to get ideas from what they see in movies or on TV. Later in my adult years, I had a neighbor who had to stop their children from watching the three stooges because they kept bopping each other on the head. My son, on the other hand, was influenced by Kung Fu and we always had his foot in our face while doing a kick. (Before readers start pointing to everything that happens is because of programs and video games I will make a comment. There very well can be ties, yet not everyone is affected by the same thing the same way. One person may see some situation which happened as being the cause of a movie, television program or a video game, yet look at how many other thousands saw or played the same things without being influenced. You can't stop something because of one person. Should a pattern arise from say, a violent video game, or music enticing people to do violent crimes, then that has to be looked at? Some people are highly influenced, and that is where the parents, family and friends need to step in and make sure the subject is removed from their availability for at least a period of time. Some people actually identify with things and without the ability to rationalize things, carry the fantasy on from there to reality. When it ends or where it might go, depends on the individual and no one can know what is in a person's mind. Most people aren't influenced at all but merely enjoy the activity or programs they are watching.

One can't even say it's the violent things that are always the culprit. A case in point is the Boston Strangler who got his ideas from the Bob Cummings Comedy Show. In this day and age, they think gun control is an answer but those people who want to do something won't stop their violent ideas. They will either make or steal an illegal gun or use knives or blunt objects which are actually rampant with attacks in other countries. The very same day we went through our tragic shootings of children in Sandy Hook, there were twenty-two children stabbed in a China grade school. In fact, that was done by a doctor! Right there shows an answer for background checks not being able to keep someone from doing something. It would not have caught a doctor. No one can figure out what will affect a person nor how they will react. You can only keep your mind alert about your own thoughts and be aware of actions or conversations of others.

Keeping those thoughts in mind, I myself went through an incident where playing cowboys almost got me in trouble and did freak me out. My cousin and I were playing in the basement, and he captured me. He tied me up and took me to a tall storage cabinet where he stuffed me in. Well, actually I helped him by hopping there because he couldn't carry me. That part was okay to me as that's what cowboys do. However he then did another thing we'd seen them also do, but I wasn't in favor of. He stuffed a rag into my mouth. I was tied up so couldn't stop him and with a cloth in my mouth couldn't yell for help. Then, he left! He went upstairs to get something to drink or something and here I was in this closet tied up and gagged. Luckily he came back, and I kept pounding against the half-opened door, so he came back and took the rag out to see what I wanted. I wanted to be untied! Since that day I've had claustrophobia. I can still be in a small space if there is a way to get out, but don't lock me in or don't stop the electricity if I'm in an elevator. Elevators these days is a place where the walls are solid and so is the door with no way to get it opened or to climb to the ceiling to get out. No place to get immediate help and very quickly!

As a kid, I had many dreams of flying high above the trees and houses. I swore it wasn't a dream but that I actually was out of my body, and I was really flying. I could see the house tops from an angle I couldn't have imagined what they would look like at that age (or even now). I remember doing a body movement like the breast stroke in swimming to move forward through the air. I had these type of dreams many times with also experiencing a different kind or type of feeling. As an adult many, many years later, I got that same feeling although I wasn't flying as if in a dream yet it was sort of a similar situation. One night I woke up to discover I was out over my bedside stand and thinking I was falling out of my bed I jerked to put myself back in. The only thing was, I was already there. (Now I hope this doesn't freak people out and probably should save it for my future book of paranormal type happenings, but 1 for some reason feel this one should be included here too.) We never see ourselves from behind, and it was very strange to see myself still on the bed sleeping next to my husband. I had that same strange feeling I could identify with, from when I was flying in my dreams as a youth. This time however, I could actually feel like being two people at once! Both had their own thought process! It was as if I was still connected at the waist and had not actually separated totally. The top half moved back in with the rest of my body but very slowly and during the process I experienced the most fabulous feelings you could never imagine. There are no words in the English language that can come close to what I experienced. I remember thinking, "If this is what people feel like when they die, they have got it made." It is fantastic, and no one can ever tell me there is no body and soul because I experienced both, separate and as one! We may have been told about the spirit or soul at church, but we all have to take what they say on faith. I know for a fact! It was such a great feeling I tried many a night to do it again by saying "body separate, body separate' but to no avail. There was yet another time I felt this same inner peace. That was when I thought I was going to drown as a kid, and I completely lacked fear of any kind. That time there was a life and death issue involved yet the same peace was there. This time, it was merely an experience, and that is why I guess I'm being led to put it here.

Over the years many doctors have tried saying when people claim they were out of their body during an operation that they've been told it was just the anesthetic. Well, folks. I wasn't sick nor was I under anesthetic! (I had something happen one more time in my life and although I won't go into that now. The one thing they all have in common is, it seems that when a person is going through a life-threatening situation, even if the body itself seems to be struggling or in great pain, the other half, the spirit or soul, feels nothing, so in reality neither does the person. The pain comes back when the body itself then becomes dominant. So anyone who has lost a loved one in any way from a drowning or accident or even murder, rest your thoughts they did not suffer. You can test this out yourself if you know anyone who has been in a horrible accident or trauma of some kind. They will tell you they don't remember anything until they 'woke' up. They may be in pain right then because they are back in the body but at the time of the incident and at the scene they remember nothing. It wasn't from an anesthetic for they didn't have anything yet. Some will say they were unconscious, but I sure wasn't. I have never feared death ever since. (Oh, just for reference. The King James Bible does also mention an out of body experience in 2 Corinthians 12:2-4)

Sometimes our memories pop up from something we never gave a second thought about at the time of their influence. One of those things was the phone booth. Phone booths were in common places on many corners, by businesses or wherever it was thought they might be needed. They were taller than the people but just wide enough to stand in with having three sides of solid glass walls and a folding glass door on the fourth to close behind you when you went in. That was both for privacy, or to block out outside noise. There was a small shelf under the phone with the phone itself being about two foot tall by ten-inch wide metal telephone which had a dial and three coin slots above it. You put in either a nickel, dime or quarter depending what the call called for. The great movie character Superman used the telephone booth to step into as he went in as Clark Kent dressed in a suit and mysteriously turn into Superman with the bright Superman outfit and gained power as he flew out of the telephone booth to fly off to stop some tragedy somewhere. Many people got rescued just because Clark Kent had a place to change and gain power.

Ya I know, there are cell phones now and you carry them with you and you can talk whenever you want without needing coins...but just how in the heck could Superman change in your phone. You've lost the power!

There are other things of the times gone by which people don't do today, or probably don't even know about. It's called darning socks. When we got a hole in our socks they were never thrown away. A six to eight inch wooden handle with a rounded top was used to place socks with holes over. There was something called "darning thread" where the thread was threaded through a big needle and you went from one side of the hole to the other, going back and forth until the entire hole was covered up. It didn't feel that bad to walk on it but the socks were aggravating when they kept creeping down into your shoes. You ended up with no cuffs at all and half the sock down inside which usually happened when you were wearing socks you were outgrowing because you didn't have others to wear.

My mother had a wooden music box in the shape of a spinet piano. I loved that piano and always wanted her to play it but was told only at special times. It was sitting there up on the shelf and could have been easily taken down when she wasn't home, but I knew I'd better not do it because I'd probably drop it and then I'd be in real trouble. I think it was fairly old even then, and is a whole lot older as it is sitting on the shelf in my home now...

Not many of the kids had a watch for a long time but when there were watches we had a stem just like there is today but had to be pulled out to not only set the time but in our day we had to wind the stem back and forth until it was tight so the watch would run in order to tell time. It had to be wound every day, and it was common to see people holding the watch up to their ear to see if it was ticking because it sure had stopped telling time. The watch left the ear and went immediately to be wound again because they had forgotten to do it.

We had a Jewel Tea truck come once a month. They had a catalog to look through for things you could buy. Most of which were things that we couldn't afford. They had foods, household products, toys, and their own pattern of dishes. The dishes were cream colored with a gold and brown design. Believe it or not, you can still find them in antique stores today and when I walk through I can spot that design a mile away!

There were also green S&H stamps people would get with the purchase of a variety of things. Supermarkets, department stores, and gasoline stations gave stamps in denominations of one, ten and fifty points. People got stamp books and tore off the perforated stamps to place in the correct place within the book. They had gummed backing to be able to stick easily. Each book had 24 pages and had 50 points per page or 1200 points per book. The stamps could be exchanged for things like household goods or other things from their catalog. Each item itself had a number of stamps you needed to purchase it. You could buy something that took only one book or save up books until you had enough to get what you wanted. (You may be able to experience this yourself as possibly in 2015 as it might be starting up again in some form.)

A real back in time scene was with the home-delivered milk. The milk man came right to the house and delivered milk in glass milk bottles. They were placed inside a small square box by the door. The bottles had thin round lids made of cardboard. You needed to make sure you weren't to be gone long after he delivered the milk, because if the milk stayed in the heat too long, it would spoil, yet in the winter if it was left out too long the lids would pop off and tilt sideways making the milk freeze into icy substance.

Sundays were a special time as the radio had a person who would read the newspaper comics to us. We would get the newspaper as soon as it came and spread the comic section out on the floor before the radio. We followed the pictures as he read. The Sunday paper also had paper dolls with clothes that could all be cut out, to play with. There were tabs on the clothes so they could fold back over the dolls to stay on. Those dolls were sort of flimsy with being newspaper substance, but there were other paper dolls you could buy which were sturdier, and even some were later made of cardboard so you could stand them up on their own in their design stand. Those paper dolls were a favorite pass time. It was imagination time at its fullest to get them to talk to one another and do things. We didn't just play with them alone, but other kids would bring their dolls and we all joined to carry on conversations and make our dolls do things. There are so many children these days who don't even know how to do that sort of thing.

There are far too many others who think it stupid! In our world, we could be anyone we wanted to be. We could be a movie star, get into a cowboy shootout, be a boat captain, or fly off to rescue someone all on the same day. With imagination, the sky is the limit.

Another item of our times but yet can be found even today, although probably not as popular now because of the computer world, was the View-Master Reels. The viewer was similar to binoculars but had a slit on top where round thin cardboard reels go. The reels had small films going around the entire edge of the reel. When you looked inside the viewer, you would see the pictures against a thick film covering over the viewer ends. There is a lever to click to advance to the next picture. I still have my reels from my childhood which now are antiques and can't be bought. I have Roy Rogers, Gene Autry, Tarzan, cartoon characters and many more. They still bring back memories of a time long cherished. The problem with having all these treasures with so much history from the "good ol' days" is the newer generations don't treasure them and when I die so will those items. It's sad because they still are useful and work as they always have from back in time.

The slinky was referred to at various places throughout the book, but if you don't know what a slinky is or what to do with them, a short lesson might be handy. They can still be purchased today, but most have been reduced to plastic and don't work as well. We had a two story house so had a long set of stairs which was perfect to set the wired spring like a slinky down and then flip half of it onto the next step. From there it does its own thing and walks down the rest of the steps by itself. Just putting it in each hand then lifting up one hand and then the other shifts the spring back and forth giving sort of mesmerizing or hypnotizing effect. None of our things were expensive but gave hours of fun over and over again.

Two things referred to at various places in the book but really never addressed are mowing the grass and our coal bin. Our heat was the baseball sized and smaller, chunks of black coal which were delivered by truck and sent down the opened basement window through a chute to the coal bin area in the corner. We had to open the heavy metal furnace door and shovel the coal into the flames billowing up inside and feeling the heat blowing out to our face and arms. The other thing I need to describe for those who didn't live in those times is the issue of the lawn mower. It was nothing like the power mowers you might walk behind these days. The power of our mowers was our own strength. Our mower had a long handle with a cross-bar at the top and at the other end were two wheels with a couple of cutting blades going from wheel to wheel and only a few rods to encase the area, at least, a little. You had to push the mower to get the blades to turn and cut the grass. You didn't move...neither did the mower...neither did the grass get cut. It was hard work, and arms and back plus legs and feet got a workout.

Chapter 6

My girlfriend came to our house every Sunday for lunch, and I went to hers for supper. When it was starting to get dusk I had to go home, so Toni walked me part way to make sure the boogie man didn't get me. We walked up the alley and when we were the half way we turned and ran as fast as we could to our respective houses. When we got home, we called each other to make sure the other had made it okay! It seems darkness carries a sort of stigma with it.

There were crazy memories that took place as close as straight across the street. One day it was raining "pitchforks and hammer handles" (an expression from those days) and we could not go out to play. That is...until we looked across the street and discovered it wasn't raining at all over there. In fact, the sun was shining. So we went across the street to play.

My mother was always telling me she thought I was put together backward. When it was snowing and cold, I did not want a hat on my head and when it was hot outside I wanted long sleeves or a jacket. She didn't want me scared of all doctors, but she wanted to break me of being so contrary, so she told me there was one certain doctor in Iowa City who specialized in taking people apart and putting them back together the right way. (I think she must have done too many jigsaw puzzles. Now she thought I was one!) Iowa City was a medical specialty center. Her wanting me to go there really didn't faze me as she never made any steps in that direction, so I continued doing my thing. That is until one day when we were across the street talking with the girl who asked my sister if she had heard that morning's news. It was on the radio that morning and was about a doctor in Iowa City who did an operation and left a sponge in the guy, so they had to open him up again to take it out! That actually happened, and that was enough to make me not to want any doctor touching my body so to leave something inside. So from that day forward I dressed according to my mother's wishes, but yet inside I was not happy. When I was on my own later in life, I reverted back to my ways. I usually don't have a hat on in the winter, (At times there are exceptions.), and when it's hot, you just may see me in long pants rather than shorts and even a long sleeve over a shirt. At night in the summer I will cover up with a blanket and my husband even says, "How can you stand a cover? It's hot outside!" (I married my mother?)

One day there was a man who was on the way to the slaughter house with a cow and had it tied up in the back of his pickup truck. He had stopped across the street for a minute first to see the people. I thought it would be fun to sound like a cow, so I mooed very loudly. I guess I was a pretty good imitator as that darn cow got riled up and started kicking and bouncing back and forth trying to get out. Everyone from their house ran out to settle it down; the man drove away...and I got into trouble...again!

Geez, no matter what, I ended up being the culprit. One day my sister, who was five years older, was constantly picking on me. We were in the front yard, and my mother was sitting on the porch. I yelled to my mother "Mom, Sandy's picking on me!" My mother's answer was "Fight your own battles". (What? I'm smaller and five years younger, but yet mom wasn't going to stop her?) So, I did what she told me to do. I fought my own battle! I went after her and chased Sandy around the house. On the way around the house, the second time Sandy yelled "MOM!", and guess what? My mother said, "Pauline leave your sister alone!" What? What the heck was that? She just told me to "fight your own battle." Now that I did what she said, I was supposed to leave her alone? (Who was it that was put together backward?)

Another day my mother looked outside to see my sister and I standing face to face with our mouths wide open. She asked, "What are you two doing?" I said, "Measuring our mouths. She called me a big mouth, and I said her mouth is bigger than mine, so we are checking." My mother shook her head and walked away. The answer was never determined but from that day forward we referred back to that day and still called each other big mouth. Even as adults, when we talked over the phone one of us would end the conversation with "YOUR mouth is bigger than mine!" and hang up. (For the record...her mouth was bigger!)

My mother had flowers and ferns growing by the side of the house and would send us out from time to time to pull weeds. When she told me to go out and pull them, I informed her "I can't tell a flower from a weed!" She said, "The weeds are the tall ones!"

Sparks

One time I took seven jigsaw puzzles apart at the same time and the pieces were totally mixed up. I tried putting them together, but I was having a real problem and got so frustrated I broke out into a sweat. I wanted to go outside, but my mother informed me I couldn't go out until I put the puzzles together first because I knew better than to do what I did. (I think maybe she just might have told me not to take them apart at the same time!) I thought I was going to be there until I died...or she did, so I could get away. My sister came to my rescue and told me to go outside, and she would put them together. (For someone with a "big mouth" she did have a big heart too!)

Speaking of big mouth, one time she talked back to my mother! You didn't talk back to any adult let alone our mother. My mother started toward my sister, and as Sandy was backing up to get away, she backed up and fell into a bushel basket of tomatoes. What a mess! (But it was also pretty funny! Especially since my sister was one of those prim and proper type of dressing.)

We had red ants in our kitchen cabinets. We did everything to try to get rid of those things. We put cucumber peelings which were supposed to work, as well as many other supposed remedies, but nothing worked. Then we used one of the ideas of putting a pop bottle cap filled with coke on the shelf. The ants would drink the mixture and apparently end up blowing up their stomachs. They were horrible to get rid of, but it finally worked. If we fixed a peanut butter sandwich and laid it on the cupboard for a second, we soon discovered the peanut butter was crawling with movement. The ants had gotten into the peanut butter which we had not been able to see before because they were the same color.

My sister and I had a little tea set and a kid's small table. We had tiny dishes and silverware. We would sit at our table with our pretend food or get a few things like the ant infested peanut butter sandwich. My dad thought he'd add to the tea party and poured some of his coffee into our tiny coffee cups. At first, we thought we were really getting something great, but that coffee was so bad it has kept me from drinking coffee to this day! In fact, the way he made coffee then and actually for the rest of his life was so bad my husband in later years couldn't stand it. Dad just kept adding more coffee grounds along with more water when the liquid got down. He never got rid of the previous grounds! Coffee smells good, but I'm satisfied just smelling it!

We had fish for supper quite a lot and when we did we had to have a stack of bread on the table. That was there in case you got a fish bone caught in your throat. That fish was full of bones, and we'd strip the entire backbone out first and then any single bones we could see, but there were always ones we'd not see, and usually you'd feel those sticking you with a mouthful, and you could pick it out, but sometimes one would be swallowed. The bread would help it go on down without being stuck. I hated fish night!

My sister might have shown her helpful side when she put my seven puzzles together for me, but there were other times she wasn't always helpful. With mom at work, we had to fix our own brown bag lunch to take to school. We were both in grade school and with getting ourselves ready for school by ourselves sometimes we were running late so was in a hurry. One day I wanted to take a hardboiled egg, but she wouldn't fix it for me. She just said, "Put it in a pan of water for five minutes." She didn't say after it boiled! At lunch time, I cracked it open and all this yellow liquid yolk spilled out and all over the table. Every kid ran as fast as we could to get outside leaving the mess for the kitchen people to clean up and to wonder where it came from. I never took another hardboiled egg!

When we were walking to school one day, I had my foot sliding along in the gutter between the grass and the sidewalk. The leaves were spilling onto the sidewalk, and I looked down there was a dirty dollar bill. My sister told me to throw that dirty thing away, but I thrust it into my coat pocket instead. That night I retrieved it from my pocket and asked my mother, "Is this dirty old thing worth anything?" She told me to bring her any one of those dirty old things I could ever find, and she gave me a clean one! (And my sister said it wasn't worth anything. She might be older, but she wasn't as smart as she thought!)

In the fifth grade, the principle of the school chose me to come to be the one to be assigned to her office and ring the buzzers when it was time for the older kids to change classes, go to lunch, recess, or tell them school was over. Her office had a wool rug with a small eight-inch border of wood around its outside edge. If you stood on the wool rug when pushing the buzzers, you got shocked. I had to stand with my feet sideways in the small wooded area to ring the buzzers without having my fingernails shooting sparks. Eventually, Miss Poggie also had me come to answer the phone when she was going to be gone for a while. I felt very important. Believe it or not, my first introduction for giving first aid came at that time too. When she wasn't there, and a child got hurt on the playground, they came into the office. I ended up cleaning wounds and putting band aids on. In fact, I even removed a sliver or two. (Another story with a sliver, but these were tiny things).The one thing I did not do was use the paddle. That was strictly for the principal. If a kid needed to be reprimanded the teachers weren't even allowed to spank but was rather sent to the principal's office where the wooden paddle was used. She didn't have the frustration the Teachers would have had because the disobedience happened with them so when the principal did the discipline, it wasn't overdone.

One day I was in the office and became the subject of a situation. Usually, people, parent or anyone, had to go the office if they needed to see a student for any reason, to get principals permission, before they were allowed to see them. Then the meeting was done in the office with the principle present. Boy did my situation miss all of that! The principal wasn't there while I was manning the office one day so couldn't give permission for anything. Except...I was the one the detectives wanted to see! That was scary! We were law abiding people and when a policeman came to see someone it meant they were in deep trouble! Here were even scarier people. Detectives! I would have had no idea what they were even talking about when they started asking me questions if it hadn't been for a conversation I had just that morning while walking to school with a girl who walked to school with me most the time. Luckily she had just told me about the incident they were there about. I always walked to school with the same kids but two days before they were late, so I had gone on. Apparently another boy who walked with us every once in a while had joined them that day. He pulled the fire alarm on a light pole at a corner and then actually waited for the fire trucks to arrive. Then he told them I had done it. I don't know why he did that, and I really didn't know the girls last name, to be able to tell them, who would be my proof that I didn't do it. I only knew her first name, and she wasn't in my class. I knew someone who did know her' so I got them to go to the playground to get her since the kids were at recess at the time. They found her, and I was thankful 'that was over. She told them exactly what she'd told me.

Well that night when I was home I told my mother about it, and she was upset they'd talked to me, and even the other girl, without an adult there but was glad everything was over. Then someone knocked at the door! It was those same detectives. I was scared all over again. I hadn't done a thing yet now they were even coming to the house. Actually, they'd just come to inform my mother of the incident and to tell us the kid had confessed to pulling the alarm so wanted my mom to know. That scare may have been my first lesson in what happens if you break the law, and I decided right then and there I never wanted to ever go through something like that ever again, and it kept me from ever breaking the law. If I was that scared when I was innocent what would it be if like if a person was guilty! I never walked to school with that kid again.

Something which happens all over the country in areas with winters snow and cold weather is some person who knows what will happen but dares or double dares a kid anyway, to put their tongue on an outdoor metal object in the winter. Anyone who has seen *A Chrismas Story* at Christmas time knows of what I speak. There's always someone who falls for it, and then someone has to rescue the person with the tongue stuck to the metal. One time a little girl at church just did it on her own as she was walking down the steps to the basement entrance. No one told her to do it, but no one told her not to either. When she got her lips stuck, she pulled back completely and left her entire lips on the rail and had to be taken to the hospital.

Someone had taken a picture of my parents with my sister and me which I found while going through some old things. If we weren't the picture, perfect family! We looked like a family in need of a handout. My sister's eyes were dark circles looking like a raccoon or a starving refugee, and I stood there in my coveralls with a brother's service hat on and the meanest scowl like a street gang fighter. I think my sister was deficient in some kind of vitamin or mineral because besides the look (which we didn't notice at the time) she used to take her apples or oranges down to the basements coal bin and rub them in it before she'd eat them. Maybe she, on some level of being, knew that's what she needed, but I just thought she was weird! (And she was the straight A student! Maybe that's the secret to brain power...and here I was, eating normal food!)

We had two female cats who were constantly chasing each other all over the house, over the furniture, around the room, and up the curtains. Mom decided they needed to be "fixed" (spayed) so they not only wouldn't have offspring, but maybe the operation would also calm them down.

Well, they had it...and it didn't. They were back home with a huge bandage around their stomachs and were back to chasing each other again. Mom had gone to work, and we kids were told to check on the cats in the basement before we left for school. When we went down the steps, not only were the cats chasing each other around, but one of the cat's bandage was coming off leaving a huge gross looking gaping hole making the cat looking like it was coming apart. We called mom at work, and she told us to bring the cat and bandage to her at work on our way to school. So here we were on our way to school, walking and holding the cat's insides together. My mother's job was sort of on the way so left it with her. You may have heard the stories where older people tell the younger generation about how soft they are because in their day they remember walking miles through a foot of snow just to get to school. Well, how many have you ever heard that they walked to school holding a cat's insides together?

My mother not only worked, made things for me to sell, but also took in washings and had a job to address envelopes for a company. She did all this so to make ends meet and not to have to go on welfare. (Another term started back in time.) Although she could have gotten help through the government because of being divorced with small children, she just would never take it. She was too proud to get a hand out if she could do something to make it on her own. The thing is, my sister and I did a lot of the work with the envelopes. My sister did a lot of the typing, and I had to put the envelopes in alphabetical order. I was still in grade school but learned how to get them in alphabetical order as to the first letter of the state but if there were names that had to be sorted beyond that I had trouble.

My dad had to pay child support, but mom could never count on the check to be there. Sometimes it was and sometimes it wasn't. In those days, a judge decided if you could even get a divorce and then when it was granted the child support check went to the courthouse where we went to pick it up. For any of you reading this who pay or receive child support, look at this. My dad had to pay $25 a month for us kids. $10 for my sister who had been from a previous marriage, so a different father to begin with, but he had adopted her, and $15 for me because I was his. I was the one who always went downtown to get the check from the Courthouse while my mother was working. You have to keep in mind my parents divorced when I was seven, so I went downtown by myself, either by bus, riding my bike or sometimes even walking, to get the check from there. I always wore either the sailor hat or army cap my brothers had given to me, and I always seemed to get the same clerk at the counter to give me the check. He had been in the service, and whenever I came in he saluted me! I liked that, and it got to the point if I walked in and another clerk might have started to wait on me he would rush forward and say, "I'll get her." I felt special and important. I called him Sargent. All of a sudden after a couple years he seemed to be or get, busy the minute I came in and wouldn't even look my way. I even mentioned it to my mother. A few months later we went to the fairgrounds for some kind of show, and there on the field was the man I'd called 'Sarg,' helping put up stage stuff. I pointed him out to mom but still wondered what I'd done that he wouldn't take care of me anymore. Another lesson learned, for I was to discover when things happen, and you think you did something wrong, that it actually might have nothing to do with you. Some people never learn why, but I was soon to find out. Shortly after the fairgrounds incident, the newspaper came out with headlines of a man from the courthouse being arrested for embezzlement. There in the picture was Sarg. His wife was very sick, and the doctor bills were mounting up, so that's when he started embezzling. He apparently felt guilty and didn't want to have me be a part of the world he wasn't proud of. (Little did I know then but I was to be with a couple other embezzlers throughout my lifetime).

I didn't mention the circumstances of my parent's divorce. We used to sit on the porch to watch for dad coming home. On paydays, he came later and stopped at a tavern to drink. When we'd see him staggering down the street, my mother sent us to bed saying we could see him in the morning, but we knew a fight was to ensue. One night I was in the living room when my dad (sober) told my mother he wanted a divorce. He had another woman. I can tell you exactly where I was and where she was to this day, even though it didn't really seem to affect me or cause any outward trauma or even inward thoughts. It just 'was'. I actually was pretty lucky with my parent's divorce, because we didn't have to choose which parent we wanted to go with. It was automatically done for us. The courts usually had the kids go with the mother. I had a friend with my same first name whose parents were also getting a divorce at the very same time, but the kids had to choose which parent they wanted to live with. That was horrible because either way they had to hurt one of the parents. It wasn't like they were abused by one so they would want to go with the other. The matter was even worse as the one parent had been married before and brought the one very small child into the marriage so that child only knew the parent as their own and was legally adopted by the other. So here were two boys and a girl who had to decide where they would go, and besides having to hurt one of the parents the kids could be separated from each other if they divided up by their decision. My girlfriend was a mess over the ordeal, and I've often wondered if it affected her whole life! (I didn't tell you all my memories would be happy ones).

The basement in our house was a story all its own. My mother did canning so we would keep food in a fruit cellar for the winter months. We kids helped with the canning by washing the how many glass mason fruit jars it took. We helped fill the jars with either the cucumber that would become either sweet or dill pickles. We grew both the cucumbers in a garden and the dill weed next to the house. The fruit was bought at a store. After the product was inside the jars a rubber ring was placed over the mouth of a jar and then the flat lid sealed. I didn't mind putting the finished jars into the back room fruit cellar with everyone being with me in the basement, but in the following months when I was sent to retrieve a jar, that was a different story. I would go down the steps very slowly with my eyes as wide open as they could go, looking out for any movement there might be from a 'boogie man'. I was sure there was. I was going to have to pass the huge furnace in the basement to get to the fruit cellar, and I just knew someone was hiding behind it in the shadows. It would take all I had to finally take that last step down and run like crazy to get to the fruit cellar and turn on the light. Whew! I was safe! Now don't ask me why I thought I was safe just because I made it to the fruit cellar without someone grabbing me because a common sensed person would know they could have just followed me in there. Luckily I apparently didn't have common sense because I thought I was safe, but now that I think about it...don't take me back there because now I don't know what I'd do!

My sister and I had to go downstairs to shovel coal into the furnace to keep the house warm, but I guess with us together we felt safer, or the 'boogey man' had to stay behind the furnace by the fruit cellar! Boy, looking at it from an adult standpoint sure makes a difference. Not a difference of re-alizing how silly it was but rather that "if someone had been there they could have followed me in" and thinking about it now, gets my blood pumping!

The basement was known for another thing. Sometimes it flooded, but then other people in the neighborhood also had the same issue at the same time. When the city sewers would back up the water came into our homes. It was sort of neat to go down the stairs to see a 'swimming pool' meet you, but unfortunately, it was water you wouldn't want to swim in. I liked sitting on the steps watching the flooded basement. I didn't have to go anywhere but on the steps so I was safe. (Guess I figured the "boogie man" couldn't wade or swim from behind the furnace either!)

One time as I sat there watching the basement 'swimming pool' I had taken a drink with me which was in a thick blue plastic glass. (That's how traumatic it was. I can still picture that glass) When I finished what was inside I took the glass and discovered that if I put it around my mouth and sucked on it, it would stick to me. That was pretty neat. I'd unstick it and then do it again. Then when I went upstairs, I passed a mirror. "Oh no!" I had the biggest blood mark there from sucking the glass. I thought I was in trouble, but I had to figure out how to get rid of it. I innocently went to mom and said, "Mom, look at my mouth." She freaked out and asked, "What did you do?" I innocently told her "nothing." Well, there is always a way to get the truth and the words "We need to call and get you into the doc-tor's office right away!" Oh, then I remembered. "Unless it's from this plas-tic glass I sucked in." She was so relieved that I didn't get into trouble, and I was relieved that I didn't have to go to the doctor, so we were both happy! I've seen kids doing that very thing even today, and that memory comes back loud and clear. Depending on whether it's a paper cup they are doing it with or plastic or glass I have warned them what can happen.

I have mentioned being a Roy Rogers fan and anything along that line was for me. Most the kids had doll houses, which I also had, but I had a farm and ranch set that when all set up took up our whole dining room. I would play with that by the hour. There were cowboys with lassos and with horses that were running, standing still and even bucking. Farm wagons, tractors, and even chuck wagons graced the scene. There was a barn with bales of hay and chickens and feeding troughs. It was awesome. Kids today sit with things like iPod, iPads, smartphones, etc. to entertain them, but the things we did took ingenuity and used one's imagination.

That brings me to another thing. We had a large tall radio sitting on the floor in our living room. We would sit around it at night listening to stories that made you use your imagination as to what was going on. Unlike television that does everything for you, you had to listen and picture in your own mind what was happening. We had programs like *Amos and Andy, Lone Ranger; The Shadow Knows/Inner Sanctum, Jack Benny*. Tom Mix, Abbott and Costello, Arthur Godfrey, Hopalong Cassidy, and Bob Hope for entertainment along with musicals, mysteries, quiz programs, sports, dramas, soap operas, and news. With the war going on there were times people seemed to be glued to the radios for any new updates. So both the days and clear up to bedtime were full days filled with active endeavors of work play and entertainment. There was always something going on.

I could never figure out how those people got into that small radio. I actually tried peeking through the sides where I could see light streaming through, expecting to see tiny little people inside on a stage. I wondered how they got them so small. (I didn't say I was the brightest kid on the block! In recent years, there was the movie, *Honey, I Shrunk the Kids* that would have fit my scenario and thinking completely back then.) However I also believed the action was going on somewhere, but we just couldn't see it. We had to use our own imagination as to what was really taking place. Boy was that not only wrong but very disappointing! The *Let's Pretend* or the *Howdy Doody Show* was coming out of a downtown studio. I was excited when I actually got a chance to go see it live. There were kids packed in seats in this big room and a stage with bright lights. A man came out who said he would be holding up signs and when he did he wanted us to do what it said. It might say clap or yell or boo. Whatever it said to do we were to do. The man we heard on the radio came out, and we all followed the cue cards and clapped and yelled. He didn't look anything like what we thought he would. He sat down on a high stool, and I waited for the neat stuff to start. It didn't. What we were seeing was it! None of the stuff we had always pictured in our mind of what was happening happened. It was all in our imagination. There was nothing there except for background sounds, the guy talking and with us following cue cards. What a bummer!

I was disillusioned again when my hero Roy Rogers and his wife Dale Evens came into town and was going to be at the Coliseum. We didn't have money to be able to go see them, but we went down to see if we could catch a glimpse of them coming in the doors. Someone told us they were already in the basement and would be going on stage from there, so we wouldn't be seeing them. We raced to the basement windows, and they had put paper over them so we couldn't see. There was one that didn't quite cover so I peered through the tear and there they were. Gross! They were so painted up with makeup they looked more like clowns not what we ever saw in movies. It was explained they had to use a lot of makeup because of stage lighting but to me, it was a turn-off. I'd follow him in movies and not want to see the real thing, which to me was fake! Boy, can a lot of lesson for life be gleaned during experiencing life as it comes, in the real world?

Although we didn't have the crimes of youth like we have today, we weren't completely innocent. Even I used to steal lilacs from someone's bush that hung over a fence in an alley and take them to school to my favorite teacher. I didn't count it as stealing because it wasn't the ones in the people's yard but just out in the alley. Then there were also the apples on a neighbor's tree. They were so red and delicious looking and all us kids would run in and grab one to eat. The people didn't pick them all, and there were so many they even fell onto the ground. That was my way of thinking, and we actually called it 'swiping' instead of stealing. It wasn't things anyone wanted but...they still were theirs. The owners eventually told us we could take as many as we wanted so we still went to get some but trying to do it without being seen had been half the fun. I never took anything else and would never steal something just because I couldn't afford it but wanted it. I did do a lot of odd jobs and saved up to get what I wanted... Of course, there were things we would never be able to get anyway, but we had to learn that was life and be satisfied with what we had. Our age went through the "why can't we have it, so and so has it?" It was called "keep up with the Joneses." We learned that not everyone can have everything they want. We also found that people who had some of those things weren't any happier than we were, so 'things' weren't really the reason for happiness. There has been a millionaire who has committed suicide even though they had anything they ever have wanted. One such news article I read was the rich man saying he had everything, did everything he ever wanted and went everywhere and yet wasn't happy. He committed suicide. Money isn't everything in life!

Chapter 7

If you haven't figured out yet how different things are now as compared to when we who grew up with the freedom, of the "good ol' days," just to be, learning life's lessons from experiences where we gained self-esteem, you probably won't see it even as I continue to reminisce. By using our ingenuity and God given talents, we overcame, thrived, and at times even excelled. That's exactly why our generation cringes at the ridiculous things the government tries cramming down people's throats that supposedly are bettering their lives but, in reality, are taking away their freedoms as well as suppressing their chance to gain self-esteem.

Picture in your mind, going to the dentist by yourself at the age of eight or nine. That involved taking a bus to town and walking through town to the maybe eight-floor tall building where the dentist's office was. I hated the dentist and took the steps up the five floors to his office rather than taking the elevator which would have gotten me there faster. The previous night I had already drawn the dentist and his secretary on a chalkboard, and then crossed their faces out with the chalk, like getting revenge on them. I was now on the fifth floor of the building heading toward their office. As I passed by some opened windows that looked down into an open type courtyard below but actually was the first floor covered roof, I noticed all I could see was nothing but a huge square of the entire buildings walls with opened windows on every side looking downward to the floors below through opened space. I never could figure out why it was built that way nor why they left the windows open. It wasn't like the opened windows let in fresh air as it was an inside area and there was also a roof. Many a time I actually gave the thought that if I jumped, I wouldn't have to go to the dentist, but then I thought of everything

I could do after the dentist was over that I would never get to do ever again if I jumped, so begrudgingly I went inside the dentist office.

They had a little kids table sitting in a corner area where they could sit to color or look at books while their parents were getting their teeth done or the kids waiting for their turn to go in. I hated the sound of the dentist drill as much as having anything actually done. If they got rid of that sound, maybe there wouldn't be so many negative thoughts of dentists.

When I was through, I skipped down the hall and went right passed those opened windows without giving them another thought but instead going directly to the elevator. I didn't mind getting down quick, now that the dentist was over for another year. (You have to realize part of my dislike for dentists, which still resides to this day, has come from experiences during various visits. One time while having had my teeth drilled and my teeth being extra hard, the drill slipped off the tooth and drilled my gum. Then was the time they couldn't get a wisdom tooth out because a nerve was wrapped around the gum three times so had to take it out in three pieces. Moving forward in time I had my jaw dislocated and another time almost drown in my own saliva from the chair being tilted back too far. I also had a piece of machine breakdown inside my mouth, so the process had to stop. "I think back to those windows a lot"!) I'd like to say that these were the source of my fear of going to the dentist when I was little, but actually, all those things happened at various times of my life growing up from pre-teen to adulthood!

When we went to the movies, we could choose which one we wanted to see, but first, it had to be okayed by my mom. The newspaper had the movie listings and the reviews given for each by the Catholic Church. We weren't Catholic, but mom knew the movies would be okay for us to see if the church said so. She sort of went by their rating but actually movies back when we were in grade school weren't that bad anyway. The Catholic Church might even give a poor rating if the 'married' couple in the movie slept in the same bed rather than twin ones, so the ratings weren't always meaningful.

Mom said we could go see *The Little Rascals* as that group of kids were pretty entertaining. How negative could a bunch of young kids be anyway, when doing things together even if they did get into mischief?

Well, this movie was so scary for me, that I had nightmares for months! Where in the heck was the movie reviews for this one? They will say you shouldn't see a movie because a husband and wife went to bed one night and slept in the same bed but they didn't care a little kid got swallowed up by a wall! Not just once in the movie, like the couple going to bed and saying good-night with then the immediate next second they were waking up in the morning, but many times in the movie one of *The Little Rascal* kids would disappear. Did they say "Don't see this movie?" NO!

The kids went into a castle, and as they were exploring it, they walked close together through the room peering wide-eyed around, afraid of what could be there. One kid after another decided to sit down to rest for a minute on this big, huge throne chair which was against the one wall. The others were busy looking around the spacious room so didn't see that poor kid get flipped around and sent behind a revolving wall. While the group was wondering what happened to their friend another decided to sit down to figure it out. The chair spun around into the wall and dumped that kid on the other side before spinning back again without them, leaving again only an empty chair. One by one, the kids disappeared leaving the others, scared and petrified wide-eyed behind. That scared the heck out of me, and I had nightmares for months. In fact, when I think about it even now I can almost bring those reactions back.

Why that scared me, I have no idea. I'd seen some really scary movies which never fazed me and, in fact, I still like scary movies. I can always remember the main plots of various movies and may recall one of the scary parts but it is always with words but never holding the same emotion or fear like when seeing it. Yet I can still 'see' the movie within my mind, of the Little Rascals Castle, and the big lobby with that big chair on the left wall and the petrified expressions on those kid's faces. My heart verifies it. (Maybe that's another thing for my 'to do list' before I die. See if I can find that movie and watch it again. I can't remember anything else about that movie but those kids disappearing behind the wall. It might be interesting to see what the whole movie was!)

I've had other movies which have affected me profoundly from my youth and of which I can also still remember, but their emotion wasn't fear. The movie *So Dear To My Heart* was about a boy who was raising a black sheep for the fair and it had to go up against all the white sheep for judging. That left me with sympathetic and caring for others emotions. I felt sorry for that boy who had worked so hard to raise his sheep but because it wasn't the same as the others, so he was being ridiculed. One of the movie scenes had a ladder coming down from the ceiling where the little boy's bedroom was. It retracted back into the ceiling when not in use. I liked that so well I had always wanted one. In later years my son had one of those in his barn leading to a play area for his kids upstairs. Seeing that brought the memory of that movie to my mind, for it was "So dear to my heart!"

Another story I was affected by was "The Boy with the Green Hair." I felt so sorry for the boy afflicted with an issue of having green hair and everyone either shunned him or taunted and laughed at him. It was sort of the same type of message from the "So Dear to my Heart" movie, and I vowed that I would never be like the people in that story but would be kind to others no matter what their differences.

A very favorite storybook of mine was "Little Black Sambo." Over the years this book has been unjustly ridiculed, protested and even at one point in the United States, taken off the market. The book has been pointed to as being racial and insensitive against blacks. As a kid, having it read to me and later reading it on my own, it had nothing bad against black people. Instead, it was a pretty neat story about this boy in India who came across tigers in the Jungle who wanted to harm him, and he outsmarted them by offering to give up an article of his nice clothes instead. (It was sort of like the story of Billy Goats Gruff.) First of all, I liked the scariness of the story because he had tigers running loose where he lived. We didn't have that here, and I couldn't imagine what that would be like. This book was far from being a racial issue. It had nothing to do with race. (I'm going to digress for a moment here before getting back to the book.)

I grew up on a street where two black families lived, which was apparently very uncommon for the times, although we didn't think anything about it. Their two houses were kiddy-corner across the street from each other. The one house was peach colored with turquoise trim and no screens on the windows. Curtains blew out from the upstairs window when there was a breeze. They had all kinds of stuff laying around their yard, and my dad was friends with them, and he and I often went there.

The other black family lived in a perfectly painted brown house trimmed in white. Their yard was neatly trimmed, and they actually had the best house on our street. The man was a Limousine driver, and we would see him getting ready to leave for work each morning in his immaculately ironed and perfect uniform. We did have to laugh though because they were black and their name was white.

Neither of the families had children, but there was a rumor the Whites may have had one who was handicapped in some way with seizures or something, but we never saw him if they did. In fact one Halloween when I went to their house for trick or treats and Mrs. White went to another room to get something, I peered around the room to see if there really was a kid there somewhere but never saw him. All I saw was a room with nice things and much better than what we owned. Her place was as immaculate inside as their house and yard outside. (Just a few years ago when my mother died in Florida,

Sparks

I found an obituary in her things of when Mrs. White had passed away. Some-one had sent it to her as they had remained friends)

One time my sister wanted me to go get something she needed from her friend's house, and she herself wasn't able to get it. I went to her house, and the girl's mother answered the door. I told her what I needed, and she said she'd go to her daughter's room to get it. Then she said something funny, which took years for me to understand. She was being polite and asked me if I was allowed to come in! I said, "ya, my mother knows you." I thought she was thinking about the talking or going with strangers' topic we kids had been taught about. They had a nice house, and although they did not have as expensive looking things as Mrs. White had had, theirs was more like our house. I was an adult before I realized why she had asked if I was allowed to come in. She had been talking about me being white, and they were black. Her daughter was the only black person in our church and played the piano for us. I couldn't figure out why color mattered. We didn't have any racial issues that I knew of in our city.

I didn't even know there was a black section to our town because we had two blacks right on our block. When I did find it out at some time, I still didn't think anything about it as we had a Czechoslovakian area too. I just thought a group of them wanted to be together in an area like us. We had only a few black kid's in our school, but everyone went to their area school so whichever side of town you lived in that's the school you went to. The one school then had more because of the section where they lived.

So then...with my background told, I will get back to the subject of the "Little Black Sambo" book. It is not racist nor was it ever to be derogatory to blacks...unless they chose for it to be! The story is actually about a child in India where the author, a wife of a physician and officer in the Indian Medical service lived for 30 years. They had two daughters and two sons. The book's setting is about the south Indian Tamil people and their culture and a place where tigers abound. The author wrote the story for her two daughters once when traveling on a train and also drew pictures. Because they were living where most the people and the kids her children were always playing with were black, she made the story about a little black boy named Sambo. I loved to hear how the different tigers tried to take the little boys clothes from him, but they weren't happy with having just the piece they had gotten but wanted everyone else's item too. Their greed ended up costing them their lives as they chased each other around and around a tree and turned into butter. The little boy got all his clothes back plus also had tiger butter for yummy pancakes. (Even the pancakes themselves made a connection with us because there was

66

a black lady who was pictured on a bottle of syrup and she traveled around the country advertising Aunt Jemima pancakes. We stood in lines for hours downtown to get to see her. Now here was a story of "Little Black Sambo" that connected two things for us.) Well, somehow the NAACP in the '30s and '40s took the story on as being racist even though it was an *Indian child* because he was black and they took offense. The word Sambo then became a slur for the black person. (Think about it, any name which would have been used would have been the slur. It happened to be Sambo. It could have been the little boy's name in *The Jungle Book*.) Actually, you would think blacks would have been proud to claim Sambo because he taught such a good lesson for life. It did a lot for me. I was so excited the little boy got his clothes back, and he got to eat those mean tigers who had become butter. I cannot see it as being against blacks but even had it been about blacks it was a story with a good moral for life. It would have been something to be proud of. However, it wasn't about blacks. It was about the child from India who was black and lived in an area with tigers.

Trying to figure this all out from a white person's standpoint may be impossible to do. Apparently there was some imagined, subhuman black juvenile who was depicted as accepting or even looking for violence that they referred to as the "Pick ninny" (means black child). Somehow this pick ninny got tangled up with Sambo the little boy from India, just because he was black. A black boy is typical for India as are tigers. How did the blacks in the U.S. link to tigers? (There may have perhaps been other artists of different renditions of the book who later got into the picture who made a derogatory issue but the "Little Black Sambo" story shouldn't suffer for that. Sambo is not racial.

There were some people, many years later, who opened a chain of restaurants around the United States, who had to change their establishment's name because the blacks again cried racism because they named it Sambo's.

Actually, the owners combined their own names to come up with the name for the restaurant. Sam Battistone Sr. and Newell Bohnett. Even though the name had nothing to do with the story, so many people thought of it as matching the storybook they'd love as a kid. The owners then picked up on it and decided it was a good theme for the restaurant so decorated their walls with pictures of the stories in the book. It was a great place for kids and for adults who had grown up with fond memories of the story. By 1979, Sambo's had 1,117 outlets in 47 states. The restaurant opened to make a place for blue collar workers to get low-cost pancakes and coffee. There was nothing racial for anyone to eat there but again, protests broke out about the name being used. NAACP once again got involved with lawsuits saying the name was offensive.

Neither the book nor the restaurant had anything negative with Negros but was something good. People's freedom to name their own restaurant had been taken away for no reason. There was not a thing racial anywhere, but merely some people's own personal views of it. By then there may have even been agitators making up stories which although not true fed the fire. It seems a lesson I was taught as a child fits here. "Sticks and stones may break my bones, but names will never hurt me." People can say anything, but they can't make it hurt you. Only you can do that. Now, treating you badly or unfairly is another thing, but Sambo was just an innocent name.

I went into one of those restaurants when they were open. Do you know what I saw? Illustrations of a favorite kid's book with jungle tigers, and a little boy watching the tigers holding one another's others tail while chasing each other around the tree and turning into butter. That's it! In both cases, in the book and pictures on the restaurant walls, was more of an honoring story of an Indian boy. However if a few blacks choose to take on Sambo as being a black instead, then they should feel the pride from a lesson being taught about how the greed of those tigers who were not satisfied with what they had, but wanted everyone else's things also, but cost them their life and they ended up with nothing. The little boy showed how to compromise and save himself from others who wanted to harm him by sharing, and outsmarting them and became the winner in the long run. A lesson I would be proud to have been a part of giving.

My mother had told me one time when I said something about niggers that I wasn't to use that word because they were hurt by it and they wanted us to call them Negro. To me, it was still the same except before it was just a simplified brief word. Like comin' rather than coming, gonna rather than going to, open instead of something. However I didn't want to hurt anyone so changed how I said it. Then it wasn't long before I was corrected again. They no longer wanted to be called Negros but blacks! I was confused but conformed again. Somewhere in here was also the word to use being colored. Perhaps African American is the term being favored now although I think it is actually mixed as to what some want and others wish to be called. None of the United States born youth is from Africa. Our entire country is from somewhere else. We are the melting pot of the world. I suppose everyone could add the prefix of where their ancestors came from to the word American, but that could get really lengthy to write and say if our two parents and your grandparents were all from different countries. Think of having to say or write, "I'm a Dutch, French, Irish, German, Czechoslovakian-American." No, I was born and raised in America, so I am an American, with an ancestry from other countries.

I grew up with having black people as ones I enjoyed seeing or hearing on the radio and television. It had nothing to do with being black but had everything to do with them being talented and enjoyed them sharing their much-wanted talent. Amos and Andy, Rochester on the Jack Benny show was my favorite time of his program, the dance Shirley Temple did with the black man was a favorite thing to watch. The black woman in Gone with the wind was terrific and the little black rascal with such impressive eyes during episodes of fear. We grew up with black singer's songs being favorite ones to play at parties and dance to as well as just to listen to. As a little kid, I saw some black dolls at the store which I'd never seen before. I wanted to get one. My mother told me I could if I wanted it but that if I got them, some little black girl who wanted a baby to look like her might not be able to get one if I took it. It was my choice, but when I saw there were only a couple black dolls and quite a few white, I decided to get a set of twins instead. I didn't want a black girl not to be able to have one who looked like her.

I've mentioned before, all the type of games we played. We also had more types of toys not stated before. There were so many things which got their start in our days and because of us, children are still finding them enjoyable. Wooden building blocks and a variety of colored chip pieces of wooden designs to make patterns with. We had Lincoln logs, tinker toys and hard plastic, one-inch blocks, which you could build houses or buildings with and even had some clear blocks you could use to put in for windows. There were erector sets and some already aforementioned card games. The card game authors was actually a learning tool because as you played the game over and over, the books and who wrote them became embedded in your mind. It was sort of played like go fish, but there was a list of the books each author wrote below their picture for you to ask the other players for.

One of my favorite poetry books as a kid was by Robert Lewis Stevenson. The one poem that stood out in my mind was about the little sick boy stuck in bed, and so he played with his soldiers all around him I can still recite some of it.

We put a lot of jigsaw puzzles together, especially in the winter. We also had a number of metal or plastic square slide puzzles where you had to slide the small square pieces around to complete either a picture or number series. There was chalk with boards, magic slates, paddleball, pick-up sticks, tops, and gyroscopes. None of these games were expensive even then, and you can still get them inexpensively today. They can still bring people enjoyment which they have no idea is available, if you can get beyond the electronics things of today. I never heard the words "I'm bored" come from any kids mouths back then and for a long time we didn't even have televisions, but then even when we did get one, there were only three channels to choose from.

We ate popcorn as the main snack while playing games, doing puzzles or later while watching TV. Back then you didn't have a microwave to fix popcorn in so had to put oil in the bottom of a pan, pour in the popcorn, put the lid on, and then as fast as you could, move the pan back and forth on the burner to pop the corn. You could feel the popping vibration inside the pan but if you went too slowly you burned it or a lot of times it got stuck to the bottom of the pan. When we thought the popcorn was done because we didn't feel or hear any more popping going on inside we took the lid off and poured it out into bowls. There were always kernels left over which didn't get popped. They were called old maids. We chewed on them too, but they were hard and crunchy.

We were not given homework in grade school. That made plenty of time for kids to explore and just be kids. There wasn't pressure for us to hurry and get homework done so we could go out to play. Life itself was teaching us more than some of the books. Learning history might have been important, but that was the past. We were making history! So what was more important? We did read aloud from our school books, and we did do flashcards with letters, addition, subtraction, multiplication and division at home, but those were like playing games, and there wasn't a set time to do them or any specific amount of time that had to be spent. Our bodies also were not weighed down by the weight of carrying so many books like kids today. The closest to homework for us was on Valentine's Day when we had to make out Valentine's Day cards for everyone in the class. The valentines were a penny a piece but if you got a whole package you got even more for your money. The challenge was to find the best Valentine for your friends and if you really like one particular boy to give him the best one of all. At the same time, we searched to find one valentine which didn't say much, to give to the least liked person in the class but everyone got one.

We got culture without really being aware of that being what it was. There were times in class when they had us close our eyes and lay our heads on the desk while listening to some music. The teacher would tell us the title of the piece and who wrote it but then it was up to us to use our imaginations as to what pictures came to us while listening. It was then followed by giving us a paper and crayons to draw what we heard or saw within our mind. It was amazing to see the different pictures each kid came up with and even though all our pictures were primitive grade school drawings, they still had individual meanings attached, and our age could see the other kids drawings quite easily.

You can see from what has been mentioned in the book so far as to why people speak of the "good ol' days" with love in their heart and a sparkle in their eye. Times were simpler, not so pressured and came with wonderful freedom. It was a time when kids sat and did things together, got to know one another and thoroughly enjoyed life. Today, even when groups of kids do get together and are right in the same room and sometimes even sitting right next to the person they are in contact with, they are on their laptop computers, smartphones, iPods or iPads, etc. and instead of talking, they text each other.

Oh, how times have changed! Another change which is quite noticeable is the comparison of differences in prices of things back then to the cost of things today. Unbelievable...but then, so too are the wage differences. Milk cost 34 cents a gallon in comparison to today's prices of almost four dollars or more. Eggs in the '40s were 45 cents a dozen, bread 8 cents a loaf, gasoline 18 cents a gallon and a movie ticket was 24 cents. The price of things might have been a little different depending on the state but in general, the prices were pretty close. Ivory soap was 8 cents, corn flakes 2 for 35 cents, ketchup 19 cents, Campbell's tomato soup 3 cans for 25 cents, gum 3 packs for 12 cents, Jello 3 packs for 23 cents; grape jams 35 cents a jar, and chicken and ground beef 55 cents a pound.

A car in the '40s was $800 and even though they weren't super like now they were simpler, easier and cheaper to fix, and they still got us where we were going. The price for an average house was $6,550. People are having trouble making ends meet on the minimum wages today at $7.50 an hour, and it's even tough for those making ten and twelve dollars an hour. Wages were 30 cents an hour in the forties. The annual income back then was about $1,900. I'm sure our parents had a tough time, and their views of having to contend with low wages and all the bills was probably a different viewpoint from those of us who were kids and just growing up in the times.

We had such a variety of candies which got their start on the market back then, and it's funny to see these same candies still are on the market today. The candy bars were five cents. There was Baby Ruth, Milky Way, Hershey bars, Almond Joy, and many more. With penny candies also being out, there was always a decision to make, whether to get one candy bar or five penny candies. In fact, if you got Kits there were four or five pieces in that pack, for a penny. Then you were really getting a bargain. There was also the long paper strip of color button candies which we used for 'pills' when playing with our doctor and nurse kits, so getting one of those was even more of a bargain. We learned to add and multiply with just the decisions we made with our candy selections. We also had Smarty's, which was another doctor and nurse kit antidote, and Pez also got its start, coming in unusual dispensers.

Candy cigarettes were another favorite. They came in all types. Long three-inch white hard candy sticks with a red food coloring tip representing fire, and there was white paper rolled to look like cigarettes with powdered sugar type stuff so when you blew out it actually looked like you were smoking. The thing is, those were just pretend and had no candy value. There were chocolate candy cigarettes that looked like tobacco but tasted good. There were even bubble gum cigarettes as well as cigars plus a licorice, pipe.

A lot of people smoked in those days. No one knew how dangerous it was. Later there were commercials on television when it came out and advertised them. There were two cigarette packs kids like to see thrown on the streets. One was for camels cigarettes. It had a camel on the front and an Egyptian hotel on the back. We kids used to ask people. "If you were stuck in the desert and had to sleep overnight, would you sleep on the camels hump or between them?" Well, the answer was..."Neither, I'd go around back and sleep in the hotel". The other cigarette pack was Lucky Strike. If you found one of those, you'd run up to someone and hit them and show them the package saying "Lucky strike, no strike back" and they couldn't hit you too. Even with the advertisements and people smoking, it never made me want to smoke. I hated the smell and even though I liked to 'pretend' I was smoking, the ads never fazed me. The closest thing for influence to smoke were the movie stars who did smoke in their pictures. The ads did nothing to entice kids but taking movie stars on as role models, did do a lot for kids to do things they did. We'd mimic them and almost wanted to smoke to be cool like them. The thing was that the smoke stunk. I don't know about the taste as I have never tried one even to this day. It was funny. When I became a teenager, and everyone was smoking, which was the in thing to do by then, to be kept from being called names and goaded into smoking, I just told everyone I was allergic to it. That was fine, and they never bothered me about it again. It was so easy. The thing is, I told that lie so many times, that apparently my subconscious mind picked up on it as being true, and now I really am allergic to it. If we picked movie stars as role models or some movie we liked and tried to mimic, I'm sure the kids today are no different. We kids even tried flying like superman and many a kid broke a bone when they jumped off their porch roof or from a tree to get some height to fly from. The problem is in our day we had mainly smoking, drinking or fast cars the stars did. These days the list of things kids see to mimic are way off the charts and go from drugs to crimes to immoral acts. I am reminded of a story called the 100th monkey. It was a Japanese experiment way back in time. They threw sweet potatoes to monkeys on an island and even though they loved the potatoes they didn't like the dirt taste from what they landed on. Eventually, one small monkey washed the potato and found it pleasing and before long the other monkeys watched and started doing the same thing. I don't know exactly how many monkeys there really were, but the story used it as an example using 100. They claimed that when that 100th monkey washed its potato too, they discovered something very strange. The monkeys on an island way off somewhere in another part of the country also began the same procedure which seemed to point that mind control is a real transmission.

A recent story of another study was using five monkeys in a cage with a ladder and bananas at the top of it, plus having the researcher sitting by to spray cold water on the first monkey to go up to get one As that monkey jumped off the researcher also sprayed the other monkeys with cold water too. After a while, the enticement was too much, and another monkey made its way toward the bananas where the repeated cold water event took place. By the time, the third monkey decided to try to get one the other monkeys pulled him off and beat him so to keep themselves from having to get the cold water again. The experimenter took one monkey out of the cage and put a new one in which knew nothing of what had been going on. He saw the bananas and immediately tried to go for one but was pulled down and beaten by the others. The researcher then took a second new monkey and replaced one of the originals. Again when the new monkey tried climbing to get a banana all the other monkeys including the previous one who had never been sprayed so had no idea why it had been beaten when trying to get a banana, beat him up. By the end of the experiment, all the original monkeys had been replaced so none of the monkeys in the cage had ever been sprayed with the cold water but yet they had learned never to try to get a banana. The experiment was apparently one with a certain meaning as a moral, but actually many meanings can be gleaned from it. One person's meaning from the outcome which leans toward their own views then isn't necessarily the right one or only one. I, myself, can see many which points to different life issues. However keeping the thoughts of mimicking our favorite stars, we can see how we could get involved with something we actually never experienced ourselves and merely respond from others thoughts and actions yet have no idea why. We see a lifestyle played over and over again on the screen and feel that's the way things are supposed to be like.

The other thing for us to take into consideration in our day was about beer. Did the commercials entice us to drink or again was it to mimic the stars we bonded with? My only reason for my not drinking was because I had an alcoholic grandfather on my dad's side, as well as my dad himself. So movies might have caused some to do it, life itself could be the cause not to. As a young kid, my grandpa was at our house and he had been drinking. He got mad at me for something and he picked up a big old stuffed chair and threw it at me. Luckily I was close to another chair just like it, sitting in the corner of a wall and I was small enough to slip behind it as his chair hit. I would have been killed had his hit me with that much force. My mother came out from the kitchen and saw what had happened and took grandpa by the collar and the seat of the pants and threw him out the front door telling him to never come back. She then went to the phone and called dad at work and told him what she had done and if he didn't like it he could leave too. This was the same grandfather who threw away my food for me so I could have some candy and the same one who was sleeping in a chair one day, with his mouth open so I thought it would be neat to put an apple in it. He about choked to death! I didn't do that again! Had I done something like that the day he threw the chair at me I might have understood why he did it but I hadn't done anything. I can't even remember why he was mad at me that day it might have been he told me to do something and I didn't. I don't know. So between that incident and the later ones of dad coming home after drinking away the paycheck causing us to be without enough household money, plus later asking for a divorce after his drinking had helped him find another woman, I basically became a tea toddler. (Somewhat anyway. I have had maybe a rum and coke at a Christmas party but it's more coke than rum.)

Impressions are one thing but how you file them within your own mind is another. Even several children in the same house living under the same exact rules and discipline will come out with totally different thoughts and sometimes so different that at times it's to the point of wondering if they ever lived together. I guess if you look for the bad and dwell there, the outcome can be different than if you experience something but then shove it aside putting it into a no longer relevant file. I've seen this with many families.

Some of the neatest commercials on television way back were beer commercials. I loved them, but they didn't make want me to want to drink. With all the commercials I'd seen over the years, one beer commercial for Hamm's beer still sticks in my mind from my youth. So again, even though I liked the ads they didn't entice me to drink, yet negative experiences did keep me from it.

There were large red wax lips we could stick in our mouth and later there were large gross protruding wax teeth. When you didn't want to use them anymore, you could chew the wax, but there really wasn't any taste to it. There were also wax pop bottles about 2 ½ inches long with colored water or a substance with not much taste yet thought of as pop.

Those pop bottles held a memory for me as when my grandmother was in the hospital, and I was too young to be able to go into her room I was left in the hall so went looking for something to do. I walked the long hall down from my grandmother's room, and as I looked into the open doorways along the way, I saw a little boy my own age with his legs in a cast and a bar connecting the two. They were hoisted up by a pulley to the ceiling. He was by himself and waved at me as I went by, so I went to the doorway and talked to him. I knew I wasn't allowed in the rooms, but they never said anything about doorways, even though I couldn't see much difference. The little boy had a pile of these wax pop bottles on the bed with him. He offered me one but I wasn't supposed to be in the rooms so couldn't get it. He finally told me just to run in real quick and get one and then go back to the hall side of the doorway, which I did. I stood talking with him, so he had me as a company for a while, and I met a new friend for a short time. In that short time, a lifetime memory was formed to bring back now, as having been special with him and those wax pop bottles.

Although the wax treats had no taste, we had bubble gum which did. We were always having bubblegum blowing contests to see who could blow the biggest bubble. Most the time the bubble would burst and end up plastered all over our face. That was especially a mess if you managed to get one blown about the size of your face. The only way to get the stuff off was to take what was left of the gum in your mouth to wipe the residue off the face. Someone got the bright idea that if one piece of gum would blow a big bubble imagine how big it could get if you put more than one piece into your mouth. Then two wasn't enough, so soon we were cramming more pieces of bubble gum into our mouth to the point we could barely chew, and our jaws hurt from trying.

We also had candy necklaces. We'd wear them around our neck for a while but at some point in the day if we wanted a piece of candy we would eat some of the necklaces. It sort of sounds unsanitary and gross now, but it seemed fine at the time. We had 'blow pops' which were the combination of sucker and bubblegum. You got the best of both worlds.

Cakes in our time were all homemade. We didn't have cake mixes for a while. Everything was made from scratch and actually was scrumptious! They took longer to make and took a lot of ingredients, but I don't think you can beat the taste even today. However the cake mixes we have now are good and sure take a lot less time, so are fine with me. When I was a young teenager, I decided I'd make a special angel food cake as a surprise for my mother's birthday. That kind of cake takes thirteen eggs. My cake wasn't even in the oven half the time it was supposed to be, and smoke started rolling out from the oven. "It couldn't be burning!" However, it was! My step dad removed it and actually was trying to scrape off the charcoal to taste it. I told him "You can't eat that. Throw it away. He said, "Well don't throw it away. At least, give it to the dog!" So I did...and the dog buried it! Microwaves first came into being in 1946, but not many people had them for quite a long time.

Other signs of the time were newsboys who stood on the street corners downtown with their newspapers waving above their head yelling "Extra, Extra, read all about it..." and then they added some headline from the paper that would entice a person to want to know more and buy a paper to read. They could choose which story they wanted to call out. It could have been a national story, sports, scandal, local story, or an investigation update just released.

This next part will be more for information of the times and what was happening, rather than my own personal memories, but in fact, they are the atmosphere in which I was living and had meaning to my life. This will give memories to those of you who lived back then and, as a backdrop of life we lived for those too young to have been a part of it. It will be a short section, but one might find the information enlightening or interesting.

There were many inventions started back in the forties which then were improved over the years and are still being changed to this day. Black and white televisions led to colored ones and then to all the latest updates we are enjoying. The jeep, kidney dialysis, aerosol spray for the hair, cleaning and medical supplies, computer controlled software, turbo engine, synthetic rubber, LSD, Jacque Cousteau aqualung, synthetic cortisone, atomic bomb, the jukebox, Tupperware, Velcro, theory of the holography and many more inventions got their start during these years. The fun things were silly putty, Frisbee, and the slinky.

The jukebox was the in thing during those years. For you readers who lived through it, you will remember these songs and they may just spark a memory for you to retrieve. For you readers who didn't get the chance to enjoy music that was music, I'm sorry for you. Maybe you can find some source on the internet that could give you a peek into the experience of hearing music from back in time, but warning, the music had meaning. Some favorite songs were "Over the Rainbow," "Oh Johnny Oh," "In the Mood," "Fools Rush In," "When You Wish Upon a Star," "Pennsylvania 65-000," "Last Time I Saw Paris," "White Cliffs of Dover," "You are My Sunshine," "Don't Sit Under the

Apple Tree," "Deep in the Heart of Texas," "String of Pearls," "Lamplighter," "I'm Dreaming of a White Christmas," "Chattanooga Choo Choo," "American Patrol," "Pistol Packin' Momma," "That Old Black Magic," "Song of Bernadette," "Stormy Weather," and "There Goes that Song Again."

The movie stars were Betty Gable, Bob Hope, Bing Crosby, Gary Cooper, Abbott and Costello, Humphrey Bogart, James Cagney, Clark Gable and Mickey Rooney. Many of these stars went to the war front to entertain the troops. Musicals and war movies were the favorites at the time. No matter what movie you went to see, they had a black and white news reel of the war with battle scenes and updates to what was happening. While it was important to the adults, it really didn't mean much to the kids. We kids just knew when it was over a cartoon came on. The only thing we were really aware of, of the war, was that for some reason we had to have these red ration stamps to get some of our food, and we were told they were more precious than money. If we lost these, there wouldn't be any way to get certain foods even if we had money.

Some of the movies from that time were *This is the Army, Heaven Can Wait, For Whom the Bell Tolls, Lassie Come Home, Casablanca,* and *The Song of Bernadette.*

While those things already mentioned might bring back memories to those who were brought up back then, these next ones will also be identified with fond emotions to even the current generations, but you will now be aware that they originated in the time the people refer to as the "good ol' days." These are the memorable Disney movies we were blessed to receive first. From our generation then, to yours. *Pinocchio, Fantasia, Dumbo, Bambi, Song of the South, So Dear To My Heart,* and *Three Caballeros.* These are but a few.

Besides Disney, other movies which were started in our time and are still enjoyed were *The Jungle Book, National Velvet, The Yearling, Miracle on 34th Street, The Secret Garden, Little Woman,* a variety of *Lassie* films and *My Friend Flicka.*

The popular songs of the times have also spilled over and flowed forward through time from our time where it got its start. It's funny, but you can tell 'real music' because it never seems to die. Music from our time can still be heard being played after all these years but what these days call music is lucky to last even the year it was written in, let alone make it over centuries. Songs of our days had meanings to them. They were uplifting, caring, filled with love, and respect. They were Patriotic and filled with hope and positive emotions. Maybe that's why our crime rates were lower then, and our youth more respectful and law abiding.

Some people of each generation might recognize at least a few of the following songs from our past. "Over the Rainbow," "I'll Never Smile Again," "When You Wish Upon A Star," "Last Time I Saw Paris," "White Cliffs of Dover," "You Are My Sunshine," "Don't Sit Under the Appletree," "Mairzy Doates and Dozey Doates," "Sentimental Journey" and "It Might As Well Be Spring." A mere token list.

So all the previous things mentioned are to give you information about the atmosphere of the times we call the "good ol' days." It shows where things we enjoy even today, got their start and grew through time into the modern day products. Today's things will also be worked on to get even better, but remember just where it all got its birth. OUR "good ol' days!"

By now the younger generation 'might' be realizing something they didn't know before. The neat things that got started in our "good ol' days" and because some of them, they themselves are enjoying some of the rewards even now. The things might have been improved since then and made better as they have advanced throughout time, but without our generation to plant the seeds, they wouldn't even exist. Even with all the modern inventions, advancements, computers, electronics, and discoveries, society and the world is not necessarily a better place. When a person's own identity is lost and their freedom to explore, learn and grow disappears, what good is life? Without freedoms, we become like robots being ruled and manipulated by a few people who crave power. We no longer can be ourselves, but what power hungry people insist we be. They tell us what to do and not do, what and who to like and dislike, what to eat and not eat, what to be and not be, who to agree with and who to disagree with. They tell us what size of drinks we can buy, or what is good for you or is not good for you, whether you like something or not, they can take it away from you. You lose one freedom after another to a point where you might as well be a puppet on a string. So think about it. Were our times, even as simple or poor as they were, worse or better than life today?

In today's society the way it is, we who were "free range kids" back in time would have been put into homes run by a government because all our parents would have been charged with child abuse and put in jail, or the kids were taken away from them! None of us would have had parents!

Chapter 8

Even though we had a YWCA, it didn't have a swimming pool, so we got to use the men's pool at the YMCA for lessons. They didn't have to do me the favor! I hated swim lessons. Getting in the water wasn't bad, but you couldn't stand down on the bottom even in the shallow end, so we hung on the wall. Do you know what they wanted us to do? I mean, do you really know? They wanted us to put our face into the water! "Say what?" Didn't they know a person can't breathe under there? Weren't they aware a guy could drown? I wasn't about to be the one to show them what could happen, so I refused to do it. One stupid kid after another got suckered into bobbing up and down under water like a fish bobber but they weren't going to get me to do it! They actually kept after me and after me until I started to cry. When I did that, they went on to the next guy. That was easy! Each time they came I started the tears and they moved on. Well, after two weeks and the lessons were over, the kids who started with me and stupidly were enticed to go under the water, moved up into a different swim class level. I went home. Thank goodness that was over! "What? My mother registered me in another class for another two weeks?" "Is she getting back at me for something? Does she really want me to drown?" I took those stupid lessons again, but I already knew what to do, and I could turn those tears on the second they even looked my way.

Well, my mother had a lot more stamina than I did because she signed me up again. In the meantime, my sister was swimming all over the place. It looked like fun but not fun enough to put my face under the water! One day my mother went with us to the swimming pool on the other side of town. She never went with us, so this was special. She was sitting on a bench on the outside of the six-foot chain length fence and could see us splashing around and watched my sister not only swimming, but she also went to the deep water and jumped off the diving board. I wanted to do that too, but my mother told me I couldn't do that until I learned to swim. "Darn!" So while my sister was having fun jumping off the board I was trying my darnedest to swim, but naturally with my face out of the water. I'd jump up paddling my arms like a dog as fast as they could go. I was actually jumping more like a kangaroo but a couple times I made maybe a foot before my feet touched the safety of the ground. My mother was excited that I was finally even trying to do something, after all those unsuccessful swim lessons, so she tried praising me. The problem is, she said the wrong words. She said, "Oh, Pauline, you are swimming!" Well, she had just told me when I learned to swim I could go off the diving board, and now she just said I was swimming! So, I immediately got out of the pool and ran to the deep water. Now remember, my mother was on the other side of a six-foot chain link fence and could do nothing to stop me. I jumped into the water and went down, down, down. Luckily I had taken a breath when I jumped, but it wasn't big enough. My lungs were to the point I couldn't hold it anymore. I looked upward seeing the sunlight streaming downward through the water from above. Although my arms and legs were fighting for all they were worth, inside I was just as at peace as could be. I was to the point I was going to have to let the air out which would mean I would then inhale water and...drown. I remember saying to myself, "I guess I'm going to die now." I had no fear but complete peace. Right then my head broke through the top of the water, and I glanced up toward the lifeguard for help. I discovered I was on my own because he was too busy talking to some girl by the guard chair. I beat my way to the side of the pool, and I was safe. Besides that, I discovered I had just gotten my face wet! It wasn't that bad, and I knew what I had to do now. I immediately went to the diving board to jump off. Either I was a daredevil, or stupid, but after all, jumping off that board had been my goal to begin with, and I came near to dying to do it! I did jump off the board but jumped close to the wall. So, there I was...swimming at last.

Once that initial experience was over, I went gung ho to advance my swim abilities. I took class after class during my future years and eventually took junior life saving. I practiced my diving abilities in my own back yard on our picnic table. I would practice the approach you take before diving into the water. One, two, three, lift. At that point I'd stop, and continue practicing it, knowing that on the lift on the actual board I would spring up into the air and go into the dive. One day I sort of forgot one thing. Anyway, until it was too late. I forgot for just a second that I wasn't on the board with the water below.

I remembered, as I was in midair, where there was nothing I could do except crash onto the grass. I jammed my wrists, shoulder, and neck. Being young, I actually came through it pretty well. Do you want to know the effects of child-hood injuries when you get older? That's another story!

I got to help as an aid for instructors with swim lessons. Me. The one who wouldn't put their face into the water was now helping to teach others to swim. I earned tickets to get into the pool free for every two hours I volun-teered. I never had to pay to go to the pool again. I really felt empowered, and my self-esteem grew.

By then my mother was the only bread winner so any money I could make took pressure off her because I could buy a lot of my own things. I got a special permit from the city to be able to work summers at the swimming pool to earn money. A teacher at our school was the pool manager, so I had someone on my side who helped get me the job. Kids couldn't get a job at sixteen without a special permit. I could only work so many hours, and only during the day, but being barely sixteen I had a job. I worked in the basket room giving out the empty baskets, then taking them to be put away on the shelves once the clothes were in them. When people were ready to go home, I got their baskets for them to leave.

The pool itself had several special memories. I got to go inside before the doors opened, which made me feel special. The job in the basket room con-sisted of giving out empty baskets for people to put their clothes in, filing them on shelves when they turned them in and getting the clothes for them when they were ready to leave. We had a rubber wrist identification ring which was imprinted in raised numbers for each basket. We had to check to make sure the basket and ring numbers matched before giving them to the people. If one was wrong, when the people came to get their basket when going home they got someone else's clothes. The look on a guy's face when he got a females bas-ket of clothes was pretty funny, or vice versa. Every once in a while there was a goof up, and people had to come behind the counter to scour the shelves for their clothes. That sort of taught the customer to do their own checking when they got their basket to be sure their ring and basket matched.

There was a cold foot water bath you had to wade through before going into the pool. No one really liked going through it because it was so cold but it had disinfectant in it to keep down any athlete's foot. It was funny watching people trying to keep from going through it by trying to press against the wall and try walking on a tiny lip of side tile running along the wall. What usually happened was they almost made it but at the last second lost their balance and their foot not only slipped into the water but with a big splash getting their legs wet with the cold water too.

When it was our break time, a lot of us climbed up and laid up on the stretcher high on top of the shelves of baskets, where we read comic books. One day I was almost dumped out as a guard rushed in and reached up to grab the stretcher. Someone had drowned, and they needed to get them onto a stretcher to get them to an ambulance which was on the way. Those of us in the basket room got the detail to take our yellow towels to clean up huge bright red chunks of blood off the deck where they had given respiration. Why there were such huge chunks of blood, I never could figure out. You usually don't get that with resuscitation unless there are head or internal injuries. Fortunately, the person did live, and my eyes were opened up to first aid challenges.

I also learned another thing at the pool. Being typical teenagers we did a lot of goofing off like teenagers are known for and sometimes doesn't come out with the best results. In the basket room during lull times, we were always snapping towels at someone else. If you wound up a towel with just the corner tip out, you could fling it out just right, and it would snap with a loud noise and whoever got hit with it jumped and yelled because it hurt. Sometimes it even left a mark. However, one time someone decided to wet the corner of the towel when they did it. That was a mistake. It ripped the kid's leg open, and he had to have a lot of stitches. That was the end of us being able to snap towels.

When I was finally old enough to work around food and longer hours, I got to move from working the basket room and advanced to the concession stand. I made more money and got to work longer hours plus evenings. I also became an assistant to swim instructors but because they were short of instructors I ended up with a class of my own. Swim lessons were in the mornings and the pool opened for people to swim at noon. Therefore, I could do both, teach and work the concession stand.

All this time, from my beginning of getting only swim passes, to the time of teaching and working the concession stand, I rode my bicycle from my SW side of town to the NW side to the pool every day.

There ended up being a funny story connected during those days but didn't show up for maybe twenty years later. After I was married and my husband was looking through a picture album of mine from when I was younger he all of a sudden gasped, "You taught me to swim!" He recognized my swim suit. To top that, we discovered my grandmother who was a nurse for a doctor who did home baby deliveries was the same doctor my husband's mother had used when he was delivered at home. My grandmother helped bring him into this world.

Across the street from the swimming pool was the Cedar River. When we were little and the weather was so hot that no one could sleep, and with no one having air conditioning we would go for a car ride to this area where the air was cooler at night. We loved those rides for two reasons. To cool off, and it gave us an excuse not to have to go to bed. However, the ride ended up lulling us to sleep on the way home anyway.

The river also had a time of year when it flooded and the roads were covered with water. That brought another car ride for us to go see the sight. It was awesome for us but I think the people in the area had a different view of it. This is sort of the way the memories in this book might be for some readers. For us who identify with what I mention in the book who also saw the "good ol' days," as it was for thousands of others across the United States the memories are great. After growing up and seeing and hearing things about civil rights issues going on at the same time in other parts of the country with others not having freedoms we had just because of their race, I guess these days I speak of with fondness aren't the same for everyone. The information within the book then becomes, for those of us who did have the awesome gift of freedom to experience it, but then just becomes information to those who didn't. Hopefully, the stories themselves will be light hearted, funny or at times to bring a smile or a laugh for everyone.

We lived in a time when mother goose, fairy tales, Aesop fables, and classics were great books to read or have read to us. They had funny things and stories that kept you glued to what would happen next, but they had morals and gave lessons for life as well as just entertaining. We loved "The Three Little Pigs" where the bad wolf came back and ate a pig. We didn't see it as any wicked story but a fun type story of 'animals' confronting one another. There were other stories that were just stories like that. There were poems similar in type of subject like "The cradle will fall" which didn't cause us to have traumas or nightmares or want to do violent things. The "Little Engine that could" gave us strength to do things and for us not to ever give up because we remembered that little engine who overcame his hard challenge. Like the flood being seen differently by some, or life's experiences of the "good ol' days" different for others, so too in years long after our childhood, someone got a stupid idea that the children's books of our time needed to be changed. They felt they were too violent. This was a different situation than the difference in views about our flood. Others were trying to change our memories and take away our culture by people because of their own personal views. Sometimes I think the people who want changes made don't even understand the stories they read. The three little pigs had to be changed so the pigs could get away and run to the others house. I have books with the original stories before people tried changing other's lives to meet their views. My books are very special for they are from a time when people were free to write and fantasize and kids to dream. A time when a pig and a wolf were animals. You know, like the things we eat every day. Oh, and how many of those people wanting to change the stories are aware...pigs can't build houses? These were pigs with houses made out of various things. In case people missed the moral to the story, each pig made their house the way they wanted. One of the pigs did a shabby job of building his house just like some build their houses these days. He wanted to hurry it up and get done so he could do something else. With that house being very flimsy it was easily destroyed by the wicked wolf. (In this day, robbers) The second pig was a little bit better and used better materials but, still, even with little more put into it, he still cut corners which cost the pig's house to not withstand an intruder either. The last pig took his time to build a sturdy safe house. That house was so strong it could not be torn down or broken into by the wolf.(In our day, build strong, locks and alarm systems) A lesson to do things right to begin with in our lives no matter what the issue, and don't cut corners, even if it takes more time to bring long lasting results. The people trying to change our stories were never looking at the moral but the surface story. Their insistence on changes being made also changed what moral it was trying to teach. With their moral would be, "Just do what you want because you can depend on someone else who did things right to be there to save you." Notice today how much is being done by one person who forms a small group, to change things to their own personal views even if it isn't the views of the majority. Many simply want to have things changed if not for any other reason than to have publicity or feel some power they want. Many riots have the very same people demonstrating for both sides for they are actually being paid to demonstrate. It's a job! Society is falling apart. Again, I ask. Whose lifetime experiences of life was/is better?

Think again about today's setting of computers, smartphones, iPods, or iPads, etc. people use. They don't have that feel of the paper in their hands and the turning of a page to see what lies beyond. They don't have the fun of using their imagination to picture anything but instead just have conversations from one to another. People today text, so can't even spell actual words correctly. The book readers see words over and over thus making them better with spelling skills. Books on tapes aren't usually listened to by the kids, even if the adults do, but listening does not sharpen their spelling and reading abilities.

I remember the flash cards we had with all kinds of things to learn from. Letters, numbers, addition, subtraction, multiplication and division. There were also ones with words. The cards weren't thought of as work but as a game and yet we learned much. Most our technical kids today can't spell worth a darn even at high school level. If the implements kid's use today and their batteries go dead, they won't be able to do anything; send a letter, look up things, or even communicate with their friends, even sitting right next to them. If electricity ended as if a power grid failure took place, communication would end but books would still be there that could be read for information and recreation. I've been in stores when the electricity went out, and no one knew what to do. They couldn't even make the change manually. Remember we have already recently had power grids quit several times causing massive electric shut down.

We had spelling bees in school where once a week we divided the class into two groups. Sometimes it was boys against girls and other times one side of the classroom against the other. We would stand against opposite walls, and the teacher started at the first person in line giving them a word to be spelled. If they could spell it, they went to the first person on the other side with a different word to spell. If the person missed the word they had to sit down and the person on the other side got the same word. That continued with one after the other with each trying to spell but having to sit down if they couldn't. This kept going until there was a winner.

We not only learned how to spell but we learned how to sound out words we didn't know. It was hard at times but got easier the more you did it, and it gave you a feeling of accomplishment when you succeeded. The one thing with that was if you wanted to know how to spell something people would tell you to look it up in the dictionary. Well if you knew how to spell it so you could look it up, you wouldn't have to look it up! I never could figure that one out, except you had to scan a whole area of the dictionary to see if you could find it!

I was a kid who had sore throats all the time. At least, three to four times a year my throat was so sore I couldn't even swallow my own spit. I had to go to the Eyes, Ears, Nose, and Throat, specialist to have my throat painted. If you've never had your throat painted, let me tell you it is horrible. Nowadays it might be different but we are into 'memories' and those reading this who lived back then will identify. They took a long thin stick with cotton on the end which was dipped into some of an awful smelling and tasting substance you could imagine. It was stuck in the back of the throat and painted the area, which made me gag. I hated those times. The doctor's view was that God didn't put those tonsils there if they didn't have a reason. Therefore, he wouldn't take them out then at that age, but told me when I turned seven and a half I wouldn't have any more sore throats, but if I did, then he might take them out. (My mother had her tonsils out when she was young, but when she had throat problems as an adult, and the doctor told her she had tonsillitis, she questioned that doctor's credentials. Well, it seems her tonsils had grown back in. Well if that could happen, why take them out in the first place? My doctor said God wouldn't have put them there if they didn't have a purpose, so I guess my mothers had a purpose, and he gave them back!) I spent many days gargling hot salt water just to be able to swallow. Then I discovered something called Aspergum which was aspirin in gum form. It was like a chicklet piece of gum but was so sour when you first bit into it, you puckered up, but it worked. I then didn't have to have my throat painted as often, and my throat never got to the point I couldn't swallow my own spit. (Apparently others also enjoyed everything that gum did for sore throats too and I would recommend it to people over the years, but not long ago I found it was no longer available. Figuring it was just our area not having it, I looked it up on the computer only to find it had ceased being made. There were a whole lot of disappointed people also looking for it.) I don't know if that doctor planted a suggestion for my subconscious mind to accept as true, or if he was just that good a doctor, but at the very age he mentioned my sore throats would end, they did. I never got sore throats like that again after the age of seven.

Other than the sore throats I was pretty healthy even though I did get all the childhood diseases. In fact, I got measles ten times. Most of them were the three-day kind but a couple times it was the seven-day ones. This was supposed to be impossible...but don't tell me I can't do something! After all, if my mother could regrow tonsils, I could have measles as many times as I wanted! (We had a slang saying about the (Czech) Bohemian people because we were strong willed at times. We were called the stubborn Bohemies, and that's what I just said.) "Don't tell me I can't have measles that many times if I want to!"

We had to darken the room and not go outside when we had the measles because the eyes could get affected. I was surprised that recently when we just got an outbreak of measles the people weren't warned about that. I wondered why. Were they wrong back in our time or are they failing to tell people things now that could harm them? It has to be one or the other. People haven't changed being people. I looked it up, and it still says people should be in a darkened room, so today they are failing to tell the people an important piece of information. Even though healthy I was also allergic to a lot of things. All kinds of soap except for Camay, strawberries but maybe because I ate so many at a time, eggs which then had me allergic to things they were in. I didn't stop eating any of the things I was allergic to but took only a bite here and there. Perhaps I build up a tolerance by doing that because little by little most of my allergies left. Pine was my big allergy, so it involved Christmas trees too... Whenever we got anywhere around Christmas trees, my eyes watered and even ended up swelling shut. I also broke out in a red rash. I couldn't see why everyone else should have to suffer by not having a tree for the holidays just because of me. So I just told them I'd sit in the kitchen at home and moved across the classroom room at school. 'Course in those days trees weren't put up for a month like can happen today, but rather three or four days at the most. Being live trees, they dried out quickly and dropped needles all over the floor which could catch on fire easily. We did, at least, have a big inch or two, colored electrical Christmas tree lights for the trees. When my mother grew up, they lit 'candles' on the tree.

So most of my health issues were not with being sick but rather from allergies. Well then again, there was always that confounded impetigo episodes. I was constantly plagued with that plus I did get heat stroke one time when I got a little older so had had to stay in the shade a lot more. That would be an issue I ran into again later in life.

At least, my diseases came from being exposed to them somewhere. My sister got hers from telling an April fool's joke. She told my grandpa over the phone that she had the mumps, and he felt so sorry for her. The thing is it was just an April fools days joke, but the joke ended up backfiring. She really did get the mumps...the very next day! The funnier part was that she hadn't even been around anyone with mumps or for that matter we weren't aware of them even going around. We had no idea where she could have gotten them!

My memories keep jumping all over the place and actually are hard to keep up with. It would be so much easier to go memory by memory for each age group but unfortunately, that's not how they come. I could write them down and then go back to find the ones that belong together but then it's an organized book of stories and not memories that pop up in their own good time.

I went fishing with my dad one time, and I wasn't very patient with waiting to get a fish. I wanted one right then! I'd throw the line in and pull it right back out. They kept telling me I had to wait until the bobber went under. So, the second I saw that bobber bob, I'd pull it in. Then I was told the bobber had to go completely under not just wave up and down with the current. Well, I continued doing my thing and all of a sudden I pulled the line in and was so excited. "I got one! I got one....I got a whole bunch!" There on my line were about seven or more fish. Don't tell me how to fish! My way got a whole bunch at once. No one else did that! Everyone was astonished and were coming to see my catch! Then some 'spoil sport' came over to where he'd had his stringer of fish he'd caught and left in the water until he was done fishing and when he pulled it up, there was my fishing line too! The lines had got entangled. Boy did I (almost) have a fish story to beat all stories!

When my parents were divorced, that was the end of us having a car. I went to my dad's each Sunday. He lived in a railroad car that was made into a house. It was sort of neat as the large doors made it possible to add an addition off from there. There were several stories from there, and the problem is they crop up at times when they might have already been covered and with there being no rhyme nor reason to anything it gets to the point you don't know if you have told it or not. I'm not the one to be able to tell because I wouldn't know if I already told it because it's always in my head. You the reader would be the one to know for everything would be new to you unless you already heard it before. Hopefully, this won't happen too much.

To get water to my dad's house, we had to take a bucket and go to the pump house. That did have an electric pump, so you had to flip the switch to turn it on and place the bucket under the spicket to fill up with water. Their bathroom was an outhouse, which any who can identify with those, knows all too well about them. It's about a seven-foot tall wooden building and about as wide as adults spread out arms could reach. It sat over a deeply dug hole. The smell, the flies, and the use of sears roebuck catalog pages for toilet paper is only a start. I could never figure out why these places had a seat with two or three holes. That beat me. There was no way I was ever going to have someone sitting next to me while going to the bathroom! These outhouses were a prime target for pranksters on Halloween. The kids would either tip them over or move them back a few feet so when the unsuspecting subject walked in the dark to go 'do their business' they instead fell in the deep hole where everyone else's business had already gone.

My dad was not real educated and in fact, couldn't even write his own name. When we went to the store to buy things, and he cashed a paycheck, he'd sign an x and I would then put my name as a witness.

So keeping that in mind you might identify with my thoughts with this next episode. My sister and I were playing baseball with some of the kids in the area. My sister was up to bat, and I was a catcher but was standing too close behind her. As she swung the bat, it came backward, hitting me on the head. A huge lump immediately came up on my forehead. In fact, it was so big that I could look upward and see it. Dad went into the house and brought out a long butter knife. When I saw him coming with that knife, I screamed. "No, you aren't going to cut the lump off." I ran as fast as I could, and my sister tried to stop me. I kept yelling, "I'm going to call mom." Well, how was I to know that my dad who couldn't even sign his own name actually knew that the silver in a knife would take down swelling. Through my screams with everyone trying to catch me to hold me down, I finally gave in when they said he wasn't going to cut it off but merely press it on the lump! It worked! Wow, my dad did know things after all.

Dad also had geese. One day I was in the garden with him when he sent me to the house to get something for him. I knew the geese were near us, but they stayed away. That is...until I started toward the house. Every one of those geese came toward me as a group of attackers with their heads down and making a racket of noise and flapping wings. They can travel fast, but not as fast as my feet took me that day! I ran so fast I actually leaped over a four-to-five-foot fence and with room to spare. I couldn't believe I had done that and just stood there looking back at the fence I'd just high jumped over. It seemed impossible. However when I got what dad wanted me to get, I walked around the fence and handed it over to him. I wasn't about to test my luck again! The heat for my dad's house was a big pot belly stove. It was made of cast iron and the sides were dangerously hot. If you got too close it was extremely hot and if you accidentally came in contact with it you got badly burned. As I got older I cut down on the times I went to his house because my girlfriend and I liked doing things together and Sundays was the time her parents went for drives.

I've mentioned before and probably will again, some of the things I did with Toni and her parents. They were my second family. We would go to the woods to mushroom hunt, and I was taught the difference between mushrooms and poisonous toadstools. The difference wasn't mainly seen from the top but with the webs when you turned them over. We also went to the Iowa corn festival. With Iowa being known for growing corn, it had a big celebration where people would come from all around the state. Many came to get corn on the cob being fixed in large vats of melted butter. The sights, smells and sounds connected with that festival almost make one's mouth water even now. People walked by with butter dripping down their arms as they devoured the corn on the cob.

With our Czech side of the city being known for their Kolache festivals, we were always eating some scrumptious food in celebration. Kolaches were a soft pastry with fruit inside. Some kolaches were open faced while others were closed so you couldn't see what was inside. Either way, they were delicious. One of the Czechoslovakian favorite fillings were prunes. When you tell that to people, their eyes widened because all they know about prunes is prune juice to be used for constipation. Oh, they are so much better than for something like that! Here it is generations later, and now I make those kolaches myself, and I always have to have prune ones along with the cherry, apricot, and poppy seed. The poppy seed ones bring a whole new dilemma because if a person got a drug test after eating one of those they wouldn't pass but would show a positive result for drugs.

That's not all about the prunes. Prunes are a favorite thing for the Czech people and our high school song, believe it or not, was called the "Prune Song." Oh, and we sang it in Czechoslovakian. No one knew what the heck we were even singing, but we sang it with enthusiasm and vigor. However, we were well known all around town for that Prune song. Even just a few years ago we went back to Cedar Rapids and happened to meet someone from back in our days but who had been from a rival school. We got talking and he, still after all these years, remembers being at a football game and their team was leading by twenty points but then our band struck up the (His words... that stupid)" Prune Song." He stated, "It was like some spell got cast and your team came alive, and we actually ended up losing to you." Our classmates rose to their feet, and the Czech language filled the air with the words we had no idea of what we were saying. I think it had something to do with a boy and girl eating plums off trees growing by the main road and the girl left him for another. That sure didn't sound like any school song I would imagine. Yet in Czech, it sounded great! (We kids had our own English translation. "Prunes are good for you; Prunes are good for you. If nothing else will do it, prunes will do it. Prunes are good for you") If any would like to hear it in Czech, you can look up Prune song / Svestkova Alej sung, on YouTube. Even if English words weren't the greatest, the tempo and music made up for it. Our local radio station's Czechoslovakian songs had great music, mostly polkas, and so even if played no one had to understand the words to enjoy the music which had a polka beat. "Beer Barrel Polka" was a favorite. The Czechs started the song, but many nationalities have carried it on. Czech people were patriotic, proud, law abiding and hardworking people. They were also very talented. My great grandfather was a chief Magistrate in Czechoslovakia, and that's where my grandfather learned his occupation as a bookbinder. Grandpa would yell at us if he ever saw anyone bending a book backward while it was being read because it would break the binding eventually. His photography was always top at exhibitions in the United States and even at times in Canada. We have relatives who are in their 80s and still active with the Czech singers in Cedar Rapids Iowa, and an uncle who was a constant first place winner with his gladiolas. Many a relative were active with their homemade crafts.

A man by the name of Antonin Dvorak was a famous worldwide known composer from Czechoslovakia and came to the United States. One time he stayed in Spillville, Iowa where there is a museum about him and where he composed some great music. He had taken a newly finished symphony with him, and the local symphony played for him. The organ he practiced on each day and wrote these famous pieces is in a museum in Spillville, and Prague Czechoslovakia gave one of only two busts of Dvorak to that town.

The Bily brothers from the same town did hand carved intricate clocks which are displayed in their museum. Neither brother ever left the town within eighty miles their whole lives. Ford wanted one of their clocks so badly that he offered them a million dollars which they refused. No clock was ever sold. None of those clocks had any nails but were put together with their own homemade glue. While we were on a trip there, we went on a rope bridge across some water. If you've never been on a swinging bridge, don't ever do it if you get motion sick. I didn't like it at all, and I don't get motion sick. I didn't even go all the way across it because I knew I'd have to be coming back again and it was bad enough returning just from where I had gone.

I think the Czech in me, after hearing the Dvorak music, tried coming alive. I don't know if I had great expectations that I could someday be a great violinist like I heard in his orchestra, but I found something like that takes a lot of work, and dedication and that wasn't me. Like fishing, I wanted it now! Then too, I had a teacher who wasn't very patient, and when I didn't press my fingers down hard enough on the violin strings, she pressed my fingers down so hard with her hand it cut my fingers. Grade school kid's fingers aren't very thick! That was the end of that!

Maybe music for me was just to listen to. I couldn't seem to connect with the fact it took a lot of practice to accomplish any kind of instrument. I tried the piano and after a while, I really didn't want to take it anymore. The only thing I liked about the lessons was if you got a star for the day the teacher lifted the piano seat, and I got to choose a prize. Those prizes weren't worth all the practice I had to do. I wanted to be outside playing, but my mother wouldn't let me quit. Well, I heard about someone who had run away, and the parents were so upset that they got more attention for whatever it was they'd run away for. I decided that was my way out to be able to quit piano. Another friend said she'd go with me. That was good because that way there would be two of us to figure out what to do. We went early enough that no one really missed us as it wasn't time to be home anyway. We went to the cemetery and saw a fire so went to my friends' aunt and uncle's house close by to tell them so they could call the fire department. A lot of good that did! Both the aunt and uncle were deaf and dumb. (Couldn't hear or speak). We managed to get the idea across but they checked it out and for some reason it wasn't anything to worry about. We finally left and went back to the cemetery. By that time we were getting hungry and hadn't thought this running away thing very well. Then to top it off it started to snow so we gave up the idea. The problem is I knew I was going to be in trouble when I got home. I didn't know how much though because my dad called and I was supposed to go to town to pick something up but because I wasn't there and time was wasting, so my mother had to go instead! Boy, was I in trouble! She didn't tell me I could quit piano like I'd hoped but instead made me practice my lesson for an hour or more every day. That hadn't come out quite as I planned Boy had I screwed up! The next week, however, she figured I'd been punished enough so to never try some dumb thing like that again and I did get to quit. I eventually found the drum and that was my cup of tea. I did like that and stuck with it. I didn't have to carry a tune, just a rhythm beat. I like rhythm.

There were things I couldn't ever figure out that even in my young age didn't make sense. The one mentioned before was the skeleton key for the house, yet everyone had one so if you forgot yours you could use theirs. So why have one? Another thing was when my mother was home, and we wanted to go to someone's house we had to ask permission first so if she wanted us she knew where we were. What? When she wasn't home, we went everywhere. What's the difference? She always said it was in the case of an emergency she'd know how to get us quickly. What would have happened when she was gone during the day?

Another thing I could never figure out was the bicycle hand signals to make turns. They were sticklers that we kids use them. Turning left was easy. You stuck your left arm out. Well, logic was to make a right turn you just stuck your right arm out straight too. No, you had to stick your left arm up into the air to indicate a right turn! Why? Well that was what the signal was for the driver of a car. (We had no turn signals on cars in those days, so the hand signals were required.) The arm up was logical for car drivers. They sure couldn't slide across the seat to stick their right arm out, but we were on bicycles! It was easy to just stick your right arm out straight! Sometimes I wonder if adults lose brain cells as they get old enough to make laws. Some sure don't make sense!

I also began to wonder about my dad too, when I was visiting him, and he had something cooking on the stove. I went by and peered down into the boiling pot. I looked inside again for I couldn't believe what I was seeing! With wide eyes, I did one more double take. "Oh gross, do you know what that looks like? What it looks like is a tongue. "Oh gross!" Just looking at that thing was horrible. This huge long tongue filled the pan. When it was done he had me taste it and, believe it or not; it was pretty good... but boy did it look terrible in that pan. At least, the part that looked like the tongue wasn't the part I tasted but the meat beneath. For those of you reading this are also grossed out like I was, you'd be surprised at what you are eating in the meats. Both my parents had worked at the slaughter house, and there were even things they wouldn't eat. I guess ignorance is bliss. Some people won't touch meat because they feel it's cruel to the animals. Apparently the creator didn't think so when he created them for that purpose. Vegetables even make noises when eaten if people only knew it.

When we got to junior high school and took biology every kid in the school had every disease we were reading about. We just knew we were going to die. Our class was a split session. We had to leave the class to go to lunch and then return after lunch. That was really appetizing when we got cows eyeballs to dissect during class. With having the packing house right there in town, they donated the cow's eyes to the four schools for classwork. There is a teeny tiny orange ball inside the eyes which is the cow's lens. They bounced like super balls and as in kid fashion, all of us were bouncing them all over the room with some getting away making us have to crawl to find them before we could go to lunch.

Lunch time was a story of its own. We had twenty-seven minutes in which to eat. In that time, we had to stand in a long line to get our food and eat before the bell rang. Kids who brought their lunches got more time to actually eat and whatever was in their lunch that they didn't want, they traded with a friend. The one thing that was common too was that kids would share things like an apple with others. One apple could go around the table with several taking a bite. My mother had cautioned me not to do that saying if someone had a cold or flu we could get it from them that way. I watched kids do that every day but luckily I actually listened to what my mother had said for once and didn't join in. One day one of the girls shared her apple with the group and the next day she came down with Hepatitis. Hepatitis was rampant all over the city and our school hadn't had a case yet. All those kids who had shared her apple had to go get shots, but I didn't because I had listened and didn't join in the sharing. To this day, I've kept those instructions with me and have never eaten off anyone's food no matter who they are.

My girlfriend's parents had a trellis over the sidewalk going to the back yard which had bunches of small grapes which we were constantly eating. They also had a pear tree, and a cherry tree which was my favorite and I could hardly wait for those to come in. They also had a red-handled pump we could pump to get water. It actually was more fun than at my dad's whose pump was electrical. I had a special knock I used when I came to their house, and they knew it was me. It's funny, but Mr. Grey recognized it even years later after I was married and living in another state but came to town without them knowing it. I knocked that knock, and he almost ran to the door, knowing it would be me.

One thing we enjoyed immensely was going across the city to a roller rink. That was so much fun to skate to the music, and somehow you felt you had power with moving along the floor, even though if you started going too fast and wanted to stop you couldn't go to the chairs to do it because the chairs weren't fastened down and you'd crash along with them. Again, what adult couldn't figure out that a group of chairs hooked together but is not fastened to the wall or floor, could fall over and hurt someone? They just kept picking kids up and giving first aid. Kids ended up falling down rather than go to the chairs. They got less hurt. We really liked the organ music they played, and we had 'singles' skates and 'couples' skates. In those days, girls didn't ask the boys, so if a boy didn't ask you, you had to sit out the couple's one. They had a moonlight skate where they dimmed the lights to skate in moonlit lighting.

I joined a synchronized swimming class in, believe it or not, the same pool where they couldn't get me to put my face in the water. By then my mother had remarried and my so to speak 'step sister' was in the class with me. We were going to put on the story sleeping beauty swim show, and everyone was going to have costumes. Ours were short one piece purple corduroy outfits with gold braid trim to represent soldiers. We had a lot of practices for the show but never had a dress rehearsal. The first time we entered the water in costume was when we were actually putting on the performance with an audience watching. That is not good. As we jumped into the water, we gasped out loud. Corduroy shrinks in the water. We were afraid to swim because we felt if we bent over they would rip. We cautiously went through our routine but were really glad when our part of the performance was over. The highlight of the evening was when a famous woman swimmer, Beulah Gundling, was in town and joined us to give a solo performance. She swam to the music "Glow-Worm" and swam in the dark with lights attached to her head, arms, and legs. It was spectacular.

We had a study hall, at least, a couple times a week where we could do free reading, study, or do our homework before leaving from school which freed up our after school activities. One day the teacher walked around to make sure we were doing something, and she came by me. She told me to get busy, and I told her "I am. I'm reading". She said, "Turn the book over. I said, "I can't, or I can't read. She said, "Turn the book over!" So, I turned the book over but then just sat there looking around. She was not happy and came back to me and said, "Get reading." I turned my book over and started looking at the book as if reading. She was really getting furious and was making out a hall pass to get me through the halls to go to the principal's office. I asked her what I was doing wrong, and she got even madder. I told her I was just reading like I was supposed to be. She said, "You can't read with the book upside down!" I informed her "That is right, but my book was bound wrong, so the cover was put on upside down." Boy, was she embarrassed! Now I would like to say I was completely innocent, but I had actually chosen that book to read 'because' of that. I thought it might cause a laugh or two from the kids, not figuring it would go where it did with the teacher but when it started that way I let it go as far as it could go without getting into trouble.

Chapter 9

Grade school was the first time I got involved with trying to play cupid. We were only fifth graders, but we adored two teachers in school whom both just happened to be unmarried. We kids decided to make them a couple and everyone did all they could to talk each up to the other. It was quite obvious what we were doing and even though she got embarrassed at times it was his face you could tell it on as his got beet red. Leave it to me; I didn't just plant seeds like everyone else. I point blank asked him why he didn't take her out. I think they actually did go out at least once just to shut us up, but if it ever went any further, we had no way of knowing.

The school bell was out in the yard and was rung to indicate the starting of school as well as when recess was over. Kids who have had recess taken out of school are really missing a lot. That is the time for kids to learn socialization and how to get along with others and share their own views and compromise. It is also a time for allowing one to release excess energy and build character and strength through exercising. Gym class has also disappeared in so many schools and again the exercise kids need for building healthy bodies and for developing teamwork skills with competition is being lost. Self-esteem plus acknowledging other people's strengths thus helping them build self-esteem that is being lost. Kids who get exercise do better in school.

Children always were active and would come up with all kinds of things to do even to the point of playing a game with the cement squares on the sidewalks on the way to or from school or walking to the movies etc. We had to miss any holes no matter how small, and you couldn't step on the crack separating each block of cement. The saying was "If you step on a crack you'll break your mothers back if you step in a hole you'll break your mother's sugar bowl". As dumb as it sounds, you'd be surprised how many kids were trying to miss those things. Then there were the sidewalk pieces with an imprinted emblem of some kind. I think it was the name of the cement company. Those you couldn't walk on at all but had to take a flying leap over or walk around. I think we kept a score and the one with the least number won. The other thing we learned on those walks home were just things through conversations. One was that if you got in trouble with the law, they threw you in jail, and you only got bread and water to eat. Where the person got their information, I don't know but for kids our age who liked peanut butter and jelly sandwiches, milk, a favorite meal, plus candy, that idea kept a lot of us thinking twice before doing something wrong.

The colorful cubby holes in kindergarten was a big thing because it was ours only and no one could put any of their things into it. You'd be surprised how feisty a kindergartner can be if you broke that rule. In the higher grades we did have our own peg to use in the cloak room where we hung our coats but by sixth grade, we could hang them on any empty one. That made it first come first serve attitude until someone switched others coats onto another peg and placed theirs where they wanted to be. The 'me, me, me', was trying to take hold.

Chapter 10

One big thing common for the time in the "good ol' days" was spankings. We can't go back in time without adding that to the memories because those of us living then know only too well that was part of life. Not everyone got spanked, but those of us who were headstrong and over testing for rules found the rewards of their acts.

It wasn't just home life where spankings occurred. Our school principal had the job and authority for punishment as she deemed fit. The one thing she had was a paddle with holes in it and if the discipline needed a spanking she used it. The teachers did not have the authority to spank because they were the ones the issue happened with and emotions might get too involved. However depending on the situation, it didn't mean you would slide from the paddling. The thing is, just the word going around by the kids about the wooden paddle with holes in it hurting more, kept kids in line so they wouldn't have to go to the office. Not many kids got it, but if one did, their punishment got known quickly among the school kids. The thing was, if we got in trouble at school we got a whole heck of a lot more when we got home. That was the second thing, as a deterrent to misbehaving. (Compare that to today where the teachers are even being beaten up in class, and the kids used to get expelled, but now they do nothing.)

Home punishments got a' washing your mouth out 'with soap for swearing, mouthing back, or disrespectful verbal comments of some kind. (Do you believe it? I never got that!) Spankings came from a whole lot of things you did and knew better, but did them anyway. (I got a lot of those!) One time my mother told us not to go over and play in the house they were building a couple doors away. I was playing cowboys with my friends, and we were hiding behind trees and bushes and shooting each other where ever they could hide. When we were shot (our imagination in those days was great) we'd fall over dead or stagger and find a place of refuge to only come out strong and alive again. One day the kids said, "hey, let's go hide in the basement of the new house." I told them I was told to stay out of there, but as I watched while the other kids made their way to the ladder going down to the basement, I wanted to be there too. The kids said, "There's nothing to get hurt with down here. It's empty." I figured if there wasn't anything to get hurt with, then how would my mother even know I was there, so I went down too. We had fun and played there for quite a while. Then, I slid under an area to hide but stood up too quickly and raked my back with a protruding board. Not only was it a scratch, but it was a deep scratch which went from the top of my shoulder almost to my waist. It burned, but I didn't dare reveal that! I was caught between two places. Do I tell mom so I could get first aid or shut my mouth because I knew what I was in for by being where I was told not to go? In my young mind, I decided when mom saw my scratch she would feel so sorry for me she would give me first aid and let it go. (Remember my running away episode. I thought that was going to be fine too. Somehow my reasoning power needs work!)I knew she was going to see it at some time or other anyway, and the thing was we were also taught to never lie. We might get into trouble but not as much as if we would be caught lying. (Sometimes I wondered how bad it could have been if I had lied, after being punished when telling the truth!)

I took the plunge saying, "Mom I scratched my back while we were playing cowboys." She saw the scratch and oh boy, she went into the feeling sorry mode. "What did you do? How did you get such a scratch? What did it get cut on?" It was working. I quietly said "Oh just a board." She came back with "A board? Where is there a board that could do that?" "Oh, oh the jig could be up" Then in a split second her mind went over the situation and immediately came up with "Did you go into that house they are building?" Oh Boy! Another dilemma. Here was that tell a lie or tell the truth issue. I took a stab in the dark, as she was feeling sorry for me. Well, when I answered, "yes," her demeanor changed. Maybe someone should change the way that word should be spelled because the middle of it is the word mean and that was the change which took place. She went after me to spank me for doing something I was told not to do. I ran. ("The wound mom, remember the wound. feel sorry for me ...oh well...") The thing is, we were in the house which had an area where you went from the living room into the kitchen and turned to go into the dining room then back to the living room. We went round and round, with me remembering the tigers in "Little Black Sambo" turning into butter doing the same thing around a tree. At that point being butter sounded like an out! I finally shoved a chair in the way as I went by and she stopped and merely yelled a lot. "Whew, I never got spanked, which was amazing, because putting the chair in her path could have added even worse but it didn't." I did think twice before ever doing something I was told not to again. Somehow some tattletale from the spirit world must do things to help us get caught. My mother always said she had eyes in the back of her head and knew what we were doing. I always remember trying to look to see where those eyes were! The spirit tattletale sounded like an option! Our generation may have gotten spanked but we were a better behaved and lawful generation. We didn't like being reprimanded but we also realized that if we did what we were supposed to it wouldn't happen. It was up to us! We were the ones who decided what would happen. People who break the law and end up going to jail are in jail only because of themselves. They had a choice to do or not to do what got them there. A person speeding in their car who gets a ticket doesn't get it because they are chosen by a cop to be given one, but rather they themselves knowing the speed limit chose to go faster, reap what they sow. Actually, that policeman could have saved them a worse fate which might have happened from their speed. An accident where they themselves would be injured or killed or where they injured or killed others and would they themselves be charged because of their speed might have taken place.

I got a ticket only a few weeks after I got my license. I was devastated and went home to hand my parents my license because I figured I was in deep trouble. Instead, they handed it back and actually was on my side and disagreed with the city. I got my ticket while going over a city bridge doing fifteen miles an hour over (get this) a ten mile an hour bridge. That was the first and last speeding ticket I've ever gotten. (Not that I'm a goody two-shoes or a perfect law abiding person...I just haven't gotten caught! BUT...if I do...it will be my own fault!)

One bit of research conducted while I was a teen was a survey of people in jail or prison and the majority were not spanked as kids and they even went further to say the prisoners themselves said had they been spanked they might not be where they were. That sort of stuck in my mind. I don't know what a survey today would be but I did find a study reported in 2010 which was interesting. Actually, one study was psychological while the other legal. 2,600 people were interviewed with 179 being teenagers. Marjorie Gunnoe was a professor of psychology at Calvin College in Grand Rapids Michigan. She stated the findings for not spanking didn't hold up as those who were disciplined performed better than those who weren't. This was in school grades, outlook on life, willingness to perform and volunteer, ambition to attend college. She said they were no more than those not spanked in the category of early sexual activity, getting into fights, or depression.

Another study, published in *Akron Law Review* (2009) examined criminal records stated that where there was a ban on parental corporal punishment the kids were more likely to be involved in crime.

While I'm on the subject, I will add another bit of information our media seem to keep from today's people. Thirty years ago Sweden banned a complete ban on physical discipline (spanking.) Since then child abuse rose 500 percent. Teen violence skyrocketed, and preteens became violent toward their peers. Their rate of youth criminals increased in 1994 six times over what it had been in 1984.

A story mentioned in the news recently where a mother of a black teen in Baltimore marched out into the riot atmosphere to retrieve her son and get him away from being involved. She was reprimanding him and using her hands to show her authority and had no idea she was even being filmed. She was doing what she felt needed to be done as a parent who loved her child and wanted him taught right. I along with thousands of others across our land applauded her for taking a stand and by all the people showing their support for her, just realize how many people feel the frustration of governments trying to take over our personal lives and how we should raise our own children. So many of us people feel she should be voted Mother of the Year! This woman represents what is right for our society. To stand behind her and for guidance which backs her up is the Bible. There are many verses which speak of the use of the rod being needed in order to keep the youth in line and states they will be rebellious.

The United Nations would like to tie parents hands with raising their children as they feel right, by banning spanking, but I need to add this, and you decide whose insights and authority is the correct one. (For those not interested in this, just skip to the next section of the book. I feel I need to add this to both defend our way of life back in the "good ol' days" when religion was a big part of our life and to bring light the violence we are experiencing today, to perhaps get things back on track. What we are doing now isn't working) Here then are the Bibles view on the subject, taken from the King James Version Bible. (KJV)

"Foolishness is bound in the heart of a child, but the rod will drive it from him." Proverbs 22:15 (KJV)

"The rod and reproof give wisdom, But a child left to himself brings shame to his mother... correct your son and he will give you rest, He will give delight to your heart..." Proverbs 29; 15–17 KJV

"Do not withhold correction from a child; for if you beat him with a rod, he will not die. You shall beat him with a rod and deliver his soul from hell." Proverbs 23:13–14 KJV

"He who spares the rod hates his son, But he who loves him disciplines him promptly..." Proverbs 13:24 KJV

"Now no chastening seems to be pleasant for the present, but painful; nevertheless, afterward it yields the peaceful fruit of righteousness to those who have been trained by it." Hebrew 12:11 KJV

"...chasten your son while there is hope, And do not set your heart on his destruction." Proverbs 19:18 KJV

"Train up a child in the way he should go: and when he is old, he will not depart from it." Proverbs 2:26 KJV

I know that in our day if a teen boy was being rebellious and out of control where nothing seemed to work they were sent to a place called Boys Town. There they were in strict and disciplined situations. They were taught respect, following rules, educated, but also taught a skill like woodworking or something. We went there to visit, and the place was an immaculate type campus. It was pretty neat, and I wondered at my young age why people wouldn't get into trouble just to go there. They ate together, and when it rained, they didn't have to walk across campus in it but had underground tunnels to travel through. The people there said it was really a rigid schedule and very strict plus being kept away from their family, so was not all it was cracked up to be. There weren't a lot of teens there, but it was a place to go to possibly stop a problem before it led to worse things.

The current generation is the no spanking rule and the ways laws lean; the parent is charged with child abuse if they do spank. Teachers even have told kids in grade schools that if their parents spank them, they can call the police. I know kids who have told their parents this making a lot of parents feel unable to control. A big part of our society problems with crime and dissension stem from this one thing.

I remember back in time when a man by Dr. Spock came out with a book about not spanking kids. It was like one man's views was God's word because little by little his words became a sort of rule for society. (However remember what Gods words really said which were just stated.)

Today there are so many on that bandwagon but in my beliefs, it's ruining our society and people's lives. I decided to look up as to when our crime rates began growing in comparison to Dr. Spock's book. I was surprised the book started in 1946. (My parents apparently didn't read it, or maybe luckily didn't believe it, as we weren't affected by the books words. We were spanked, and while not liking it, we came out the better for it.)

The crime rates started picking up in the late '60s, early '70s which actually would correspond with the timing of the non-spanking issue, for the kids would just be becoming the age of rebellion without early reprimands. Now there were two sides of the issue with Dr. Spock's books. Some swore by them and were glad to have them as a reference book while raising their kids. However, there were also many areas of the book which told parents what to do for a variety of issues, making that part itself being very helpful. Many kids came out just fine with being raised with Spock's theories.

However, there was the other side of the issue. Those people who saw his book as being the cause for great harm and disrespect for their parents, authority, and even patriotism. Spock himself changed his own book with each later edition and at times mentioned the people as misinterpreting what he said. Dr. Spock emphasized people needing to give their children what they want, when they want, and should cater to their feelings. (Now, what kid wouldn't want that?) Instead of the way life had always been up to then, he was against giving children chores to do or making them eat things they don't want or like. (I hated things as a child but had to eat at least one spoonful anyway, each time we had it. I don't know if the taste advanced with age or I got use to them from having to taste it each time, but I eat foods now which I hated back in time. In fact, some of those are things I now love. How many of you have seen kids who don't eat things they don't like...or think they don't like?)

Spock's idea was that kids were supposed to have freedom of expression without any stops, which brought up self-centered, outspoken demanding and defiant kids. (We had freedoms, but there was no way you would ever say or do things which were unacceptable.) We did have limits. His comments started the kids attitude that it was their right to get what they wanted. (Starting to sound familiar?) Dr. Spock was totally against self-denial of things, and the kids were to be given an over the sense of importance. This has brought the overabundant belief of self, beyond anyone else. When not getting what they feel they should have, they look upon it and treat themselves as a victim. What is happening today? Groups demand changes to their wants and wishes because they want it, not that it is the thoughts and feelings of the majority of the people. These groups are made up of those self-gratifying mass of undisciplined grown up kids.

The big issue was with spanking. Spock himself even admitted his first book contributed to an increase of permissive parenting. The man who started the no spanking thing and from where our society has fallen to where making spanking deemed as child abuse, has actually caused great harm. While his words didn't exactly come out with the words, they were understood as he stated them. He told parents when children misbehaved they were merely unhappy not morally disobedient, so giving them what they wanted would make them happy. This went on from issue to issue to a point where kids who wanted only self-pleasures weren't able to see that other persons deserved to be happy too. Children have murdered playmates; there are shattered lives, broken and unrepairable relationships as well as marriages. His comments on spanking came as "I'm not particularly advocating spanking, but it's less poisonous than lengthy disapproval." He also told the world perspective that undermined the need for any kind of physical discipline of the sort commonly known as spanking. (So there it is). You can look this up for yourself, but you need to look through many places as he had his grip on the nation who never looked further into his life. If people did, many people would not agree, now after it is too late. In fact, I was surprised to also see others saying Dr. Spock is to blame for what we are going through now. I thought I was the only one who was questioning it. Apparently even in the '60s Dr. Norman Vincent Peale stated that the U.S. was paying the price of two generations that followed Dr. Spock. So it started even earlier than I thought.

President Regan (1981–1989) made a comment about our young people losing their patriotism, and we need this to be turned around. (How much had we changed from the "good ol' days?")

Now to defend part of Spock's instructions was that he had changed life from going from withholding touching and affection or not responding to the child's tears, and fathers are not playing more of a role, to rather including these things, plus having understanding and respect. Well, you can do all of this without turning kids into outspoken, demanding and self-gratification monsters.

By the 1960s under Spock's influence people watched their kids becoming contentious, sassy and belligerent. The rise of juvenile delinquency rose, and SAT scores in schools went down. Student protest and the hippy movement with having no personal responsibility took over. Spock himself marched with the monsters he had created, to protest government authority which coincided with his views against the family authority. He was arrested over twelve times as he took stands while being in protests. He was a socialist and a pacifist and with his way of thinking, a child was just unhappy and not morally disobedient, so it excused the kids from guilt or moral responsibility.

Chapter 11

Socialism—A belief that the government should run the social programs to help the people, and the programs should be taken out of private hands. Too much of this leads to no one helping one another but allowing the government to take over everything in our lives and how we live it because we aren't smart enough. I found an example used to explain socialism on the internet and will give a short version here. A professor decided to grade on an average for the class, so no one got an A or an F. After the first test everyone got a B. The ones who never studied were happy but the ones who did weren't. The second test came and the ones who didn't study had company because those who usually studied, studied less. The average came down as all got a D. Everyone started bickering and accusing others claiming it was their fault. By the third test, no one studied, and they all failed. Socialism then is when there are rewards people will work hard to accomplish things, but if the government would share equally with those who do nothing, no one tries.

Pacifist—A refusal to bear arms on moral or religious grounds (*Are these things beginning to sound familiar in our own country today?)

Capitalism—ownership and means of production, distribution and exchange of wealth are made and maintained mainly by individuals or corporations.

Communism—all property is held in common and actual ownership is with the community or state.

Republic—The supreme power rests in the body of citizens entitled to vote and is exercised by representatives chosen directly or indirectly by them.

In a 1968 *New York Times* interview Spock admitted he would be proud if his books were the cause of idealism and militancy of kids and raising them to his goal of an adulthood of defiant attitude toward authority. (Well, folks, we're seeing just that, right now!)

In our day, politics seemed to be summed up in "You vote for Democrats if you are poor and Republicans if you are rich." There didn't seem to be any other scale to base your vote on. Unfortunately generation after generation seems to stay with those words. I've actually overheard conversations in restaurants and stores where people were asking whom the other was going to vote for, and that same sentiment still came up. Their grandparents voted that way and so did their parents so they would stay with that too. No one had any inkling of what kind of person was running, or even what they wanted to do for the country or change the things that even they might want to be changed, but was just for the other party. I did manage to get out of that mode but had also been in that mindset when I first started to vote. I now look and listen to what the persons running have to say about the issues of our country and then decide which party to vote for.

This reminds me of the example of the monkeys in the cage I mentioned earlier. Those new monkeys had no idea why they shouldn't go after those bananas, but they just knew it was bad. They had not actually experienced it for themselves and just reacted to others examples. Here we are doing the same things now. We vote a certain way because our ancestors did, but have no idea why. Young blacks take on the hatred for slavery personally, although they themselves never experienced it first hand, yet respond as if they had. They don't allow themselves to become aware of how much better things are, even if there is more that can be done. The young generation or millennia's are a mixed group, yet still carrying on the monkey example. Some were brought up by their parents who had no influence of Dr. Spock, and they fall into their parent's ways of looking at things while those raised with the influence of Spock and his socialist and pacifist ways in their parent's lives, trickled down to be influenced by their ways. We all have to figure out that if the 'bananas are there and it up to us to see if they are worth reaching for from our own experiences. We might find out our own experiences are way different from the ones we've been led to believe. We also might just find out they are good!

In Spock's 1957 edition he tried to remedy the over permissiveness of the parents by telling them the need to set standards, but by then other supposed 'experts' had taken up on the bandwagon and his efforts were lost. I found a quotation from him on the internet toward the end of his life which I'd like to share. "I was brought up by stern, puritanical parents," he said, "Against whom I tried hard to rebel—to be pleasure seeking. And isn't it ironic that I have come smack back into what my stern moralistic mother brought me up to do that I have ended up finding just the kind of stern, moral issue my parents would have approved of."

(That's great, but look at all the mass of kids that are left behind who grew up under his rules so will never have that kind of roots and beliefs to return to.)

This is information I got off the internet, however if I think back to Biblical times where the world was so full of out of control, violent and sinful people, that even God was fed up with them, so HE sent the great flood to wipe them all out. He left Noah's family behind with whom to carry the world on from there.

It appears we come into this world with Self Gratification, Selfishness, Greed, and even lust emotions which are actually needed to get attention from the adults as a new infant to be able to communicate because they can't do a thing for themselves. Everything has to be about them. From then on it's up to the parents to wean them away from thinking only of themselves and how to share, give, learn and progress in life. The Bible doesn't leave parents totally alone with the task because suggestions guidance can be found within it. Non-religious people need to pick up from tried, and true life experiences, laws, others in society and what comes naturally for there is a spark of truth within us all.

Everyone is to progress from their baby stage of total dependence to self-sufficiency and learn self-control. Self-control is what says no to those old natural drives of self and stops us from murdering, stealing, and committing adultery. Not doing anything but demanding food when hungry, moves on to helping to get it by working. There's a bible verse (2nd Thessalonians 3:10) which says "... if any would not work, neither should he eat."

As this book has shown so far, our generation did all kinds of things to get money in order to buy food to eat and to put a roof over our heads. If we sat back to get just the minimum the welfare would have given us, which my mother was eligible for but too proud to take, we wouldn't have had the other things and varieties we gained by doing for ourselves. However, that still wasn't even the best of it. Self-esteem comes with working hard for yourself which gives a person a fantastic feeling of gratification and accomplishments. It is nothing that can be bought, or given. It only comes from inside, when earned. No one can describe it as it is a feeling but is very special to each person and worth receiving. It can only be experienced by you yourself.

Besides the spanking issue, there was one other issue of those days which was, eating what was on your plate. (Maybe Dr. Spock would have said you didn't have too, but my mother wasn't Dr. Spock, and she said, we did!) There were things we didn't like, but we had to learn to eat anyway, which for me in the long run, did pay off. There were times we didn't want to finish eating so we could go play but the rule was 'finish the food on your plate. We never got a dessert until all our food was gone. (If we had dessert!). With food rationed during the war and some things hard to obtain it set a pattern of food hard to get and you couldn't waste it because it was so precious. This was always in the minds of the parents. So even after the war was over the rule stayed the same. You didn't waste food. Here is a famous quote for those who grew up in those days. How many recognize this? "You need to eat your food. There are starving kids in other countries who would love to have food." Here's another one of those adult comments that never made any sense. How was my eating my food going to help some starving kid in another country? Were they going to get it through osmosis?

One day I actually said, "Well, let's send it to them!" (How many of you are laughing because you said the same thing?) Our grandparents and parents would roll over in their graves if they saw how kids fill their plates these days and then throw half of it away. This is a very wasteful Nation, and I find myself thinking my mother's words, but I change it to "We have kids in our own country who are hungry and don't have food to eat. We need to be helping them, but not by eating our own food but by helping them actually get the food they need. Here again is our government interference because without them an answer to actually doing something about it could be found. Our minister had been living in a different town and saw how much chicken was being thrown out at the end of each day by Kentucky Chicken. Nothing was wrong with it; it was just left over. He asked them if he could take it and put it in a refrigerated area he had and then feed the poor and homeless lunch the next day. They agreed, and he got things from them, and people who had no food got a good meal once a day. That is until the city or county health department stepped in and said they couldn't do that. It was illegal. There was nothing the minister could do but tell the people it was over. Those people could go 'dumpster diving to retrieve the very same products, but that then got thrown into heaps as garbage and had to be picked through among the other things thrown out. That's okay, but things kept clean and refrigerated and then heated for them to have a nice meal is a no-no. This isn't an isolated case. We were in Florida recently, and a beach in Miami had a man who once a week had food he served to people who needed it in the area. He was always being harassed by the government because he didn't have a license and...get this...no restroom facilities! There are restrooms on the beach! There is so much thrown out every day into dumpsters behind grocery stores and restaurants across our country which is still perfectly good and could be picked up by organizations to use at shelters or nursing homes, but no, they have to be thrown away. Every town where these places have unfortunate people who are in need but one area or another of our government steps in to ban something. If churches or organizations would be given the okay to gather these things they could do a great service to their communities. It wouldn't be just someone taking things to then resell to make a buck, but genuine groups who are helping a cause.

It's funny how something from our "good ol' days" brings up ties to today's world and causes further discussions of just who had it better. So far I think the score is tilted to back in time as being the winner, except for maybe medical advances and the computer, but even those started either before us or with us. The computer may be a great invention with many positive aspects about it but has some real negatives stemming from it too. It may not be as positive as it could be, and in fact, could be a great harm in many ways. Cars are fancier now but if you look under the hood of the new cars they are one mass of intertwined and jumbled pieces and parts that when something is wrong and needs fixing half the other things have to be removed first just to get the one you want. The old cars of our day had a pristine simple amount of parts and home mechanics could fix things most the time themselves. The cars of those times were the Buick, Austin Healy, Cadillac, Chevrolet, Desoto, Chrysler, Dodge, Ford, Hillman max, Hudson, Jaguar, Lincoln, Mercury, Nash Rambler, MGA, Oldsmobile, Packard, Plymouth, Pontiac, Renault, Studebaker, and Willys. Each of these brands also had many styles to choose from and there were many extras from fancy chrome, to tail fins or stripes down the sides. Gas in the '50s was 18 cents a gallon and jumped to 25 cents in 1959. (Don't you wish we had today's wages and the '50's gas prices?)

Chapter 12

When I started writing this book, I was simply in the mode of revealing what life was like while growing up in the "good ol' days." Besides the way, life was back then with recognizable inventions and ways of doing things I've thrown in my own personal memories of happenings within our life. I'm sure many reading them may have a spark go off in some way from one of my stories and although yours isn't exactly the same it was enough to have you to recall something. There were a couple things which I already knew about as having lived through it at the time but thought I might look up information on the modern day invention called the computer, to see if I might retrieve the information I may have forgotten to mention.

I got the information about Dr. Spock, which verified my own thoughts as to the possible source of our crime rate and other problems with the society we are experiencing today having started back then. I had personally remembered him.

I was surprised I was not the only one with the same thoughts. I mentioned the music we had at the time and because we had gospel music in church too I decided to look up the name of the songs written by black composers to give you an idea of just how much their music actually is known by almost all. What I found was information about at least twelve black composers of whom studied at various universities and Institutes of art. The one who caught my eye was Harry Thacker Burleigh (1866–1949) who graduated in New York at the Institute of Musical Art, directed by Antonin Dvorak, who had been influenced by Negro spirituals when he composed pieces like his Symphony No. 5 "From the New World." I mention Antonin Dvorak elsewhere in this book, and he was like myself, Czechoslovakian. He had been in Spillville,

Iowa where the Dubuque Symphony played Dvorak's newly written E-minor Symphony "From the New World."

We had a disease called Polio going around when we were young and was a great concern to everyone. I just knew I was going to get it and freaked out anytime got an ache or pain, none of which were even near the symptoms for it. I remembered hearing and seeing people going through it and saw them confined within an oblong casket looking type of thing with only their head sticking out. I decided to look up any more information I might add to better explain that time we went through. A very dangerous time. (Mrs. Grey's isopropyl alcohol hand washes were a very important part to try keeping from attracting it. Everyone was worried.) In 1952, there had been more than 21,000 Americans who had contracted the paralyzing form of polio and about 3,000 died from it. It was connected to the inability to breathe on your own. People had to be put in those things which were actually called iron lungs. The round tube like the machine was made up of negative pressure ventilation. It was constantly displacing and replacing the air inside the machine to compress and depress the person's chest. There was a mirror above the tube opening where the head was sticking out so the patient could, at least, see the people behind them, but they couldn't do anything but lay there. For the most part, children spend a couple weeks in it if they were lucky. The patient was laid on a sliding base and shoved into the tube where the electric pump, gauge, and valves were. A collar was placed snugly into place so no air could escape, and the switch was turned on for the machine to start its work. The patient could speak only when the machine exhaled for them. I have claustrophobia just recalling the scene. It reminds me of going through a tube for an MRI and until now I never connected the two. That's why I have such a phobia about that! It's like being buried alive! Well, this reporting of memories doesn't stop here. I wish it did! While looking up the information, I found something very disturbing. There are still people in those iron lungs from that time!... NOW! In 2004, there were probably 39 people still using iron lungs and by 2010 about a dozen. There is a picture on the internet taken in a hall at Herman Kiefer Hospital where dozens of children are lined up right next to one another in their lungs! Apparently they later came out with a portable positive pressure ventilator so some can leave the respirator but those devices cause a lot of inflammation and worsen asthma caused by post-polio syndrome. Those devices are also difficult to keep clean and could introduce bacteria into the vulnerable system. All this was new news to me and from a woman still using the big lung after 61 years now.

Now is a very scary thing. We stopped with the childhood diseases which were common place as we grew up but eventually there were shots to take so here in the United States those diseases have almost become nil. I don't think we got shots for polio but think the medicine for that was given to us by placing it on a sugar cube. I remember standing in long lines to get it. However with the illegals today coming over our borders, the guards have run into swarms of people with measles. They try to say they started at an adventure park in California but where did that person come into the first contact? Soon the United States began the new onslaught of the disease. Because we hadn't had any measles for so long many our own citizens hadn't been getting their shots so when this late occurrence broke out, the measles has spread quickly. Why I bring this up now, is that while I was looking up the information about the Iron lung, it said polio has been found in Syria and other areas right now so could be getting started again and with people trying to escape the fighting, they could be spreading it too. Is this the next to come over the borders? I hope not. So while this was to be a look back in time, I hope it doesn't become a look into the future! Little did I know when writing this book I would be surprised by stuff I knew only part of and found updates I didn't know about.

The war was something else going on during our youth. I've mentioned it a little before, where we saw the black and white war news reels at the movies, and we did things like savings bonds or going to patriotic events plus having ration stamps to use for certain things. I'm going to go a little further into those things now, as after showing the iron lung information you may like to hear more of the information about the war efforts and what people had to go through too.

The stamps were small red individual stamps but in a booklet. With the economy concentrated on the war efforts and war production, consumer goods weren't focused on as much. Every member of the family, no matter what age, got a certain amount of stamps each month and there was no replacing them if they were misplaced or lost. Each person's book then gave exact details as to what they could be used for. It differed for each age group. Uniform coupons were for things like sugar, Point coupons or stamps were for processed foods, meats, fats, and cheese. Differential coupons were for gasoline, fuel, and oil. Certificate rations were for tires, cars, stoves, and typewriters but these had to first be applied for to show the need for having them. While writing this section my husband came up with his own memory that can be added here which I found interesting. (This is exactly what I'm hoping is happening to you reader, that the book might spark one of your memories too).He said his uncle ordered a brand new car just after the war, and it was delivered to Cedar Rapids but was without tires. He had to try to get some of those himself.

I remember being given stamps to go get sugar with and it came with the strict warning not to lose them as we couldn't get any sugar for another month if I did. We had just so much of a certain food for the month, and we had to use it sparingly.

Gasoline was rationed, and people turned in old tires, gloves, rubber boots or shoes, garden hoses or anything else toward the war efforts. There was also a ration on anything metal. Scrap metal drives took place for recycling. Scrap paper was collected for packing weapons and equipment to be shipped overseas. I saw these things happening but was too young to really grasp it all. It was just stuff you did. Apparently the fat wastes and grease were also taken to the butcher shop who paid for it and then resold to rendering plants to be processed into explosives.

People grew gardens to help with food. Corn, potatoes, cucumbers, peas, tomatoes, lettuce, kohlrabi, and beans graced our tables both fresh and saved for later months by being canned. We also had rhubarb. That stuff was so sour my mouth puckers up just thinking about it, but I'd go out and grab a stalk and eat it raw.

As I shared some of my stories with others while writing this book, I was met with wonderful memories of theirs which added to the subjects I covered. This is exactly what I'm hoping is happening to you readers. My girlfriend recalled how we would call home from a pay booth and let the phone ring in a code number of rings to indicate to those at home we were on our way. We would let it ring and then hang up before anyone answered so, therefore, our money would be returned in the coin return because the call hadn't been completed. I'd forgotten about that. Another recalled knowing people who knew someone in an Iron Lung and if the electricity went off they would all go to manually depress and keep the rhythm going. I had no recollection of that myself but found it very interesting. So while I share and help others recall, they too make their stories interesting for me to hear. Hopefully, this can take place among your friends and relatives. (Maybe someone with their handheld machines could be texted a story they might like to hear.)

Chapter 13

At the age of seven, my parents were divorced. With my mother having to work, we kids had household chores to do, but that wasn't really much new for that day and age. Dusting furniture and floors, setting and clearing the table of dishes, washing and drying dishes (by hand) and putting them away, were just typical things kids of our days did as being part of the family. My sister and I also shoveled coal from our basement coal bin into the big furnace to keep the house warm. During canning season, we spent time with mom in the basement canning sweet and dill pickles from our cucumbers in the garden. We put up fruits which we bought from a market. Our washing machine was also in the basement and my sister who was five years older, and I did the wash. It was surely different in those days. We had a hose attached to a faucet at a wall sink and used it to fill the washing machine as well as another tub. We put the clothes into the washing machine along with the soap and turned the machine on, looking down into it as the clothes swished back and forth. After a while when the time was up, we turned off the machine and moved the wringer into place between the washer and the other tub we had filled. We pulled the lever to start the rollers of the wringer and then picked up a few clothes at a time to feed through the moving tubes. We had to be careful because if we got our hands too close to the rollers, they pulled our hands through too. It's funny how flat your hand can get! There was a safety feature, though so that if your hand or too thick a group of clothes went through, the rollers would pop open and you'd have to reset it. As the clothes passed through the wringer, it squeezed out the soap and headed to the other waiting tub of rinse water. Even though the clothes went through and were dropping down into the rinse water, we still had to guide them downward because sometimes instead of falling down into the water they simply kept going round and round on the roller.

Once the washer was emptied of clothes and now sitting in the rinse water, the roller was repositioned between the rinse water and an empty tub. The procedure was then repeated to now wring out the rinse water. Once the clothes were through the final wringing, they had to be flipped into the air to get them out of the tightly squashed state they were in from the wringer.

Next, they were taken outdoors to be hung to dry on a clothesline with using wooden clothespins. We hung towels and sheets on the outside lines as well as shirts and socks. Being kids, we didn't want people seeing our underwear so put them on the inside lines! Once dry, the socks were paired up and rolled together and reversed so the cuff put them into one ball. Clothes that would not be ironed were folded. That wasn't many as we didn't have permanent press clothes in our day. The last part was to place things that needed to be ironed into a laundry basket. Because of our not having permanent press clothes, everything was nothing but one mass of wrinkles. Although mom did the most of the ironing, she got some bright idea one day that we were old enough we could iron at least some of our own stuff. I don't know where she kept coming up with this stuff.

Now I didn't mind putting up the wooden ironing board nor plugging in the iron which you had to pour water into in order to make steam to iron with, or even filling a pop bottle with water for sprinkling clothes. (The pop bottles original tops were put back onto the bottles after they were filled and holes were punched in them so to be used as the sprinkler. The clothes could be dampened before ironing so to help get the wrinkles out even if using the steam. The steam could shoot out in a straight stream of boiling water from time to time, but it would usually sputter first as if in warning to stay out of the way. Just dampening the clothes with the water from the pop bottle was safer for us kids.

Mom told me I could sprinkle several pieces of clothes at one time and then roll them up and place them into the refrigerator where they would keep damp. THAT part was a good idea to me, and I had no problem doing that. However, I learned that it didn't stay damp forever! I re-sprinkled my clothes.... many times! Then I finally had to give in and iron them. I discovered something else. You can't be slow about it when you have that iron on the clothes, because if you don't move it fast enough, like with the pan of popcorn, you could actually get a yellow scorched area on your clothes with the same exact imprint of the bottom of the iron, so it had to be re-washed! (....but then at least, you got to stop ironing!)I guess it could have been worse because if I'd left it any longer, it would have had a burn hole instead.

Boy—is today's laundry day a big difference? We all have one machine that washes, rinses, and spins dry. We have permanent press materials so that when placed in a 'dryer' they come out wrinkle free! (On top of all this new improved stuff, we are now retired, and my husband does the wash! Where was he all those years ago?!)

There were things kids could do to earn money if they were willing to work. A lot of the jobs were hard jobs. Most kids these days who sit all the time with handheld devices and don't get exercise wouldn't last. We detasseled corn earning a small amount of hourly rate, but it was money. Picking bushels of beans took a long time but was a bit easier than doing the corn. I did both. I also used my bicycle to throw handbills on people's porches for our neighborhood store. I made fifty cents a week. I sold tags on street corners downtown for several different organizations and made a tiny percentage of whatever I took in. I stayed out there all day just to make as much as I could. I asked "Do you want to buy a tag?" so many times in the day that by the end of the day I was asking "Do you want to buy a tig?...do you want to buy a tag?...do you want to buy a tog?, do you to buy a toc?...do you want to buy a...what are these things called?" I made a good amount of money for me that day, but boy was I tired.

You can see I was always looking for some place to make money. The jobs didn't come to me, but I had to go out looking for something. They didn't always pay well, but it was more than I had to start with. Something is better than nothing. It actually did several things. It made money for me to use towards things I couldn't get otherwise, and it kept me busy. When you are busy, you don't have time to get into trouble. It also gave me great self-esteem because I was able to do things for myself and felt proud of my accomplishments. I've mentioned all the things my mother made for me to sell. Even though she was eligible for welfare, she refused to take it but instead did two jobs and made me a family salesman with stuff she made. With everything already mentioned, over 350 of her sock monkeys got sold. They were very popular. A lot of people made them, but hers seemed to have a personality in appearance and were favorites, which was good for us. Little by little we got things we could never afford before.

We had a record player that played 78's size records. You can't get them anymore unless in an antique shop. (Or in the box at my house). The record player had to be manually wound by a handle to get the motor going fast enough to spin the record around. If you didn't crank it totally before starting the record, it wasn't long before the record started having words get mumbled and moan. You had to quickly turn the handle to speed it up again, and it came in loud and clear. As it started up again, it was like someone who had drifted off into sleep and then quickly woke up and started talking again. Later records came with smaller 45's with a big hole in the center. We had to snap a plastic insert into those to fill in the hole to play them on the thin spindle which was meant for the 78's.

Records seemed to be the best way for me to enjoy music and for those around me to enjoy it too. I would love to be able to sing, and anyone sitting next to me has that same wish. The first indication where I found out my voice wasn't as good as I thought, was when I went to the "Strand" theater for a movie. It was not unusual for the movies in those days to get stopped every once in a while and even burn an actual hole through the film. If the film didn't move fast enough, you actually could witness on the screen the film melting a hole. I guess fast was the keyword to things back then. Ironing, popping popcorn and showing a film through a projector. This one day, just after they fixed that issue, the electricity itself went out throwing us into darkness. That wasn't an unusual happening, but usually; it was fixed pretty quickly. This day it wasn't working. Out came flashlights and a person on the stage tried to keep everyone busy to see if it would come back on soon. They turned it into a talent show and with flashlights being used as spotlights they had kids come up on stage and tell jokes or sing.

Someone I was with dared another friend of mine and me to go up and sing. We finally did. That audience was quick to respond. We got booed immediately! My voice reminds me of the freckle-faced Little Rascal (California) who sang all the time and wasn't cared for either. Anyway, my singing career started and ended the very same day. However, there still remains that wish of mine that I could sing, and when I am singing with others, they still have my same wish...that I could sing! I may have the rhythm for the song, but that's it. Playing drums may have helped with that, but even with that, I was always kiddingly told to "take my drum and beat it." At least, I thought they were kidding! But then again...! I asked for a drum set for Christmas one year when I was older. We had a bit more money by then but not enough for my request. I was hoping I might get at least one part of it. I was excited because while snooping the few packages under the tree I tapped one of the packages which had my name on it and low and behold it sounded like a drum. I was really excited, and my imagination went wild. I had wanted a shiny sparkling blue drum, and I had it pictured in mind. Had the lesson about not shaking or peeking into the Christmas presents under the tree been followed, it would have saved me the disappointment that was to come. I wouldn't have even had a hope had I not touched that package, to then dream about. On Christmas, they made me wait to open that one, so the excitement went higher. I knew they'd saved the best surprise for the last. It was sort of like Ralphie in the Christmas story with his Red Ranger Rifle. Then there it was. It was time to open the prized possession! I quickly opened the box and had to try to be excited about the joke gift. There was an entire set of drums, which I had asked for, but it was a kid's toy set. I never did get an actual set of drums nor even a single one!

When real little I felt self-conscious and I didn't want anyone talking to me. In fact, if anyone looked at me crosswise I would cry. I then got called a crybaby a lot so one day I just decided on my own that I wasn't going to do that anymore and no matter what anyone said I wouldn't let myself be hurt by it. That worked but then I used something to hide behind. I laughed, joked, or talked a lot to keep the situations light. I found that if I was ever in a situation where there were people but the air was empty with no one saying a thing, I fought to think of something to bring up to fill the silence. By saying something it usually gave others something to join in with. I just felt everyone was uncomfortable with not knowing what to say or talk about so I would instigate the conversation. I would remember those times when I was little and felt intimidated, and I didn't want others to feel like that. I found I could easily get a conversation started, and the others then joined in. Anyone who knows me knows I haven't forgotten that trait. They not only wished I could sing, but they also wished I would shut up! Oh well, I am what I am. If I hadn't built my self-esteem so well it might bother me, but it doesn't. I wasn't the only one who liked to talk a lot. There were so many of us that one teacher wrote some verses for those who didn't conform to her rules. If she caught us with gum or talking, she put our name on the board, and we had to stay after school and write her stupid verses twenty times. Those caught with gum had to put the gum on their nose for the rest of the class period. I can't quite remember what that verse was, nor what the other thing she had a verse for, because I never had to do those, but oh do I remember the one for talking. "If a talking twerp I want to be, on the board my name you'll see. If I don't soon mend my ways, I'll be writing this for days." (...and I did)

My sister was a straight A student all the way through school. She never got even an A-. Try following that through school. I was an A, B and C student but no matter how hard I tried I could not make the honor roll. I missed it by a fraction of a point several times. If a teacher had given me an A- rather than a B+, I would have made it. I only mention this here because perhaps a reader has found disappointments in their lives and have feelings of not being good enough or have feelings of 'what's the use', so they need to see other people have gone through it too. I had other talents, which my sister didn't have. Even though she was so smart, I was the one always selling things, and I became something my sister couldn't come close to. Our school had a candy sale of 'The World's Finest Chocolate' candy bars, and not only did I sell the most for my grade but for the entire school. The company gave a special two and a half pound candy bar with the person's name under the words "made especially for" on the wrapper for the person who sold the most for each class, and then also for the grade itself. On top of that, there was a whopping five pounder for the best in the school! Guess who was the one who got all of them! (...And somewhere I still have those wrappers along with all the other things I've mentioned I still have somewhere from back in time. Don't you pity my kids who have to clean it out when I die?) Another time we sold light bulbs which wasn't as much fun to sell, but I also sold the most of them too.

We had a thing called an interurban that came down as far as a block away from us. It had tracks in the street and a line overhead. For us, it was fun just to see it as if it were a train. I only got to ride on it once, and that's just because it was ending its course and going out of business. Even though it was short lived the memory seem to linger on. That corner seemed to be a busy place. A big truck carrying I think meat (not sure) tipped over and was on its side. I remember whatever it was, everything was all over the ground so they ended up giving everything to the people around there, as otherwise it would spoil and not be good for anyone.

I remember going downtown to take my brother to the big train station to go back to the army base. That was a special time for us to go to the station and see the big trains. I liked those old trains, but even that train station became a thing of the past. I also remember another time with a train as the subject, but it wasn't a good story, especially for one man who worked at the packing house where my dad worked. The trains came in to the area with cattle, and a guy had somehow gotten caught between two railroad cars that came together pinning him at his stomach. They couldn't pull the cars apart because he would have died by being cut in half. The only thing keeping him alive was the two cars apparently kept his bodies functions going. I remember him talking with no problem, and he asked for a cigarette even though he knew he was doomed. I think he was waiting for his family to arrive so he could say good-bye. It was funny about that situation because it didn't have any real emotion tied to it for us seeing it. It may have been because he had no blood and was not only talking but smoking a cigarette. It didn't seem to give us any kind of negative emotion or trauma. However, we kids were taken away from the scene at that point, so the ending was left only in our imagination. Needless to say, not all my memories are uplifting ones, yet for some reason, they bubble up to become a showing on the movie screen of the mind.

It's funny what things are so imprinted within the mind that it records things so well you can remember exactly where you were to this day. One such example was when they added "Under God' to the pledge of allegiance to our flag. I was in the upper section of our junior high school auditorium on the left-hand side and three-fourths the way up about three seats from the steps. Why is that so significant? Darned if I know! Maybe because I missed saying it the first time!

That same auditorium had many other memories too but the one which still affects me to this day is from a gym class we had on the stage area. We didn't have enough gyms, so the stage was used as one. We had a tall pole in cement with a tire. It had an area where to clip our volleyball net, and the entire class would then pull the net across the stage toward the wall which had a steel round ring in it. That end of the volleyball net had a chain which was pulled through that ring and then came back to be fastened onto itself. As the entire class pulled the net tight, the gym teacher and I fed the chain through the ring on the wall, and she told me not to let go until she said to. The only thing was, she didn't follow her own words and she let go! The clip that was supposed to go back onto the chain instead latched onto my hand between my thumb and index finger. We could not get it off! It was stuck tight. The class pulled on the net again to see if it would release some of the tension but my hand was stuck tight. I finally just jerked it out with my poor teacher cringing at what she was seeing. There was this white pinched up center between two holes in my hand. I don't know if the hand was so numb, I was tough or stupid, but I went ahead and played volleyball. Eventually, the numbness wore off and then, it hurt! Another time in gym class I also went up and over the huge cage/medicine ball we played with. People don't ever do that ...but I did! I didn't get hurt, but it was weird to be caught just right to have my feet lift me into the air and flip me. That poor teacher hated to see me coming.

We played tennis on other days, and that should have been tame enough, but the end court was by the street. It wasn't the street that was the problem. Our junior high school was on a long hill. If you missed the ball and didn't run and catch it fast enough, that darn ball started rolling down the hill and could go for many, many blocks.

Our house was at the bottom of a hill like this, but one block over. One day one of the kids at school forgot his activity ticket, and we had an assembly that day so he rushed back home to get his ticket and sped off as fast as he could with his bike. He had to go down the hill past our house. My eight-year-old cousin was walking to the grade school with his friend about that time, and they were walking across the street when the boy from our school was careening down the hill. His bike had no brakes. The other kid went on across the street, but Dickey went back. When he saw his friend had gone on across, my cousin switched back to join him. Just then the boy on the bike was upon them and hit my cousin. The other boy went on to school, but my cousin went back up the hill to his house. As he entered the house trying to tell his mother what had happened, he started throwing up. She raced her only child to the hospital where he died on the operating table. He was killed by a new kind of bike which he had wanted so badly, and they were planning to get him for Christmas. He was an uncle to my other cousins at school and during school, they came to inform all of us about the accident.

Our relatives joined others at the funeral home, and we kids went into where the casket was with our parents but when they went on out to be with the other grievers in the lobby, all us kids decided to go back into the room where Dickey laid in the casket. So here we were, maybe five or six kids standing in the doorway peering over to where he lay. Then we got a little braver and moved in closer. It was funny, but death didn't seem to freak us out, or we just didn't get the whole concept. We really thought he could sit up any second to scare us like in the little Rascal type movies would do. Then I saw something. His eyelids moved. I gasped and said to the others "Did you see that? His eyelids moved!" All the kids looked closer. Sure enough, not only did the eyelids move but we all also saw him breathing! We raced into the crowded lobby excitedly yelling. "He's alive; He's alive. We saw him move his eyes, and he's breathing! He's alive. Go get him out!" You should have seen the look on our parent's faces. It wasn't exactly ones of astonishment, happiness, joyous and exciting moments! No, instead our parents said the last word to the grieving parents and then whisked us all out of the door to leave. I kept saying, "You can't leave. He's alive. Go get him out!" Once outside we were informed we were 'just seeing things.' It was from staring so much, and it was merely us seeming to be seeing something. They told us they always do a procedure called embalming, and there is no way the body can be alive. Well, I tell you what! They better cremate me because I don't want to be buried alive!

We had a couple other things tragic things occur during our early years in junior high school. One of our classmates died of Leukemia. He was a really tall large, muscular kid who looked healthy as an ox but was diagnosed and gone within weeks. That was scary because if he could get something as strong as he was we could all be vulnerable. We also had two girls who were best friends, and each had a brother who was also very close friends. Both the boys' names were Bob. Whenever you saw one of the girls, you saw the other, as was the same with the two boys. The girls were together one night and driving over a railroad track. A train was coming, but the driver tried to beat it and lost. The one girl was killed, and the boys no longer could even be around each other. The one blamed the other for his sister's death. Every time they saw each other, a fist fight broke out, and they actually had to fix it so they wouldn't be in the same classes together.

Luckily those type of events were not the normal ones, but there was one that was sort of normal for our football team with an out of town rival team. Every time the two teams got together it didn't seem to matter which team won there was always a fight that ensued between the schools. One day I was sitting in front of a football player who had been in one of those fights after they won the previous weekend. Oh, gross! Not only were his eyes blackened and swollen but the whites of his eyes were blood red, and, in fact, it was a goopy jelly looking red with not one speck of white showing anywhere.

I might as well continue along this line to get all this type of memories out of the way. (Or at least, most of it). In later years when I was dating and although I had recently stopped going with a boyfriend yet were still friends, he went through a real tragedy. He was then living in a small house where I had actually babysat for the previous owners. This guy's mother had disappeared, and no one had a clue as to where she went. After about a month there was a woman's body found floating in a river and we often wondered if it was her and especially after the next incident happened. Jim's bedroom was right at the front of the house. When you opened his door into a hall, the front door was right there to the left. One night he heard the backfire of a car out front of the house and thought some friends had come over. He opened his door but was met with a horrible scene. It hadn't been the backfire of a car outside at all. His father had put a sawed-off shotgun into his mouth and blew off his head. It was splattered all over the walls and ceiling. We often wondered if he had killed his wife and that when they found her body in the river, he knew he would be caught. That was merely the thoughts several of us had but was never verified.

By now the book seems to have taken on a morbid tone so let's get back to the other lighter emotions. There really are some! My friend's grandmother was a janitor/cleaning lady for the school. One day she said, "Let's go into grandma's storage closet where the supplies are and scare her. She always goes there at the same time every day. Being kids, I never thought we could give her a heart attack. We'd been scared by people a lot, and nothing but freaking out happened. We went into the tiny room, and there was long narrow space between the wall and the room where we could hide. It was just wide enough for each of us to squeeze through behind each other. There was a sink with a mirror above it on a wall we could view from our hiding place. All of a sudden the door opened but we were petrified. It was a teacher! What the heck was a teacher doing in the storage closet? If we got caught, we were in deep trouble. We moved back into the shadows and tried holding our breath so she wouldn't hear us. We could see her in the mirror but then realized that if we could see her, she could also get a glimpse of us in the mirror. She washed her hands and checked her teeth. We held our breath! It seemed forever before she turned off the light and left! We got out of there as fast as we could. Heck with even thinking of trying to scare her grandmother! We had enough of 'scaring' for the day…and we were the ones who got scared!

It was actually this same teacher who was in that closet that I eventually had for Algebra. She was an old teacher that actually my mother had had. She had blue hair and had a permanent but never combed it out but left the tiny rings of hair from the permanent. She also spit through her teeth when she talked. On top of it all, she couldn't teach worth a darn. We had a straight 'A' student in our class who couldn't even understand what the heck the teacher was trying to say. She had an uncle who was the other algebra teacher in school, but she couldn't get help from him as he had been diagnosed with Leukemia and wasn't at school but in the hospital or in treatment.

Our teacher finally decided to put the entire work for each problem on the board except for the answers. She said if you got the work below you would get the correct answer above. That was her remedy for not being able to teach. We all copied the things on the board onto our papers. Then good ol' Pauline came to the rescue for the class. Because of me, the entire class passed, but none of us had any clue as how to do Algebra! My desk was butt up face to face with the teachers. How I got to have enough guts to do this, I don't know, but I guess frustration with her not teaching us made me brave. We all had the work copied from the board, so all we needed were the answers. I took care of that. I waited for a few minutes and then actually asked the teacher for the answer book. "Miss M….I'm done, and I think I got them right. Can I check your answer book for sure?" She actually gave it to me. Remember I was sitting face to face with her yet she wasn't watching me but either looking down on something she was doing or over at the board writing on the board. I quickly wrote the answers at the top of each problem and then passed it behind me so that person could copy them. It went over the entire room, including to the straight 'A' student. I'd hand the book back and either tell the teacher I'd gotten them all right or just missed two. She was so pleased! However not as pleased as my classmates! I did that not once but every time we had work to do! How the heck was I able to do that and get by with it. She was probably just thrilled the class was doing so well from her teaching abilities!

Chapter 14

When television first came out, the picture was full of what we called snow. It looked exactly like a snow blizzard and you sometimes couldn't see anything but that, while other times a picture might be barely visible beyond it. It was from air wave's interference. People had to get TV antennas to put on the roof of their house and turn them around to try to pick up the correct waves. The people inside the house would watch the picture on the TV and call up to the person on the roof as to when the picture was coming in. Sometimes it had to be repeated on a different day for another position. We then got to a point when we could add an inside antenna too. That way once the roof antenna was adjusted we sometimes could bring it in better just with adjusting the rabbit ears inside. They were two thin rods sticking out of a small disc center which set on top of the TV. They could be lengthened or shortened, moved in various directions, closer together, or spread wide apart, depending on what worked the best. Just because you got one program in pretty well didn't mean that same adjustment was the one for the next program. We spent a lot of time standing by the TV to make adjustments. By adding tin foil to the tips of the rabbit ears, we found it also helped bring the picture in better. The TV's sometimes got sensitive with an even later invention. Before, you had to get up every time you wanted to change channels, but with only having three channels there was a chance you might have what you wanted on the same one for at least a couple programs. Eventually, though many years later, a remote control entered the scene but we found if someone was leaving the house and extracted their car keys from their pocket as they walked by the television, the sound from it could change the channel.

However the funniest was when the kids were playing on the floor in front of the set, and one screamed because they didn't like what another kid had done, like taking a toy away. That sound could even turn off the TV and the look on the kids face was pretty funny when we told him to scream again. We all tried yelling, but our tone wasn't the right key!

We had programs like *Jackie Gleason, Honeymooners, Ed Sullivan Show, Jack Benny, I love Lucy, Mickey Mouse Club,* westerns, *$64000 Question, Merv Griffin, Beat the Clock, Dating Game,* and so many more. The TV commercials were sometimes as entertaining as the programs themselves. The Hamm's beer commercial with the bear standing on a rolling log in the water was a favorite, and I can still see it. There was Black Label beer, Band-aid, Raid, Maxwell coffee, Lucky strike and Camel cigarettes, Tums, and one I remember so well, as then I was a young teenager and found it embarrassing; a Playtex bra commercial. The program had Bert Parks, who also advertised Van Huesun shirts. That is, until one night they added the very first bra commercial on TV. A bra commercial! The young girls cringed. We couldn't believe it. Back then the women's bras could only be shown on a half body and headless statue but still...a BRA commercial! How embarrassing! Boy have things changed with the commercials today!

Our pop bottles came in glass bottles. Today they call pop, sodas. The bottles were washed and filled at the bottling company and then when empty were collected and sent on for refilling. People would throw bottles away along roads or wherever they finished them but to some of us and especially the kids those thrown away bottles became a treasure for us. Any bottles we turned in we got three cents for and later, five cents. Boy, what we could buy with that kind of money plus the streets got cleaned up. The glass bottles did have one issue which will make you younger readers say "What?", while others will say "Oh gross", yet others will say,"Ya, unfortunately, I remember that!". Although the bottles went through an emptying process and then the sanitizing process before bottling, it didn't always get the bottles clean and free of things. Smokers had a bad habit of placing their cigarette butts into the bottles and sometimes you got bottles filled with pop which still had cigarette butts in the bottom! However, that wasn't all. I found a swollen peach seed, a rusty needle and even...get this...a mouse! Needless to say, anytime I got a bottle of pop I held it up to the light to make sure there wasn't anything besides the pop inside. Today glass bottles for sodas are coming out again and whenever I happen to buy one, guess what I do first. Yup, I hold it up to the light!

Today if a person wants to get their ears pierced they go to an ear piercing place usually in the mall. The person places a quick piercing gun to the ear and after a click, the process is over within a second. You make your payment, and you are on your way. Well, a lot of time we had a cheaper way of doing it. Maybe not as sanitary or modern but the end product came out the same. We simply had someone take a potato and after sterilizing a needle over the stove, placed the potato behind the ear to use as something to accept the needle when it went through the ear. They pinched the ear lobe to deaden it, but the lobe doesn't have much pain anyway, so that didn't take much.

Speaking of no pain, I need to reveal to those who didn't see this for yourself but in our day no blood was ever shown after someone got shot as in the cowboys and Indian programs. They could have been shown having all kinds of bullets riddling them and the victim wiggled and did all kinds of theatrics, but there was never any blood. The one thing that did bother kids, at least bothered me, was I really got into the stories on television so when the character you seemed to really like, died on the show I got really upset. My mother had to tell us they really didn't die, it was only an act, but I knew better! "What do you mean they didn't die? It showed it right there!" She explained it was just a part they were playing, and I would see that same person again on another program. Sure enough. Either she was right, or we saw a miracle of life after death.

Tattoos were something I was very interested in. I'm sure they were around way before my time, but when my brother went into the Navy, and he got one, I wanted one too. I constantly asked to get a tattoo, but whenever I see tattoos on a woman today, I think of those days and am sure glad I wasn't allowed to get one. Some woman's bodies really look gross, and the bad part is it's there to stay.

We got sheets of removable tattoos at Easter time to put our boiled eggs for decorations over the color. Instead of putting them on the eggs I decorated my body. By using just a few at a time, I was able to stretch out a number of days I could have tattoos. Each lasted a week if you were careful not to wash them off. The ideal thing for today's people who would like to have tattoos is to have a kind that would only last a couple months. That way if a person is tired of one design they can get a different one the next time or if the female is going to be in someone's wedding they can time their markings, so tattoos don't overtake the gown being worn. If people eventually decide they don't even want tattoos anymore, they could just become tattoo free.

Cameras were way very different in our time than they are today. We thought our cameras were so advanced over what they had been in the years before us. I'd see pictures from back in generations before and thought how old fashioned they were. They had big cameras set on a tripod with metal clips

127

which were placed into the camera where the picture to be printed on glass slides and the flash was a powder placed in a grove on a handle to go off for light. We had come a long way.

We had a brownie box camera that used paper film. It came on a spool, and we had to put it inside the back of the camera and stretch it across the camera from the full spool to one which was empty. The paper had a tab which had to be inserted into the empty spool and then wound a couple times to make sure it held before closing the camera back. If you didn't get it in just right, it could tear, and the entire roll would be wrecked. Once you got the film threaded you closed the back and turned the film advance until the number one appeared in a thumbnail size window on the back. You then could look through the view finder and take a picture.

That was simple enough however if you wanted to take another picture you had to first remember to twist the knob again to go to the next number. IF you forgot to do it or keep track correctly, you ended up with the new picture being taken right over the previous picture, and you had images from both at the same time. You could actually get a whole lot of pictures on the same one which was called double exposure, or triple, or quadruple, depending how forgetful you were. If you ever got a real ghost, you would never have known because that's what they looked like with the extra exposures. They had weird outcomes.

Many pictures were ruined in those days for different reasons. When the roll hit the last picture, you had to rewind it back onto the original spool. Failure to do it would cause the entire roll to be exposed to light when you opened the back to remove it, and you lost everything you had taken. I was thrilled when a newer camera came out which even had round flashed cubes for a flash attachment. First, the cubes were large and round, the size of a fifty cent piece but later there were smaller ones. Sometimes they didn't go off when they should, and you spent a lot of times readjusting the bulb or wetting it with your tongue before reinserting it. Just after graduation and I had a job, they came out with the first Polaroid camera. You could actually get the picture back right after you took it. The picture was only about a 3x4 black and white, but you saw what you took right away and could take another one if you wanted. There was a tube of a setting substance the size of a chap stick with a funny smell, which was used to rub over the print to keep the picture image from disappearing.

I had a whole new respect for my grandfather's prize winning photography after having all the issues with my camera misadventures. His patience of waiting for 2 ½ hours for some horses to get into just the right position before taking a picture was still not me. That picture won sweepstakes and appeared in all kinds of newspapers and magazines all over the country and even went to Canada, but he deserved any recognition just for waiting that long.

At school, we were given names and addresses for kids to have as pen pals in other countries. It was fun to get letters from other kids, but I think they were just as lazy as we were because they also liked getting them. It seems no one wanted to write them! Writing just wasn't quite as much fun. I had one correspondence with a girl in Hawaii which lasted the longest, but even that one phased out too.

The postage stamps at the time were three cents while postcards were a penny. Among all the other things from back in time, I also have a couple of those canceled stamps in my collection. (I think I won't put them into an album, though. I remember the fly my brother swallowed while doing that!)

The average toys for girls in our day were doll houses with furniture and little dolls inside, dolls, and tea and dish sets. The boy's usual toys were guns, farm and ranch sets, erector sets, Lincoln logs, blocks, and cowboy stuff. Somehow our family was mixed up as my cousin liked the dollhouses and was upset when he didn't get one like the rest of us for Christmas, so they had to get him one afterward, and I liked the stuff the boys were thought to want. (My mother said she always thought I was put together backward but was speaking about how I dressed in the different seasons. Maybe I was, but for a different reason. I liked the boys stuff. It was more challenging and places for using the imagination and dexterity. That's why kids may identify with their opposite sex during their growing young years even now because their talents and skills reside with the challenges of the subjects the opposite sex are usually identified with. It's not they need to become the opposite sex but instead be given the ability to explore the subjects that they seem to be drawn to. Remember nurses used to be only females but now we have male nurses. Mailmen used to be only men but now are also women.

Groups of people have created something they may know nothing about. People try making society change for things they are actually only wanting to be changed because of their own thoughts and are caught in that 'monkey with the banana syndrome. They may think they are doing others a favor but may be the culprits for causing a life of misery for them. Instead of allowing each to explore the subjects of anything that interest them people want kids to believe they are the opposite sex to a point of being listed as bisexuals or transgender. Allowing them to use the opposite restrooms and dress the opposite way may be just something they could outgrow. If someone only wants to explore a subject where their inner talents and skills lie, but then is told they have to use

129

a different restroom because of it, what does that do to their mind? Dressing is one thing but changing their name or using the opposite restroom could be a problem. I'm an adult and still have the western theme in my thoughts but quite enjoy being female I am. I was the biggest tomboy round. I just wonder what is going to happen when these children are given in to and go through years of living that way, as the opposite sex identification in restrooms, but then outgrow it. Will they feel they have to stay in that role? If so, will it cause a whole new issue to their lives? If they switch back to what they really are, will the return, bring issues of what people would say or do, where does that lead? Until a person is an adult, those decisions should not be made.

There is one issue which may be the reason for some kids to think about and act being the opposite sex and really feel their entire life they are the wrong one. Most people are not aware of this, but there are hundreds of babies born each year where the sex can't be determined. The decision has to be made by the physician or by the parents for the doctors to do. If they make the wrong decision for what it really should have been, then the child can have these inner feelings of being in a wrong body. Sometimes a child of both sexes remains as such until as a teen they make their own decision because of how they feel. I personally knew of such a case. These people are truly not to blame, and medical procedures need to then be made for them to be what they should have been all along.

While this book is to be memories of my life and of the times of the "good ol' days" sometimes because of a memory something seems to pop up to add tidbits which tie in yet are more information and things for thoughts.

I played with dolls and had several of them. Dolls back then had a soft rubber stuff for arms and legs, and while they made them feel more real over the previous hard ones, these got gummy if you forgot them out in the sun. They stuck together without any way to ever get them apart. The hard material then seemed to be better even though they didn't feel real, but those arms and legs cracked if left outside in the heat.

My sister and I played with tea sets and I played with the paper dolls but give me my cowboy stuff, my guns and holsters, my farm, ranch and western stuff to really make me happy.

Our cereal boxes had prizes in them which were a good selling point for the company in order to make money, but it also helped parents get kids to eat things they should. One cereal had state metal license plates and to collect them all, you had to eat a lot of cereal. Especially when you could get several duplicates ones if you got the wrong box and you never knew what one was inside. Kids would get together to exchange their duplicates, so that helped a little. Remember we had 48 states. Those license plates were fun just to look through at the different designs and colors but also were placed on bicycles and wagons. Course I used my bicycle as my horse and who ever heard of a horse with a license plate?

Cracker Jacks also had toys in them and in those days they were pretty good toys. You still get them today, but the toys aren't very good. Most of them just something out of paper. If they'd take a lesson from their own history back in time and start putting good things in them again, they'd find out their cracker jacks would once again be on the want list of the new generation of kids.

Chapter 15

There were so many things we had to do in our day that there was no room to be bored. However many of those same things have come forward in time so kids today also could have them, along with their computers and smartphones, but yet, kids say they are bored. This again points to the self-gratification theory of Dr. Spock and what seems to be showing up today in negative ways. Kids don't seem to know what to do to make themselves happy with simple things. Expensive things and fancy gadgets last just so long before they have to have a new model because last years are too old. Think of it. Today's people are over last year's things and yet our things have come through generation after generation and people who will allow themselves to try them will find much enjoyment.

We chased butterflies, explored ant hills, looked for insects and bugs, skipped rocks over water, played hide and go seek both in the neighborhood and in a cemetery, flew kites, played marbles, or Chinese checkers and put jigsaw puzzles together. Etch a sketch had come into the world, and we spent many hours trying to make pictures other than straight and wavy lines. I could draw actual pictures. We played red light green light; Mother may I, Tag, Rover, Rover, come on over, and Marco Polo.

Our evenings were filled with listening to radio programs where, unlike when TV came into being, we had to use our own imagination as to what was happening in their words, sounds and the music used to set the mood. The variety of shows ranged from westerns to mysteries or suspense, adventures, and comedies. The list given here will mean nothing to younger readers but will bring back so many memories of those who lived the times. *Ozzie and Harriet, Amos and Andy, Arthur Godfrey, Ellery Queen Mysteries, Blondie and Dagwood,*

Cisco Kid, Edgar Bergen/Charlie McCarthy, Father knows best, Fibber McGee and Molly, Gene Autry, Gunsmoke, Inner Sanctum, Let's pretend, Lone Ranger, Little Orphan Annie, Ma & Pa Kettle, Red Skelton, Roy Rogers, Tarzan, Tom Mix, The Whistler, plus many more. It was good we had good imaginations to picture within our minds as to what was happening because if we had seen that the music and sound effects were mainly all that was really going on like I disappointedly discovered one time, it would have wrecked everything.

Comic books were a favorite pastime and to save money, Toni, our neighbor man, and I had saved money by exchanging our favorite ones with each other to read. There were many others we bought and if the other person didn't have we let them read ours. Besides the *Gene Autry, Roy Rogers*, and *Tarzan* ones there were *Little Lulu, Casper, Superman, Lil' Rich, Reggie, Henry Aldridge, Lassie, RinTinTin, Lassie, Chip 'n Dale, Reggie*, as only a few to mention.

To add to the lists of the things we enjoyed in our time and which are actually still available today, were games such as *Chutes and Ladders, Candy Land, Cootie, Clue, Monopoly, Parcheesi, Pick-up Sticks, Scrabble, Dominoes, Chinese Checkers*, regular checkers, *Operation*, and card games. The card games were rummy, old maid, crazy eights, go fish, and authors. Slide puzzles with numbers, which later appeared with pictures too, were among other favorites things like tinker toys, Lincoln Logs, dice games, Ouija board, tidily winks, jacks, Slinkys, yoyo, silly putty, ant farms, and marbles. My toy animals and people for farms and ranch sets and western towns were spread out over the floor for hours of play to be played myself or with others. I could spend an entire day alone with my entire set up.

The hula hoop was both fun as well as a frustrating thing to have. Some people were able to work those darn things very well but those of us who couldn't master that hip or leg or whatever it took the movement to get them to work found only frustration. The frustration came from not only not being able to do it but seeing others who could. Most the time I managed to get it go around my waist once or twice before spiraling down to my ankles. I finally did master the hula hoop! I put greenery around it at Christmas time and added bows and colored electrical lights and enjoyed it as a Christmas wreath!

Clotheslines are something of the past for many people, but they are still around in small towns and with country life. The clothespins used in the "good ol' days" had a round top to them and although they can still be found there are also pincher type clothespins which open up wider to more easily catch a thicker piece of material. The round top ones were fixed so wouldn't budge if the object you were hanging was thicker than the clothespins space opening. They often times broke if what you were hanging was too thick. We needed to hang shirts upside down if we didn't want to have the pin markings on their shoulder making them look like lumps, but seeing as we didn't have permanent press clothes it really didn't make much difference as they still had to be ironed. Small or heavy rugs which couldn't be thrown into a washing machine got a good cleaning by being thrown over the clothes lines, and rug beaters were taken to them and beat them for all they were worth. The dust and dirt just flew out of them, and we coughed and sputtered until we figured which way the wind was blowing and changed place. That was a good job for someone if they were frustrated and wanted to let off steam.

The one thing those round head clothes pins were good for besides hanging up clothes and playing the Drop the clothespin game was to make airplanes. By putting together two clothespins together, they made great airplanes play with, and we had many a flying battle with them.

We had sleds we used to carry things we bought from stores in the winter and delivered Christmas packages to friend's houses, but a wagon took the place for carrying the groceries in the other times of the year. Without a car, we made do with what we had.

In our days we were very polite and called our adults Mr. or Mrs. Men and boys opened doors for the girls and women, allowing them to go in before them. Men walked on the outside of women by the street and children, girls or boys opened doors for the older people. We were respectful of our language, "Yes or no, ma'am, or yes or no, sir! We didn't talk back. (Or if we did we realized real quick why we shouldn't have)

Music was a big part of our life with a variety of kinds to choose from, but all of it was an upbeat type of wording without any derogatory suggestions like today. It might have a mood of sadness when a love was lost, but even then it was a clean emotion not one of revenge.

There were crooners like the superstar Bing Crosby and other popular singers of Cab Calloway and Eddie Cantor. The bandleaders Dorsey Brothers helped launch careers of vocalists such as Frank Sinatra whose vast appeal was with the "bobby soxers" and became their first idol. Big swing band could be strictly instrumental or accompanied a vocalist. The music was loud, brash but with rhythm. However, there was another side. Lawrence Welk played a softer and melodic type of music. The most notable of swing bands were Glenn Miller, Benny Goodman, and Artie Shaw. World war ll rapidly ended the swing sound as the musicians were sent to the war and there were travel restrictions. Glenn Miller was killed in a plane crash on the way to a USO show in France. Jazz was rekindling itself and the blues with Ella Fitzgerald and Billie Holiday came to national attention. Louis Armstrong and Nat King

Cole were top Jazz artists.

Other music coined as folk or hillbilly music became blues or cowboy and western songs, which brought country music with singing cowboys like Gene Autry and Roy Rogers. Soon another style joined in and became known as Honky tonk, which was a combination of western swing and blues rolled into one. By 1949, music did start to change to tragic themes of lost love, adultery, alcoholism, loneliness, and self-pity. Soon Rock and Roll music came into the spotlight.

While again, these names will not mean anything to the younger people who may be reading this book they may bring special memories to the older ones.

The one thing with the modern technology is the old generation can hear it again and the new generation who would like to hear what it was like, can both find it to listen to on the internet.

The artists of the days were: Johnny Mercer and Margaret Whiting, Dinah Shore, Burl Ives, Judy Garland, Guy Lombardo, Buddy Clark, Eddy Dunchin, Glen Gray, Andrews Sisters, Hugo Winterhalter, Gene Kelly, Gordon Jenkins, Benny Goodman, Les Paul and Mary ford, Perry Como, Vera Lynn, Rosemary Clooney, Pat Boone, Ames Brothers, Nat King Cole, Eddie Fisher, Peggy Lee, Sammy Kaye, Mills Brothers, Patti Page, Johnny Ray, Guy Mitchell, Eddy Howard, Jo Stafford, Mitch Miller, Frankie Lane, Teresa Brewer, Tennessee Ernie Ford, and so many more.

The music played on jukeboxes which were both the source for the loud or sometimes even soft and moody music but the maybe 5 ft. tall and 3 ft. wide box lit up the room with colors dancing and chasing one another around the trim to draw attention to its place. Some of the lighting actually had bubbles affect in the colors. Later small silver tabletop jukeboxes adorned tables in restaurants. The records within the jukeboxes had a number corresponding to each song and people put in their money then punched the correct button to hear their favorite tune. The lever moved back and forth to the songs location and dropped it to be played.

There are far too many songs which were popular to even try to list. I will mention a few so those from our time may reminisce a bit. Some could possibly even be recognized by the younger generation as some of them have drifted forward over the years. "I Walk the Line," "Blue Suede Shoes," "Oh Lonesome Me," "Rock Around the Clock," "How High the Moon," "Love Letters in the Sand," "Who's Sorry Now?," "The Wayward Wind," "Mack the Knife," "Love Me Tender," "Canadian Sunset," "Tennessee Waltz," "How much Is that Doggie in the Window?," "Mocking Bird Hill," "Do Not Forsake Me,"

"Rawhide," "Standing on the Corner," "Catch a Falling Star," "Just Walking in the Rain," "Music, Music, Music," "Why Don't you Believe Me?," "Walking my Baby Back Home," "Moments To Remember," "This Ole House," "Mona Lisa," "Secret Love," Whatever Will Be Will Be," "Goodnight Irene," "Rock and Roll Waltz," "The Naughty Lady of Shady Lane," "Oh my Papa," "Sincerely," "April Love," "Don't Forbid Me," "Round and Round," and "Singing the Blues." Again, I could go on and on.

We had barbershop quartet music plus another music which was a big part of us was the music at church. Our hymns had a variety of songs and many of which were negro spirituals. They were in our Methodist song books and I loved them. As mentioned elsewhere in the book I had no idea, there was even an issue going on between whites and blacks until later when I was almost an adult and was visiting in a totally different state. I couldn't understand the signs at a restroom or drinking fountain which read "Whites, Only." What the heck was this? With negroes living on our street and a couple black kids in our school, it didn't seem any different than what we just saw on TV with the people in South Carolina who were together as one, blacks and whites. In our case, it was not a mass of people as was shown in Charlestown S.C., but our friendliness, back in our time, at least in our neighborhood, was the same. Those people in Charleston are to be admired for the way they reacted to such a terrible tragedy. (So many of blacks were killed in their church by a white man.) They are truly the people who can change the race relations in this country by what they showed with their actions and strength and restraint under such horrible conditions from a situation caused by a racist white man. With the loss of nine precious very productive and skilled people, not one family chose violence. They are to be commended for displaying what it is like to be a real Christian and living God's words. I have to admit that I am not as good as they are for I would have had trouble forgiving the murderer as they have done. (It shows me I need work!) With people of high offices in our country almost seeming to want to cause a racial issue to divide us thus taking us back in time, the people of South Carolina have instead done something which stands strong in people's minds giving us the feeling of needing and wanting to pull together. What the Ferguson and Baltimore riots undid, South Carolina people shot us ahead to a future of hope.

(Without trying to make this a book on race I will add one thing here. I feel sorry for all the blacks who are not the trouble makers the media seems to show when covering the riots in various places. There are a whole lot of people there in the same locations who don't agree with the situation at hand nor do they riot themselves and yet can themselves be hurt physically, emotionally or

136

even financially, plus be put in the middle just because of their color.

The moral for us all is to treat each person, black or white or any color or ethnic background as the one person they are. If they deserve being shunned or chastised verbally or in thought or thrown into jail, then do it. You will find that for the most times you will be amazed at how many people are really great people.

While the music we sang, and still sing, were written by slaves pertaining to their situation, which I had no idea of, those songs were so well written that they had much more meaning to them as they could also touch and reach people not being in the situation. The songs touched any who needed the Lord in their lives too, for we all are in need. Some people these days, feel no one should sing the songs but black people, but realize, the younger blacks never actually experienced the situations the songs were written during either, so they sing them with much the same feelings we all have as with the needs for God in our life. I'll bet people reading this will not know some of the beautiful songs we have sung which were given us from the spirituals. Here are a list of the more popular and recognizable ones. "Amazing Grace," "Bye and Bye," "They Crucified My Lord," "Down by the Riverside," "Dry Bones," "Give Me That Old Time Religion," "He's Got the Whole World in His Hands," "His Eye is on the Sparrow," "Walk the Lonesome Valley," "Joy to the World," "Joshua Fit the Battle of Jericho," "Kumbayah," "Lift Every Voice and Sing," "Nobody Knows the Trouble I've Seen," "Peace in the Valley," "Rock of Ages," "Swing Low," "This Old Time Religion," "Will the Circle Be Unbroken?," "We Shall Overcome," "Were You There?," and "When the Saints Go Marching In."

So now you the readers whom lived the "good ol' days" may have had at least a few cobwebs swept away from their minds to relive memories from things mentioned in this section of things you'd almost forgotten. I hope you enjoyed. Those who are of the younger generation who stuck with all this rambling might have gotten a tiny bit of information or, for those whom may have just skipped this section altogether, you too can now enjoy....that it is over!

Another big difference from our days to today has to do with telling ethnic jokes. In this day and age a person would be in deep trouble, called names, given titles of some sort, ostracized, or perhaps even at times get caught up in media involvement if they did half of went on in our day. For us, it was almost an everyday occurrence. Today someone might even be threatened or hurt because this or that is said. Everyone is so uptight these days they seem to be obsessed with trying to find something to object to, because they don't like it or don't agree and feel their view is the only right one, without any thought for others views to be considered. We are all being choked and losing one free-dom after another. Let's then look back to how it was in our day. (A lot of the young generation will cringe when they read this. However I doubt that many from our day who are reading this book will, they will just fondly remember.)

We had jokes that were constantly putting down another group of people. We had Polish jokes, Italian jokes, Catholic or other religious jokes. There were jokes about fat people, short people, skinny people, and naturally, the dumb Blonde jokes. We were Czechoslovakian, and we were also the brunt of the jokes.

Now there may have been someone somewhere in the country who was hurt in some way by the jokes, just as today someone is offended by something every day. Yet the majority of the people knew they were jokes. We knew how to laugh at ourselves, and we knew the jokes were not actually being directed at us personally nor singled out our own ethnic background because the same ex-act joke would be told somewhere but with a different culture being replaced. There may have been a few which fit only one group because it was strictly their ethnic motif, but those were even funny and, for the most part, the peo-ple even laughed at themselves. People went so far as to buy joke books with the put downs in them, so to have them to use at the drop of a hat. We were always laughing at each other knowing it was in fun. To make a joke, it has to be about something or someone to make it funny. It doesn't mean it's serious.

We had a group of singers and movie stars who were close buddies and were labeled the "Rat Pack." It had Dean Martin, Sammy Davis Jr. (who was black) Frank Sinatra, Joey Bishop, and Peter Lawford. They were really funny, and Dean used to hold celebrity roasts that were hilarious. Some person was chosen to be roasted and then the putdowns went on for an entire evening which was shown on TV. Even Sammie Davis brought in stuff about being brought up black. There are some of the roasts still available, yet in today's way of thinking some people would find them offensive and some might even want them banned.

Luckily the put downs are still alive and well, at least among my friends and relatives who can take a joke and live life with laughter and light hearted-ness.

They don't have to be three line put downs like the jokes, but merely pok-ing fun at one another. You can almost hear the wheels turning from a person trying to come up with something smart to say. (These are an example of the same type of joking around we did as a youth which continued far into later years as an adult and is still quite alive today.) I had an Indian friend who came to visit one day. My grandson loved Dancing Wolf and did all he could to get recognition from him. Dylan found a stuffed animal which was in among our Christmas decorations to take to show him. Dancing Wolf took it from him and said, "Oh isn't that nice. Is that Rudolph?" Dylan got a strange look on his small face, and I said to Dancing Wolf "You call yourself an Indian and you can't tell a moose from a deer?" He looked at it again and then with his usual twinkle in his eyes responded "Well you white people have got us so mixed up we don't know what things are anymore!"

Another time an incident happened at the Catholic nursing home where my mother was. One of the residents with whose daughter I became friends with happened to be a nun. I'm a Methodist, and we were always jabbing each other back and forth about religious views. One day she, her mother and another close resident friend, were sitting off in a side room playing poker. The resident was one whom at times would take guests through to see the complex. While they were playing cards, someone else was taking guests through, and Agnes said "Oh dear...and here I am playing cards. What am I going to say if they come in here?" I was told the Nun never missed a beat as she came up with the answer! "We'll just tell them we're Methodists!"

We all need to get back to a lighter, happier, less uptight life, filled with laughter and the ability to not only laugh but even at ourselves and not take things so serious and personal.

Comedians these days are being stifled as they are being told by this group or that group that they can or can't say this or that. If they say the wrong thing, they have the media after them. It is to the point that many comedians refuse to go entertain at some colleges because of the student's rules, for people can't take being laughed at as a group of people even though no individual is pointed out alone. It's not personal...it's a joke. If people would look up the word joke, it says, absurd, not serious! The freedom of comedian's talent to make people laugh and teach them to lighten up and enjoy life without being so offended by things is being threatened.

If you fear being called names or being given some title because of something you say or even in fun, then the freedom of speech is fading also from your life. How does it feel? Is today's life better, or do our "good ol' days" sound more inviting?

Chapter 16

We lived at the bottom of our hill and by then we did have more books to take home for homework. Even though we did have homework now, it still wasn't like kids have it today. Certain classes had homework on some days and other classes on others. That kept the load down for us. Those names people had for various ethnic groups didn't leave our Czech people out. They called us 'flathead Bohemians' and I remember us kids walking down the hill with our pile of books balancing on our heads trying to see if it was true. "Son of a gun, it was!" It was amazing how far we could get down that hill before the books started slipping. However, it might not have been that our heads were flat but merely that we held our body in perfect posture as we walked but because we were trying to see if the title given us was true we felt it was that.

Not too far from our school was a Czech cemetery we all knew about but it wasn't until only a few years ago did I find that there was also a Muslim cemetery right next to it and divided only by a chain link fence. We had a black cemetery in another area with one of a mixed group of nationalities or Catholic one across the road. So even though we were mixed together and also had our own areas too, we also had our specialness to be with loved ones even in death.

Even as teenagers, we had the church as a power point in our life. Because of the church, we still had the family together as one, no matter what age and anyone whose parents might not come would join in with the friend's families that did. We had youth group activities alone but also still had church ice cream socials where people from all over came for ice cream and homemade cakes. Besides the cakes to choose from to go with your ice cream, people could also buy separate pieces or entire cakes which gave them scrumptious treats to take home and our church made money. But again, that became a sign of the times as it wasn't long before the local government said because they didn't know the kitchens which were used for baking the cakes, to protect the public from any unsanitary places, homemade cakes were no longer to be made and sold. So, it began. It's moved forward to the point where we have so much more government interference concerning our foods and now today, even them reaching into our private eating habits.

Church had a lot of games which included all age being able to play. We had musical chairs where a group of ten chairs was set back to back and a group of eleven people walked around them while music played. When the music stopped everyone scrambled to sit in a chair, and the one who didn't get a chair had to go sit down. Another chair was removed, and the group repeated the walk. Each time a person without a chair sat down and another chair got removed. Soon it ended up with one chair and two people. The last one with the chair was the winner, but actually, everyone watching the whole thing were the winners as there was a lot of funny, laughable moments.

We had our own version of pin the tail on the donkey. Sometimes it was pinning something on a different sort of picture. There were donuts hanging from the long doorway on strings. One person stood beneath each donut hanging slightly even with their eyes. There was a contest to see who could eat their donut first, but the thing was, they had to have their arms behind their back while they did it. Therefore, the donuts would swing back and forth and get away from them, making them have to catch it with their mouth.

As I mention these games, I am also telling how they were played. Not only will it sweep back the cobwebs of the minds from those from our years but will also give ideas for people of today to play at parties or churches who might wish to restore the games in their own activities. I have already given the instructions for the cotton ball game and the drop the clothespins in the bottle, which in our day we had a glass milk bottle. We had taffy pulls and one game where a marshmallow or bubblegum was slid down to the center of a long string. (We had to put a hole in it with a needle to get it to slide down) Two people, one on each end, had to chew and get more of the string into their mouth and keep going to be the first one to get to the prize in the middle. The church evenings always had skits and plays.

When we had outdoor days, we held other types of games. Sack races with people standing in potatoes gunny sacks (or similar) and racing by hopping to the finish line. There were three-legged races where two people were partners and stood next to each other. Their inside legs were tied together, so they had to coordinate their running together to a finish line. You can't list games without including the egg toss. Everyone formed two long lines and stood across from their partner with one of them having a raw egg. At the start with each person standing very close, they tossed the egg to their partner who caught it and then the entire line took a step backward and tossed the egg back to the first person again. Each time the egg was tossed the one line took a step backward. Naturally this got the partners further and further apart, and the chance that the darn egg was going to be caught wrong and smash all over the person became inevitable. When it did break the two partners were out of the game, but one was messier than the other. Everyone else kept going until the last couple was standing. Every partner knew while playing the game that one of them was going to get it, but each one felt it was okay if it was their partner. One of them did get their wish. There was a lot of tension, screams, and laughter with that game.

Movies of our times were great ones which will bring back fond memories to those of us who were there to see them come into being, but many will also be recognized by even people of today, as their popularity continued on through time. Who can forget *Cinderella, Alice In Wonderland, Treasure Island, Peter Pan, 20,000 Leagues Under the Sea, Painted Hills, Lady and the Tramp, Davy Crockett (King of the Wild Frontier), Old Yeller, Shaggy Dog, Sleeping Beauty* and *Around the World in Eighty Days*?

Television shows were also good back then, and many continued for so long they made their way into our world generations later. *Gunsmoke, Have gun Will Travel,* and *The Lone Ranger.* Comedies of *I love Lucy, Red Skelton Show, Jack Benny, Jackie Gleason show, Danny Thomas* and *Colgate Comedy Hour* which gave us a clean light hearted laughs. A sample of other shows included *I've got a secret, Bet your life, Arthur Godfrey, Dragnet, Wyatt Earp,* and *Wells Fargo.* Other special programs included *Leave it to Beaver, Rifleman, Maverick, Real McCoy's, Father Knows Best, 77 Sunset Strip, The Price is Right, Wanted Dead or Alive, Perry Mason, $64000 Question, Alfred Hitchcock, Perry Coma Show* and *The Millionaire.*

With Disney being very popular the other top stars of the times were Bing Crosby, Nat King Cole, Frank Sinatra, Pat Boone, Guy Mitchell, Dean Martin, Perry Como, Sid Caesar, Robert Montgomery, Polly Bergan, Patti Page, Gisele Mackenzie, Loretta and Robert Young, and Captain Kangaroo.

Our dress for the period is mentioned elsewhere in the book, but perhaps more information of facts would be interesting especially to the younger generation to compare our different worlds. The girl's dresses and skirts had to be below the knees. We were not allowed to wear slacks or jeans to school but on the bitter cold winter days, we could wear them under our skirts or dresses so to keep our legs warm on the way to school but had to take them off and leave them in our lockers until we went home. Although later on short shorts did come in style but Bermuda shorts were the first popular fad with knee socks and saddle shoes. Pearls, mustard seed necklaces, circle pins and although pretty costly also charm bracelets. Girls' hair styles were pig tails, pony tails, or pixie cuts. Hats, scarves, and over the shoulder purses were worn outside of school.

The boys wore denim jeans or chinos (twilled khaki cotton pants). Their shirts were oxford shirts with button down collars or unbuttoned shirts with collars standing up. They had neat looking crew neck sweaters and at times t-shirts and leather jackets. For church, concerts or performances they wore suits. The guy's shoes were either black sneakers, white bucks or penny loafers (which had a slot in the front top where you actually slipped a penny in.)

Other things started from our times were things like the credit card, glue, power steering, video tape recorder, Mr. Potato Head, bar codes, diet soft drinks and, the hydrogen bomb was made. Radial tires, the music synthesizer, the black box flight recorder, the transistor radio by Texas Instrument, oral contraceptives (the pill), nonstick Teflon pans, solar cells, optic fiber, computer hard discs, hovercrafts, liquid paper for mistakes, lasers, hula hoop, pacemaker, the Barbie doll and the microchip. There may have been more, but this gives you the idea that the "good ol' days" was also good for the current generation. Much of your day's influences are because of ours.

This generation is going through the controversial topic of legalizing marijuana. There are pros and cons to it as it does help many people with debilitating health issues and gives relief. However just using it recreationally is starting to show through research that it is harming people's brains and thought process. We sure don't need a world of those type of people wandering around. I have to laugh, though. As teens, we used to walk through marijuana fields where it was just growing wild. No one thought anything about it. That apparently has changed recently when the officials couldn't figure out why there were so many tourists in Iowa, which isn't a real tourist area. Then they found the people with the maps to the marijuana fields. That got fixed fast. In our day it was liquor. Iowa had liquor by the drink which meant you could buy a drink but couldn't take an open bottle with you. If you were found with an open bottle in your car, you could get arrested. One evening when I was dating Carl (my future husband), we went to a restaurant and there sitting on the floor next to his chair was an open bottle with almost nothing out of it. He wanted to take it home to his dad but knew that was going to be a scary project as we first had to get it out to the car but then had to make sure he drove very carefully to not have a policeman stop him for any reason so to then find the open bottle in the trunk.

In summers, the teenagers looked for places to get a job to both help out the family but also for their own spending money. Detassling corn was a hard hot job but was a common thing to do. There were other jobs, but one popular job for the girls was babysitting. For those who babysit these days or have to pay a babysitter now, think of our day when we charged fifty cents an hour and that even covered more than one kid. It eventually went to seventy-five cents and then a whole whopping dollar, but that took a long time. We thought we were millionaires.

A few funny recollections popped in which has no category but were still memories which gurgled up from the depths of years gone by. We had an old piano, and we used to tell people we had a hairless piano. They were as puzzled as I'm sure you are. It was a Baldwin. (Bald one!) That was actually its brand name. A funnier situation happened with my grandfather on my mother's side. (Yeah, I know it's called maternal grandfather but unfortunately not everyone knows it.) I don't know if he was pulling our leg or being serious because so often he did or said stuff that was comical yet he showed no emotion to keep us wondering and guessing. I had a yellow figurine of maybe eight inches high, and it held a fire hose in its hand and had a red fireman's cap on which was removable. The sign on the hat read "Remove this in the case of fire." Well, it was a joke, and we could hardly wait for someone to do it. My Grandfather removed the hat only to be met with the other sign which read "Not now stupid, in the case of fire!" He didn't laugh and only said," If there would have been a fire you would be thinking you could get help and not be told in case of fire and called names....if it was a fire then what? We didn't dare laugh but tried to explain it as being a joke. It reminded me of Toni's grandmother who was also Czech and didn't understand New Year's Eve celebration and came downstairs when the noise started thinking she had overslept."

As kids, we did not have money to go out to eat at a restaurant, but my mother finally had enough to take us to a really nice one as a special treat. We could finally get something we couldn't usually afford. My mother was really feeling good about it...until my sister and I wanted a hamburger! Here we were in a fancy place, and we wanted a common hamburger. I think that was also the last time she took us to a fancy place to eat. Most the time we ate at the restaurant next to where my mother worked whenever we got to actually eat out. It was just a simple hole in the wall place but great for my sister and me who only wanted hamburgers anyway. However one day my hamburger was really good because I got two hamburgers all in one bun. My sister's wasn't as good, though. She didn't have any hamburger at all. Just a bun! That was the same restaurant which had 'fly sticks' hanging above the table to catch flies. Imagine them being allowed to do that today, but it was normal back then. (And guess what, we never got sick or died from it! It didn't even gross out the adults as it was normal to see. We kids were thrilled to see the flies zoom in and then get stuck. It was really neat!)

I guess going back in time wouldn't be complete without bringing in the Coca cola image. Actually, for the younger generation who drinks cokes today, it might be good to know the background of it. It actually was invented by a pharmacist in 1886. He had been in the civil war so then afterwards was looking for something to make money with. He'd tried other pharmacies ventures, yet nothing panned out, so he decided to do the beverage market. The soda fountain was beginning to rise in popularity so making it a fountain drink made sense to him but with having no idea how to advertise another person came to help and wrote a slogan "The pause that refreshes." The inventor died in 1888 so never saw his dream come true. Another person entered the scene by the name of Griggs Chandler, who became sole owner of the company. He went all out with doing advertising by plastering the logos onto calendars, notebooks, posters, and book marks plus he hired traveling salesmen. He went as far as getting a patent on it as a medicine which would get rid of headaches and fatigue. However, Congress passed a tax on all medicines, so Coca-Cola decided to become a beverage only.

Coke came in 6.5 oz glass bottles to start with and cost only five cents. Then bottling costs went up and by 1946 depending where you were in the country it went up to six to ten cents. It continued moving up and by 1960 the five cent coke was gone forever. The pop was at the top for sales. Everywhere you looked, there was something with the Coca-Cola logos on it. Commercials brought sound to the advertisement to even get more attention. We had clocks with the image. There were red tables with either bar stools or regular chairs, pop dispensers, ice chests, fountain dispensers, large pictures in frames or tin signs with the bright colors plastered everywhere. It cheered up anywhere where it was seen. The ad signs changed constantly depicting different types of people enjoying a coke. Even Santa Clause got in on the act. There were teenagers, house wives, men in uniform, girls in their poodle skirts, guys together. The ads were endless. For those who would like to relive them look up Coca-Cola on the internet and you'll be able to bask once again in their memory. You younger generation can see what we grew up with and what you still drink to this day. Everywhere we went as kids to congregate, had the coca cola products as part of the place. There was music, double dip ice cream cones, ice crème floats, juke boxes, and, coke.

When Pepsi hit the market and started giving Coca cola a fight for the money, Coca-Cola came up with larger bottles and then even up to family size. I still have some of my own products as signs and other things mixing the "good ol' days" with coke as a reminder of the day, but mine are replicas rather than the real things.

Why this memory or trick of the days just popped in at this time is beyond any reason. It has nothing to do with the subject we just left, and it was back to the day of doing laundry. If there was something with a stain on it or needed a bleaching out, the item was placed on the grass where the grasses chlorophyll build in properties, did the trick. Today there are actually areas such as many cities across the United States which ban the use of clotheslines as they are unsightly and offensive to some. (Imagine....you might see the neighbor's underwear hanging out for the world to see! Do they not know the trick to hiding them by the way you hang the clothes?) Instead, we now use dryers which cost electricity and money to use. If the power goes off, they are useless, but those with clotheslines have no fear. Clothes have a fresh air smell when hung on the lines, so you don't need some piece of cloth to throw into the machine to get it.

By now I had taken a job during my lunch hours, at a store across the street from the school. I skipped lunch to help wait on the kids whom either brought their lunches and wanted chips and a drink or who bought sandwiches and things at the store rather than buy school lunches. With a total of only two and a half hours a week because our lunch periods were so short, I didn't make a whole lot of money but enough I could buy my own school supplies and not have to take it from my, by then, dollar a week allowance. I could use the whole thing for something I would want.

Chapter 17

The "Freedom of the '50s" was the start of teenage freedoms. In fact because of all the teenagers at the end of the war the term teenager was coined. With the war over there was more money, so the parents started giving kids an allowance. Those younger generations reading this may have great amounts of money in mind. Mine was a big whopping dollar! That's why I took a job at a store across the street from school during lunch time. It was a couple years before I was finally graduated to two dollars a week and mainly because I informed my mother the other kids were getting two, and it wasn't fair I only got one.

Parents wanted the kids to get things they had been unable to have as kids themselves as is the thoughts parents in every generation seem to carry on. (Coming from my generation and seeing what kids have today, I have trouble seeing why the next generation needs any more.) Before the war, the males were expected to go into the service and get jobs to help the family out or be able to take care of their own future family. The females were brought up to be domestic dutiful housewives and raise children. The '50s' teenagers changed that. Television and AM radios became freedom for us to be able to listen to our new Rock and Roll music. We started setting hairstyles, clothing trends, and new ways to dance. As with all generations, the parents didn't like the new music and felt it was corrupting us, causing or leading toward juvenile delinquency. It had nothing to do with the music but rather that we had freedoms and money we hadn't had before and were feeling our oats. It calmed back down by the time we turned twenty. That music is still popular to many people even today. The music was an identification with what was going on in our lives, and the singing artists were people our own age who could identify

147

with our issues. Loud music, beats to dance to, yet other slow ones to get close to your date, and fast cars, etc. We had places to gather with other kids to be sociable and listen to music. There were ice cream parlors, malt shops, pizza places, and, of course, restaurants similar to ours during my childhood preschool years, with juke boxes like we had.

We went to movies, to peewee golf courses, bowling, recreational areas with in ground trampolines, plus pin ball machines, among other things to choose from.

We also had drive-in theaters which were nothing but a big parking lot with posts holding a large speaker with a cord, spread throughout the lot depicting where the cars were to park. These speakers were to be put into the driver's side car window rolled up almost to the top so the lip of the speaker could hang over it to hear the sounds of the movie being shown on a huge movie screen down front for all to see. The drive-ins were great. We could go to them as groups of girls, guys, double dates or by ourselves with our dates. People even gathered the little kids and took them in their pajamas to a movie. That way when they got home the kids were usually sleeping and were ready to be put into bed. Teenagers also used their cars as a place to neck or pet with their dates. (Sometimes the movie next to you was better than the one on the screen.) There was also a snack bar where you could go to get things to eat. The two things which are memorable of drive–in's was first getting there. To save money kids would ride to the movie with friends then just before they got there, would climb into the trunk and sneak in so not to have to pay. The other thing memorable of drive-ins was when it was time to go home, many times people would pull out to leave and forget to remove the speaker. More speakers than could be counted were pulled out with the cord left hanging from the window. They finally put an ad up on the screen to remind people to hang the speakers back up.

In our day juvenile delinquency wasn't like todays drug dealing or drive by shootings but was,...get this...chewing gum in school (not guilty, but talking in class was another thing)talking back to parents (not very often. I knew the consequences) and souping up a hot rod car. I didn't have a car but rode with kids who did. The one thing that was a dangerous thing to do was to play chicken, which was where two kids would be a long ways apart with their cars facing each other and then start their engines. They would race toward each other and whoever swerved first was the loser. (In my eyes...the winner...they weren't dead!) I read the books Street Rod and Hot Rod, which even though they were merely just stories, they described the crashes in gross details. That book was enough to keep me from even riding in a car with anyone who liked doing stuff like that.

I guess my images of the '50s when looking back, would be poodle skirts, drive-ins, bobby soxers, malt shops, sock hops, letter sweaters, juke box, rock and roll and black leather jackets.

The media in all generations seems to be either helpful or the culprit for what is right or the cause for what is wrong with society. It is always being mentioned today as it was back then. Media can sway.

We had the movies *Grease* and *Pleasantville* and television shows like Leave it to *Beaver*, *Ozzie and Harriet*, *Happy Days* and *The Donna Reed Show* to name a few. All family type shows. There was also, *I Love Lucy*, *Jackie Gleason*, *Gunsmoke*, and *The Ed Sullivan Show*. However, there were things like *Rebel Without Cause* and *The Wild One* which seemed to be the favorites for kids who felt unhappy, directionless or even feelings of being lost.

Way back in time the woman was in control of whom she would date. Apparently before the '20s and especially in the more affluent families, a man would, what they termed "call" on, a female and present a card to the maid. (A maid? Our class would have never gotten someone to call then...we didn't have a maid. Unless the guy just handed the calling card directly to us who were the maid!) The woman could accept or make up an excuse to not see the guy. The poorer people did other things called 'courtship' which led to the title of dating. With dating, the male dominance took over, and it was improper for a female to ever ask a male for a date. That's the way it was in the '50s with us... Girls could do anything they could think of to be asked out by a guy they were interested in, but if he wasn't interested it did no good.

By then blacks and whites because of growing up together were more understanding of the views others had. Our music tastes meshed together too. A small list of the black artists of our day whose music we listened or danced to were Marvelettes, Crystals, The Supremes, Dixie Cups, Shirelles, Royals, Mills Brothers, Platters, Covers, Flamingos, Doo Wop, Dominoes, Moonglows, and so many more. There were also other black singers of Nat King Cole, Chuck Berry, Ray Charles, Aretha Franklin, Little Richard, and Sammy Davis Jr.

It is impossible to list even half the singers and music of our time, so I give just a sampling of a few, for those who grew up back then might connect with: Edie Gorme, Doris Day, Nancy Sinatra, Brenda Law, June Valli, Rosemary Clooney, Jo Stafford, Gogi Grant, Kay Star and Dinah Shore. Bobby Darin, Paul Anka, Frankie Avalon, Pat Boone, Elvis Presley, Neil Sedaka, Fabian, Roy Orbison, Bobby Vinton, Jimmie Rogers, Ricky Nelson, James Darrin, Conway Twitty, the Crewcuts, Beach Boys, Everly Brothers, 4 Seasons, Letterman, Jordanaires, and The Diamonds. Anyone who would like to listen to the music itself can probably look it up on the internet to hear what we enjoyed back then, or if you are from back then, to hear it again!

Things identified with the '50s are also so many they can't all be listed. The ant farm where ants were squashed between two pieces of glass with dirt in them, and you could watch the ants as they made their tunnels. The Frisbee was started and even to this day is enjoyed by people of all ages as well as the dogs that now also play with them. The hula-hoop, Pez dispensers (discussed elsewhere), and the boomerangs which became another craze. The boomerangs, when thrown correctly, were thrown away from you, and they returned. Mine didn't! My yo-yos went down and didn't come up but tangled the string, the hula hoop didn't keep circling around me but ended up at my ankles before stopping on the ground, and my boomerang left, and I had to go find it! (If you find one...it's mine!) Some inventions! (Add this to my inability to sing, you might think I'm not too good at anything. If you've read this book so far, at least, I've got a chance)

There was telephone booth stuffing, to see who could break the record of how many people you could get into a telephone booth. (Try that with your cell phone!) We had drive-in burger joints and diners where waitresses' roller skated to your car to get your order and deliver your food. There were pistols that shot potatoes plus we enjoyed black jack chewing gum, 3-D movies, hats made from raccoon skin and fur as the image for the frontiersmen of Davy Crockett and Daniel Boone. They were called "coonskin caps." (Now, at my age we live in a different state and only about a half hour to Davy Crockets birthplace.)

The cool guys had what was called "duck tail" haircuts which was the hair combed back ward on each side with a plastic comb forming a ridge in the back and was kept in place with grease called Brylcream. I remember part of the jingle for the ad. "Brylcream, a little dab will do ya. Brylecream, you'll look so debonair. Brylcream, the girls will all pursue you. They love to get their fingers in your hair." A lot of times the guys had black leather jackets and side burns which grew an inch or more below the ears were also part of the look. The movie stars James Dean, and Elvis Presley were the instigators for those.

There were also letter sweaters where sports award logos were placed, and it was common for girls to wear their boyfriend's sweater or jacket to show others they were dating a jock. Other people got logos for other things too, like the band, etc.

Girls wore poodle skirts which were wide swing skirts with a poodle appliquéd on it. The other styles popular for the time were sack dresses, two piece bathing suits, bobby sox, short shorts, poodle hair styles or pony tails, or even wore pants outside of the house. We had a dress code for school. Girls were not allowed to wear tight sweaters, but we did get to wear the fad of twin sweaters which was a slip over, and an opened up button down, as long as the slip over was not tight.

Pink was a fad for a while of clothing for both men and woman. I remember seeing men with pink shirts with gray slacks and always loved that look. It was really the in thing for a while.

There were panty raids that were popular in the '50s, but they were with the college kids.

Our times were a mixture of things like Disney type pictures and the Biblical Ten Commandments and then others with switchblades and cars leaping off cliffs. Television executives tried to meet their audience with the least amount of offensiveness. There were westerns, comedies, quiz shows, soap operas, sports, and political conventions or Presidents speeches. Something for everyone.

Chapter 18

With girls learning to cook and sew in school for one of the classes my mother decided to fill in at home with other things woman liked to do as domestic housewives. She tried to teach me to knit, but I couldn't master that at all. I was willing to put the big skein of yarn over my arms for her to take a strand and keep winding it until it was a big ball, but taking needles to knit, no thanks. If I couldn't do the bigger yarn, I sure wasn't going to do a smaller thread to crochet. There was one thing left, and that was cross stitch or needle point. That sort of looked interesting as the pictures afterwards come out pretty neat. I liked that. I was so proud of myself, and the picture was showing up pretty good as I stayed well on the lines where I was supposed to. Then my mother who was so excited because I finally was doing something domestic, took my work to admire it more closely. I guess she couldn't believe I was actually able to do something. Well, her doubt was real! She felt something was not quite right and turned it over. There all over the area were colorful loops of threads everywhere! (She didn't tell me I had to pull the thread completely through until it stopped, so I was just dipping the needle inside the thread and then kept going... Well, that ended my mom ever trying again to make me a homemaker.) School wasn't that much better. We took sewing class and made hot pads on the sewing machine. You were supposed to keep going around the square until there were many lines outlining the entire area from center to outside edge. I think the lines were supposed to be straight, but I sort of liked my wavy effect. Now for those of you who are reading this and sew. Have you ever sewed on a treadle machine? We had to move our toes to heels and back and forth constantly on a large foot peddle area to get the machines needle to go up and down to sew. Well, it wasn't that easy because if you got in the wrong rhythm in the middle of what you were sewing, even though the material had been going away from you it was now returning back to you and going back over what you had just sewed...but not necessarily on the same lines! We did have a couple machines that weren't treadled, but we had more kids than machines. I was willing to give mine up!

Our gym classes were classes where you got a lot of exercises. They could be jumping jacks, pushups, or twists and turns of the body with arms outwards or bending to touch your toes, climbing on things, kicking the medicine or cage ball, climb things or high jump. We played basketball, and softball, volleyball, and tennis. We had to hit the showers after gym class before returning to classes and kids would try to say they took a shower but didn't, so we had to put our towel over us while wet and turn around butt naked so the teacher could mark down you had taken a shower. I have to brag about my basketball skills. (I have to brag about something. My homemaking sure wouldn't do it!) I played guard in basketball, and I could guard so close without fouling that the other team hated it when I was their personal guard. I did play forward at times and one day we had seconds left to play and we were so close, yet losing. I was in center court and made a shot toward the basket. That darn thing went in, and we won! Everyone was amazed, but so was I. That's it, folks! That was my moment of fame. Never did it again, so I have to hold on to that one.

We had science classes, biology, English, history, art, math, algebra, band, literature, cooking and sewing, music, gym and later in the new high school, swimming. (The boys got woodworking and shop) In grade school, we had learned to read and write, add, subtract, multiply and divide. If we didn't learn it in the one year, we stayed back a grade until we did. They weren't concerned with our feelings about not learning it to begin with but was more concerned they did learn. You never can use something needed for later in life if you were just passed through.

Again, a practice from our time that leads to today's practice was we had winners and losers. We worked harder to become winners if we had previously lost, but we did learn how to lose without being scarred for life. In this day and age, it seems child psychologists, or parent's who don't want their child to have to suffer defeat, don't want winners and losers but merely play the game. If those parents would know their child would win then, they'd probably would have been okay, but they can't stand to think of them being a loser. (Didn't seem to bother my folks. I had a whole lot of things I couldn't do. Can't ya just see all the things people would have had to change to keep me from being hurt and feel I couldn't do something? No music would be able to sung, boomerangs and hula hoops would not be able to be used, and all domestic type endeavors would have to be curtailed. (I did find what I was good at! Not being able to do things!) So much is lost both in developing skills and self-esteem when life is so padded. It's not going to be like that in the real world. (In later years when my own children were on swim teams they had place ribbons where each child got a different color ribbon depending on the position they came in during the swim meet. That was the best of both worlds. Each person got something but yet the competition was still there to be the best you could be. However when my one son was going to swim, we knew he wasn't yet good enough to come in anything but last, so we kept pumping him up to get a brown ribbon. Well, that was great but when they got onto the starting blocks one person wasn't going to swim. My son did come in last, but now the last place would be a green ribbon. When he got the green one, he was upset because it wasn't the brown one. We had to tell him he was even better and got a green one this time. From that time on we just said, "Get a ribbon." Not allowing a child to try doing his best and compete to do better than others, takes away those children's talent and skills. While others are trying to keep kids from getting feelings hurt, others abilities are being stifled. Give me the "good ol' days!"

The other thing of our teenage years was because of the new found freedoms and money. Dating was becoming looser and things like kissing, hugging, holding hands in halls at school, necking and petting became common. The schools showed educational films to the kids, but usually, the boys and girls times were separate. The films had teenage actors but with their adult's messages, which reminded the kids of customs and certain boundaries in dating and warned of serious consequences if they violated the rules. Even with all the looseness, virginity was still a virtue, and the kids themselves seemed to be the ones to keep one another in line with their own peer pressure views. The boys were expected to be the ones to pay for their dating expenses.

Chapter 19

Our family was going to be moving from the city into the country. That meant leaving behind all those memories made in that house. The winters snowy days of loading Christmas gifts for others onto the sled to trudge along taking them to their houses. Those memories of the neighbor's car with the rumble seat which was outside the back of the car. The smell of the stench in the air that floated to our house from the Penick and Ford Company only when it was going to rain. It never failed. We knew rain was coming when we smelled it, but we always said: "Grandpa took his socks off again." My dad's father worked there. We had a teacher who lived right next door to us and was mean. We didn't dare step on her grass when we were playing, or she'd open the door and yell at us. One day our ball went into her front side of the yard, and she ran out and grabbed it. My mother happened to be home, and she came out and said to us. "That's okay kids; she must need a ball. We'll get you another one." With that, the teacher's door opened and she tossed it back! We wouldn't miss that.

The days of playing Halloween pranks and soaping windows would be gone, even though the one store actually gave us the soap to use because it was the type that cleaned the windows when washed off. Other soap would be hard to remove.

We were leaving behind the memory of the cats who had been our alarm clocks even though now were long gone. Those cats knew exactly the time we had to get up because they put two and two together when that noisy clock sounded the alarm, everyone got up. Alarm clocks in those days had to be wound, and there was no sleeping through their noise. The cats decided to get us up a lot more quietly and would jump on us and knead their clause into us

155

until we got the message. If they happened to be outside, they actually jumped on the screen and made a loud racket until we got up to let them in. It was always at the same time just before the alarm went off.

Now with moving, I had one thing I was sad about. My uncle had given me the entire series of the National Geographic from their beginning to that present time. They were stacked several feet high all around the walls of the entire front screened in porch. Now we were moving, and I wanted to take them with us. I thought it was neat to have such a collection, but we weren't even going to have a house to start with so nowhere to put them. We were going to live in one side of a man's house who lived across the road until our house got built, and with us building it ourselves it would go up only as fast as we could do it. I didn't want to throw the books away, so I gave them to the school. I took them little by little up the hill in my bicycle basket. What a job, but at least they would be in a good place. I had a couple spare books from the first years so do still have them in remembrance of all the ones I had at one time.

Toni was driving and said she would come out to our house so we could still go places together, so that took care of that aspect. The good thing about it was even though I was moving I wouldn't have to change schools as the country school only had grade school. I was now in Junior high. When the country school added a grade I had moved up a grade and they didn't have that one yet so I kept one grade ahead of their grade progress. There was a school bus that would take us to our same school. That meant we did have to get up early to ride the bus for a half hour or more so finished our sleeping on the bus. Little did I know there would be a whole new slew of memories waiting to be made but there sure were, and it didn't take long for them to start.

With still going to the same school I would be with the same kids I'd been with since grade school so that part wasn't much different. I did have homework but nothing like kids today are stuck with. We still had time for ourselves. I did my homework on the school bus on the way home, so I had time for myself once I got home.

My step dad was building our house across the road, and I helped. He laid blocks, and I helped bring the concrete mud to him to keep the wheel barrel full. I also was taking driving at school even though my first driving experience had come with Toni's dad who unknowingly taught me to drive. I mentioned that episode earlier. One day when we were coming home from the town, my own mother pulled over to let me drive the country roads home. I was excited, but my mother got more excited when after a very successful drive home I turned into the driveway and the engine started roaring making the car speed up with almost making me hit a telephone pole. Mom started yelling at me, but I told her it wasn't me ... the gas pedal stuck! (Like she believed me!) However, it was true! She should have been glad I was good enough to miss that stupid pole! When she drove the car next, she discovered I was telling her the truth and got it fixed.

I took a course to teach handicapped and mentally retarded kids to swim. One house over on the rich side of town had a pool in their house and offered it to be used to bring in the handicapped kids. We each got one of the children to work with. The little boy I had had no arms but had artificial ones. He was about four, and he informed me I had to take his arms off first before going into the water, or they would rust. Another little boy who had one leg half as long as the other also had a brace as well having an issue with his arms, laughed when we took my little guys arms off. My little guy just looked at him and said, "You're not in such good shape yourself!" I had to laugh. These kids would always have to have help in the water, but I could teach my little one to be able to roll over to his back and roll again and kick a ways before rolling over again. The scariest part was to pick him up in the first place. We don't realize how beneficial armpits are until there is nothing to hang on to. I had to push inwards on his body real quick to keep control of him. That was a very interesting course. During that course, they blindfolded us and had us swim the length of the pool. I very carefully put my hand with each stroke right in front of me knowing I was going really straight and soon was touching the wall. I removed my blindfold and found myself only half way down the pool where I had turned and was at one side. Try it sometime. It's not as easy as you think. Our main issue with the mentally challenged was we had to keep the boys and girls at opposite ends of the pool, as they might have mental issues but physically they had the same drives as anyone else their age. We would have had a problem had we allowed them to get together.

Chapter 20

The old man we lived with had a telephone that was as old as that "cowboy" candlestick one of my younger years. In fact, it was more ancient in technology, as our phone had a dial we could use to call someone. His was a wall phone, and you had to lift the receiver to tell the operator whom you wanted to call. It also had several others on the same line so you might pick up the receiver only to hear the line being used by someone else and until they were through talking, you couldn't call anyone. If you got a long winded person, you could pick up that phone for an hour and not get through. When someone called you, you had a special ring. Every ring sounded in your house but also to those houses on your party line. You only answered the one with your own special code, but it wasn't unheard of to have someone nosey also pick up their phone to listen in. I guess more than one person was told to get off. They did, but sometimes you could hear the receiver slowly lift to listen again. Our ring was two long rings and a short. If there was a fire someplace, the siren sounded all over the area, and everyone would go to their phones to pick up the receiver where the operator told everyone at the same time where the fire was. Because we had volunteer fire department everyone who could go at that time went to help. The head of the department was the sheriff and also the town barber. If the fire alarm went off, he had to stop everything to get the fire truck and go. One year the alarm rang, and before long it rang again. Then our neighbor's field caught on fire, and he called the fire department, but they were still on the last call. I ran over, and he and I were able to get the field fire out just as everyone else finally drove in. Seeing we had managed to get the fire out the barber smiled and said, "Oh good. I guess

I can go back and finish that haircut".

One night while we were still living with Morrie the fire bell went off, but we didn't go check out where it was this time. All of a sudden we heard a knock at the door and as we went to answer it, men started rushing in. Cars were pulling in one after another. What the heck? It seems someone was driving by and saw a fire in Morrie's own attic and called in the alarm. Some of the men's wives also showed up but came in and sat down with us. Now does that make sense? The attic was full of volunteers putting out a fire and us women sat in the kitchen to talk!

Even though Morrie was pretty old, he still walked the one to one and a half miles into town every day to play cards with the other guys. They played for candy bars which he brought home and gave to us. For the first few months, we were thrilled, but it got to the point I couldn't look at another Three Musketeers, Milky Way, Snickers or Forever Yours. Sometimes he won a Mounds or Almond Joy and I raced to get those. To this day I cannot eat one of those others, except in the last four years, I have managed to do Snickers again.

He had a horse which I thought was great and wanted to ride it. I knew boys from town would come to ride it from time to time but wasn't aware they abused it by pulling back so hard on the reins it made a callous in its mouth. You had to ride bareback as he had no saddle. One day I decided to go for a ride and everything went great. That is everything was fine as we went away from the barn toward the cemetery. However, when I turned the horse around to go back toward the barn again, the horse also thought that was a good idea and decided to get there faster than I'd planned. He took off running, and when I pulled back on the reins, I soon found out what those boys had done to its mouth because it didn't react to pulling on the reins at all. I also learned it didn't understand English as when I yelled "Whoa," it didn't! Maybe he was deaf, so I yelled louder. No matter how loudly I yelled "Whoa" the more, it ignored me. Now remember I was speeding along in a full run, not just a gallop and I was riding bareback. No saddle horn to hang onto. I had only its mane. As I was sliding back and forth from side to side trying to keep from falling off and breaking my neck, I noticed one thing in the path ahead right where we were going. "Oh no!" I couldn't believe it! Where we were heading was a five foot barbed wire fence. I cringed as the horse jumped into the air. I just knew I was about to become dead meat, and I wondered who or when someone would finally come find my broken body! Would I be dead or broken to smithereens? How I ever stayed on that horse to even be able to tell this story now, is more than I can ever know. If there are Guardian Angels, I sure had one that day. That was my first and last ride on that horse.

There was a cemetery at the end of the pasture where I had been riding. Sure glad it hadn't become my resting place as an outcome of my 'last ride". One day a line of cars pulled into the cemetery for a funeral. All of a sudden gun shots rang out. With my usual quick comments although I wasn't really thinking about it, I came up with, "Hmmm, guess they weren't sure he was dead yet." Actually, it was a military funeral and somber, but it just hit me funny when you put the funeral and sound of guns together in thoughts.

I was lucky another time that I didn't end up taking up residency in that cemetery. In fact over the years, I've become to think myself as a cat with nine lives but haven't kept track so hope my last one isn't up yet. I'd hate to think I got this far with writing a book and keel over before I get it finished! When I watch *It's a Wonderful Life* at Christmas time I think that I singlehandedly have given a whole lot of Angels their wings!

My sister was married by then and had come out for a visit. Actually, they had some news to deliver. My sister was going to have a baby. The words hardly left her mouth when wind blew up, and we laughed and said, boy was that startling news but not enough to cause a storm that bad! Then it really started to pick up, and as we turned, we saw a bad storm roaring toward us from the down the road. My sister and brother-in-law jumped into their car to leave before they got caught in it and we ran into the house to close windows. The front door of the old farmhouse was crooked and didn't fit very well when closed. I took a butter knife to slip into it and fill in the space to make it tighter. As I turned to walk back toward the kitchen, the wind hit really strong, blowing the front door wide open with force. It sent that knife I'd just placed in the door to wedge it shut, sailing past me and just barely missed stabbing me in the back. As strong as that wind was, had the knife hit me it would have killed me for sure and probably gone clear through me. I've seen flimsy pieces of straw get sent clear through the wood of a barn from a tornado wind. This was a solid, sturdy knife! The storm was over within a few seconds. We went across the road to see if any damage happened to the house we were building. We had the cement block walls up but hadn't yet begun to start the roof. We got over there to find the entire back wall laying on the ground inside the house. The blocks were so close together they appeared as if they had been cemented together purposely and laid that way. That quick wind was actually a tornado which had come through. Talk about a cat with nine lives. If that was true for me, I just used up at least two in the short time we were living in that old farmhouse.

We continued working on the house but then had to redo what had come down before finally making it to being able to put up the roof. I helped work on the roof and pounded nails right alongside with my step dad. I was becoming a jack of all trades. (Except for homemaking skills!) We put up the partitions inside the house as to where each room would be, but none of them were into actual rooms yet. Therefore, it was just open rafters when my sister and her husband came again for a visit. With us not having anywhere for them to stay in the old farm house with us, we put up a bed in the house we were building. They could sleep there. The roof was on, and the windows were in. We gave them a lantern to use for light, but when our cat climbed on the rafters, it cast humongous shadows like a monster clear across the room. While they were sleeping my brother-in-law reached over to my sister during the night and touched her head. There was that darn cat sitting on her head. He was mad and reached out and grabbed it and gave it as hard a throw as he could. The only thing is, it wasn't the cat! My sister's hair was done in a ponytail, and he about threw her head off the bed!

Once the house was finished, we had many new episodes to add to our book of memories... We had a cat get a paralysis causing her to walk with only the front feet while dragging the back. It wasn't long before it reversed and the cat's back feet worked but the front ones didn't. The veterinarian had some name for it but said the cat would die when the paralysis returned to the back feet again. Both happened. It almost seemed to be like what we saw in later years of something called "mad cow disease."

Our luck with cats wasn't real good. Another cat ran up an electrical pole and then walked out on the wires. Had it gone on any other combination than what it did it would have been alright but the ones it chose electrocuted itself and shut down all the electricity for miles around. That wouldn't have been as bad, but there was a dairy farm down the road that usually used electric milking machines for the cows and with them needing to be milked right then were going to have to be milked by hand. There were a lot of cows so others came to volunteer help. However, the farmer figured how to hook the milkers' to the tractor source. It took them a while to find out what had happened but when they did it came to be at our property and our cat being the culprit.

We also had a dog, and none of our animals could ever go without memory or two being made. Those reading this who have animals can identify with that. We were sitting on the back porch one day watching the farmer behind us plowing his field when all of a sudden we smelled a skunk. The dog was lazily laying at our feet, and my step dad said, "If you weren't such a lazy dog you'd go get that thing!" We weren't really paying any attention so were unaware that the dog had left, but all of a sudden it came back. It had that gosh darn awful smellin' skunk in its mouth and went over and dropped it at my step dad's feet. We all ran away as fast as we could, into the house. The dog was gagging and spitting, and sputtering and my step dad had to give it a bath in tomato juice to get the smell out. By then he himself didn't smell too good either! That taught him not to call the dog lazy...and especially not to tell it to go get a skunk!

Not all our cats had negative experiences to report. We had one cat that loved corn on the cob. In the summer, we ate things from our garden for supper. Tomatoes, cucumbers and corn on the cob. When we threw the cobs into the bucket on the floor, the cat jumped into it to clean up the kernels which had been missed. One day we had a photographer friend of my mom's over to eat, and he worked for the newspaper where she also worked. He saw the cat eating the corn so grabbed his camera and the picture ended up making the local newspaper but then also traveled with the associated press across the country.

I used to go into town to friend's houses for slumber parties but never found out why they ever came up with that name because none of us ever slept. We also had sock hops which were dances where we danced in our socks rather than shoes. I decided to have one at our house, so I set out to make it special. I got huge sheets of brown meat paper from a meat market that had rolls of it, and I hung them next to each other on the wall from ceiling to floor. It was perfect to make a scene on. I painted a Hawaiian scene with palm trees and moon light and water. In front of the mural, I had a three tiered plastic dish type water fall. We had lei's for everyone to wear and everyone dressed in a Hawaiian shirt or outfits. By then we had a better record player that no longer needed to be cranked and had all kinds of the 45's records of our favorite music. Our new house was perfect for the dance as our living room was right off the kitchen with no division between them. The living room was 21 feet long with the kitchen area itself being another 24 feet. The kitchen cabinets were along one end, so there was a wide open space where to dance. While we were dancing, we heard a knock on the door. It was two boys our age who informed us they had brought grandpa home so if we saw lights on at his house across the street it was okay. That was strange. We didn't even know Morrie had been gone anywhere.

The next morning we saw a whole bunch of kids piling out of the house, and my step dad and I pretended we were working in the garden so we could get closer to the scene where I wrote down license plate numbers of some of the cars. We contacted the sheriff who came out and went into the house. The place was a total mess. The kids had wrecked the place and even killed a sheep in the kitchen. The first clue was that the kid had said they brought grandpa home. It was Morrie's own grandson who brought kids out to the party because he knew his grandpa had been taken to a nursing home. With that information and the license plate number we gave him, the sheriff didn't mess around. Within an hour, parents were pouring into the driveway with their kids in tow. The sheriff made every kid clean up the entire house and the yelling and screaming being done at the kids by their parents made us quite aware those kids hadn't seen the last of punishment yet to come. We knew they were in even more trouble when they got home. I'm not sure what charges were also given them, but kids were never just smacked on the wrist back then. They were shown it didn't pay to do things against the law. In fact, when I was very young I'd heard that if you went to jail, you only got bread and water to eat. That was enough to make me never want to do something to end up in jail.

School events and my experiences continued even though I was now living in the country. With me playing drums in the band I was put into a situation that to me was pretty funny even though I about got into trouble. Most the band kids disliked the band director. His attitude of strictness and being unwilling to bend made him a target. One time some kids stuffed all the drums in a special place under the floor, which I never even knew existed. Another time the director got ready to direct the band and couldn't find his directing baton. He was furious. He looked everywhere...but up. It was stuck in the acoustical ceiling holes right above his head. The day I almost got into trouble I was simply playing the drum. The director stopped and told me I was playing too loud and needed to be less aggressive. He started the band playing again, and the same thing happened. He again stopped the band and was emphatic that I was playing too loud. He told me to get a smaller bead (tip) drum stick. I got a tiny bead, but then he stopped and said I wasn't playing loud enough. I informed him if I played that loud with the small bead it would break. He was getting furious. We started again, and the culprit for this whole situation reached out the cabinet behind me and took my drum stick and slammed it into the closed hinge of the door to break the tip and then handed it back to me. When I wasn't playing at all, the band director stopped again, and I held up my broken stick. He clinched his teeth and said to get another stick. One more time I simply started playing as I was supposed to do, but Jerry sitting inside the cabinet, just went wild and started beating the drums as loud as he could. By this time the director was furious and was barreling down the area weaving in and out between the other players. I wasn't about to get sent to the Principles office when I was innocent. As he approached, I simply opened the cabinet door where Jerry was just beating away for all he was worth. The whole thing caught the director by surprise and Jerry was taken from the cabinet, and everything returned to normal.

Our high schools were both junior high as well as High schools. We had too many kids to keep those going as both, so two new schools were built. One for both sides of town and they would be only High schools. The four other schools we had been using, changed to becoming strictly junior highs. The new schools weren't ready for us to move into yet, but we did go to each other's Junior High school for some classes to intermingle until we were finally together when the school was finished. We finally got into our new school. We had a large swimming pool and with all my swimming experience I became an asset because they didn't have someone who could guard for a coed swim after school unless I would volunteer to do it. Remember me, the kid who wouldn't put her face into the water during so many swim lessons. Boy, do things change!

There was a senior life saving class being given at the school, and I already had it but renewed it again. When you are rescuing a person during practice, if the victim wants the rescuer to let them go, they tap the rescuer on the hand or arm, and they are to be released. At least that is what is supposed to happen! One day during class one of the people who was supposed to be the Rescuer, had the victims face too low during a cross chest carry maneuver, and her face was under water. The victim tapped the rescuer who didn't get the message so kept going. With the cross chest carry being used, the victims are always told to try getting out of the hold as a real victim being on their back would do. The rescuer's job was to keep control and not let them get away. That part of this event was a plus for the rescuer because she did keep complete control. The bad part of it for her was that her victim actually was really drowning, and it was the rescuers fault. The victim's face was below the water...the struggling was real...she was drowning. The teacher yelled to the rescuer from the side to tell her to release her victim, but the rescuer was so busy trying to keep control she didn't seem to hear. Then all the classmates began yelling too. I think the rescuer was feeling they were actually applauding her for being so in control. I couldn't believe the teacher wasn't doing anything, so I raced past them all and jumped into the water and separated the two and pushed the victim to the side to safety. The incident was over, and everyone was thanking me, but all I could think was "Why didn't the teacher do something?" With being in the new school, we were with new kids from the other school who combined with us. The new school hadn't gotten done fast enough for us to be in it for even a half year before graduation but in that time we made friends. One of those people eventually became my husband, but who was also in a band with me.

We went on bus trips to march for different events. One day we were going to Pella, Iowa for their world known Tulip festival. They had people dressed in Dutch outfits and wearing wooden shoes which made a very colorful event to be a part of. The entire town was decorated with beds of colorful tulips everywhere. On the bus ride the kids did their usual singing of songs to liven up the ride. This one kid on the bus from the other school kept watching us and looking at my cousin sitting next to me. I'm not sure if he thought those of us from the other school were nuts or he was interested in my cousin. We got to Pella and got our instruments ready for the march down Main Street. In those days, white buck shoes were the fashionable footwear for kids to wear, along with saddle shoes and penny loafers, but the white bucks were also part of our school uniform.

The town people had done everything they could to make their place presentable for all the expected tourists for this time of year. The tulips were absolutely breath taking so there was plenty for people to see but the town wanted everything perfect. In fact, they had just redone the streets black top only the day before. That...was a mistake! It was a very hot day! Our uniforms were hot to begin with and the sun beating down on the blacktop made it even worse. Then when it was time for the parade to start and we took our position to begin our march down the street, all of a sudden we were stuck! The whole band was stuck! The tar from the street had become so hot it was sticky and as we marched our shoes stuck like a suction cup and we were coming out of our shoes. There was no fancy strutting going on as we marched. The funny stepping we were doing was just us trying to keep our white buck shoes on our feet so the black tar wouldn't claim them. Band trips were always fun, and so were any events we did together. I usually played just the snare drum but once or twice during orchestra practice I did play the kettle drum, tympani, and even the cymbals.

One night during a performance I had one cymbal crash to make at a very crucial time to emphasize the piece being played. ONE single crash of the cymbal! The music built...I waited for my solo which was about to be heard by everyone in the audience. I watched the music...I listened for my time... and...I missed it! The others continued on, but you should have seen the look in some of their eyes and the grin and smiles around the sides of their mouth from the instrument they were playing. I couldn't believe it! (That memory could have stayed hidden as far as I'm concerned!)

Our group of us girls who hung around together did all kinds of things together. We went on picnics and walks. We went roller skating, to events, and had slumber parties. We went to amusement areas, fished and played miniature golf. Sometimes we just got together for fun at home. One day one of the girls was having a very special birthday, so her parents rented the Kappa Ann boat which went on the Cedar River at Ellis Park where the swimming pool was. The girls could invite their boyfriends if they had one, or any boy they wanted. The person I would have wanted to ask had already been asked by another, so I didn't know who to ask. It was still not totally away from the boys being the ones to ask the girls era and although it had broken away from that a tiny bit for times as this. My cousin told me to ask that kid from the other school who had kept looking at me on the bus trip to Pella. I quickly corrected her by saying "ME? He was looking at YOU!" Well, she convinced me it was me he had been looking at. (Hmmm, I should have paid closer attention!) I told her I didn't even know his name, so I had to ask someone from the school he'd come from. They told me his first name but then added his last name. "Pretzel? No, Petsel." What a dumb name. (Don't ever put anything down, because you just might end up eating your words. I once said I wouldn't have a dog when I got married. Then, when I got married and had a dog, said I wouldn't have a dog in the house. Then when it was an inside dog, I said it would never be allowed to sleep with us on the bed. Well, we've had different inside dogs who've slept on the bed! So now here was the first of many episodes like this as I thought the name was funny and I eventually ended up with it!) Anyway...we were setting up instruments for a concert and my cousin came up to me as he was walking through the same door as we were, and she loudly said "Did you ask Carl yet" I could have shot her! Now I was stuck because he said: "Ask me what?" So that was the beginning of my dating of my later to be, husband.

For a long time, it was only the boys who asked girls out. It was aggravating because there were so many girls who were interested in a boy but could only wish they would ask them. In our days, we didn't just date one person at a time but rather went out with any who might ask if we were interested. It was called 'playing the field' and was done so you would get to know others before deciding that special one you wanted to be with. If two of you wanted to make a real commitment to see only each other, then the boy would ask you to go steady and give you some kind of jewelry or ring of his. In Senior high it might be his class ring. We also had some rules which were just floating around but sort of got slightly overlooked when just going out. Catholics were to only date Catholics, Lutherans with Lutherans, Methodists with Methodists, whites with white and blacks with blacks. I guess we never asked why it just was.

Right now comes one of those memories which have jumped ahead in time but seems to at least have a connection this time. Carl was a Lutheran, and I was a Methodist, which made a difference to Carl's mom. He was supposed to date Lutherans, and she tried to break us up in many ways. I was also a year older than him, so I had two strikes against me. She point blank told him not to date me, and he couldn't get the car to drive, so figured that would help the cause. I actually had to drive into the city from my house in the country to pick him up. He then drove my car until the date was over when I then had to drop him off at the bottom of his hill and then drive back home myself. Doesn't that sound great? Those type of stories themselves would fill a book. One evening we went to see the movie *The Ten Commandments* when it started snowing. That is a very long movie and half way through they stopped the movie so they could announce that the snow was getting heavy, and some of us might wish to leave. They would give a ticket to come back at a later date. We stayed. Another announcement came again saying parents were calling and concerned about their kids, and the theater manager again mentioned a free ticket for a later date. We thought it was stupid. It couldn't be that bad.

It had just begun to snow when we came in, how bad could it be? We stayed for the entire movie but then we saw just how bad it could be! It was unbelievable. The car was snowed in, and we had a heck of a time getting it out. There was no way I could drive the highway home alone so after dropping Carl off I went to Toni's house to stay in town and I called home only to find our phone wasn't working. I had to call our sheriff in town and ask him to drive up to tell my parents I was okay and where I was staying.

Carl's mother finally gave up about our dating, but when we talked marriage, it started all over. He was Lutheran, and I was Methodist! He was too young. Not just too young for me, but too young. She said, "No one should get married until they are 28, and then they are crazy if they do." This scenario was to continue but not right now.

We had the German Amana Colonies right near our town. They had the Amana refrigeration plant there along with seven separate colonies yet still a part of each other. Each colony had their own specialness with a couple of them offering restaurants where people could go eat. One colony had a meat market while another offered a different specialty. The one we went to was the Colony restaurant which was in the same colony where they made hand-carved grandfather clocks and had the woolen mills. Like our rules about who dated who, and who could marry who, those people also had even more of a separatism within their churches. The men all sat up front of the church with the woman seated in the back. Each colony was responsible for themselves, yet if one fell behind in funds, the others pulled them through. They were a strict society which like all of the society has changed and loosened up over the years. We started going there as a treat when we were kids. Carl and I went there when dating and later we even had our wedding supper there. Many years later we traveled there again when visiting back in Iowa as adults and believe it or not after all those years some of the original people we'd met were still there and recognized us and even called us by name.

I guess everyone had some kind of rule or restriction with growing up, but some were worse than others. However although I welcome some of the changes that have been made over the years, I can also see the pendulum is swinging too far to the left where no rules are setting an atmosphere for people losing themselves and the inability for developing their much needed self-esteem.

Somehow the rules we had as kids, or the laws we were to follow, or the way we were free range kids who figured things out on our own, had something to do with the characters we build. I remember finding an envelope on the school grounds which had a lot of cash in it. There wasn't anyone's name with it, and that money sure would have done a lot for us, but yet, I put myself in the shoes of whoever lost it and thought "What if I was the one who lost that much money? How bad would it be for them and what could happen without having it?" I admit it was a tough decision. Even if a name had been with it, I still could have taken the cash, and no one would have known. However when you build up self-esteem you also have something attached to it. A conscience. Even if not one other person ever knew I took it, I would know. To always wake up remembering the money you took caused another family a hardship is a guilt trip I sure don't want to carry. I turned it in to the school and the girl who lost it was in tears when she found out it had been found. She was supposed to make her mother's house payment after school. I can imagine how hard that would have hit her family. Now if I found an envelope of money on a street somewhere with no indication of where it belonged, I might watch the paper to see if it appeared in the lost and found but I wouldn't put it in there unless the person had the exact amount they lost. I know everyone, and his brother would try claiming it otherwise. A funny thing happened concerning that very issue a couple other times in my life. We were in a parking lot and a family got out of the car to go into a mall. I saw a wad of bills drop onto the pavement as he left and called out to him. I could have just gone to get it and been richer, but again I put myself in his place. Remember "What goes around comes around" is a truer statement than you think. Karma isn't something to mess with. However, with that said, there was another incident where a man had just gotten out of his car and was going to the trunk of his car to get something to take with him into the pool. I saw him get out, and I did not see anything drop, but there between his car and mine was a dollar bill on the ground. Now I could have asked him if it was his and whether it was or not he would have probably have said yes even though I had seen him while getting out and didn't see anything drop. So that time I said nothing, but merely kept walking to the car and with my barefooted toes and without missing a step, picked up the bill and once inside the car reached down to retrieve it from my toes. Carl looked at me wondering how the heck I got money from my toes! No, I wasn't a bank and no I didn't have any more.

Maybe I got the idea about money being so important to others, and we should never take what isn't ours from the incident of the March of dimes collection on our city streets when I was a kid. (The problem with the way memories float in in no special order it is hard to remember if I've already mentioned it. This is probably okay to repeat here if I already have, though, as in a way it sort of connects) There were long boards between chairs or barrels along the curbs of the streets down town that ran down for entire blocks. People placed coins and bills on them, and the money was for the March of Dimes to be used for child birth defects and issues. It would have been so easy for people to go help themselves or steal the entire thing but no one touched it. (Try that today!..today they'd even take the chairs and boards) Maybe that left an impression in my young mind and was carried onward into life. I guess a good lesson to keep close.

One of the weirdest things we did as kids was to play with an Ouija board. When we were little kids, we did our version of fortune telling with plucking flower petals, saying he loves me he loves me not, or the magic eight ball that had a set up answers to our asked questions and with both if we didn't like the answer we just kept doing it until we did. With the Ouija board, it was different. Two people would put their fingers on the flat plastic pointer and ask a question. All of a sudden the pointer started to move and go to the letters around the board to spell out an answer. It felt creepy when it moved, but we always figured the other person was moving it. Of course, everyone denied it and thought it was us. It always left us with that mysterious feeling as to how it worked. The one thing,we were always instructed never to ask was about our own or anyone's death or anything hurtful. It was feared someone would take it as true and upset us. We were always told it was just our minds making the thing move. Well, now years later, there are different views about it. Some still feel it is a simple, innocent game to play while others who are into spirits say the board is actually a place where low level spirits can come through and shouldn't be used. It never phased us in any way then, but perhaps that's where my interest in the paranormal got started, in later years. (I have another whole book worth of those type of things I could tell and which are more currant experiences or encounters, but those will be a totally different book for another time, another place!)

Chapter 21

I liked to go back to school to help teachers do anything they could give me to do, on their 'teachers' day' where they worked to get meetings and other things done while we had the day off. I had a couple favorite teachers I really liked and felt good that I could do something to help them.

The one teacher who had gotten me the special permit to work at the pool to earn money years before apparently had some issue he couldn't deal with and he ended up committing suicide. I couldn't believe it. Many, many years later I was to find someone who committed suicide, and my first thoughts went back to this teacher. (Man, embezzlers, slivers, and suicides...they keep playing repeat performances in my life.)

With living out in the country, we traveled many snow covered roads in the winter just to get to school or work. One day on the way home we slid into the ditch and I braced myself which was actually the wrong thing to do because we slid in pretty smoothly but because I braced myself I wrenched my back and still have some issues with it today. (Of course, that adds to my stupid diving issues with shoulder and wrists from diving off the picnic table! I'm lucky I can still even move!)

We had a collie dog when we moved to the country. Our driveway was very long, so when the mailman came, we had a pretty good walk to get to it. Our dog figured out the routine, and when the mailman came, she knew I would be coming out the door. That dog took my wrist lightly but ran me to the mail box. People walk dogs, but I guess dogs run people!

Even though we were in the country we still went back into town to go to church. After graduation, we still went there but became a part of the adult groups with their own activities. We did things both at church as well as dreamed up special things to do somewhere else. One such thing was a Halloween party planned out in the country at one of the member's brother's cabin. It was a perfect place and atmosphere to hold a scary setting with all the decorations. We had a great evening and cleaned everything up so not to leave the brother a mess when he came in. The next day we got a shock. Her brother came home and was tired and fell asleep with a cigarette in his hand. The cabin burned down with him in it, and they found only his feet, still in the bed.

Tragedy comes in many forms, and although I didn't know the person involved, I did know his cousin. We had invited friends to our house, but they called to say they'd be late. There had been a farm accident. People don't realize all the things farmers do where they can be injured or killed. Those big bins you may have seen in the county (city slickers may not have a clue) have corn in them (or grains). Some farmers silo bins had the corn still on the cob and should someone fall into it at least they have a chance to work their way back out because there are air pockets. It isn't the same with shelled corn (when it's only corn without the cob) that is a very tragic and dangerous situation should someone accidentally fall in. Then the person slips down into the corn like quick sand and is almost impossible to be retrieved fast enough before they die. That's what happened that night. One slipped while trying to dislodge something and he fell in, and the rest was history. So not all memories in the book are happy ones, but God didn't promise us a rose garden.

On a happier note, our graduation party was held in the hay mow of a barn. There were several other parties going on elsewhere, but we had the most fun. Of course, while we were dancing to polka music (Czechs love Polkas) where we were all over the room up there, we had to be careful not to get close by the hay door and fall out.

We've gotten beyond the childhood memories by now. The images of the "good ol' days" were fading a bit, with products and life itself starting to make drastic changes with some good and some not so good. The age of the freedoms and innocence was slipping away but the wheels for unusual or more memories to be made seemed to keep moving on. After high school, I stepped out into a new world of sorts. I had been working a variety of jobs my whole life since childhood, so working wasn't itself the issue. The new phase was a job to make a livelihood myself. Luckily I was still at home until I got my 'training wheels off before being totally on my own.

I worked several jobs along the way before taking one as an elevator operator at Killian's, a five floor department store. I had been a soda jerk making milk shakes and malts, I packed meat at a grocery store meat market and still worked at the pool, plus I baby sat. I then became an elevator operator. The elevators in our days were different than most today, but I liked them a whole lot better. I didn't have claustrophobia in a big way yet then, but anyone who does now and fear elevators, you would prefer the old one like I operated. They had three solid walls, but a see-through metal gate that opened and closed by hand for the front. The gate was slid closed for safety as you went from floor to floor but you could see the wall going by. When you got to the floor, we manually opened the gate to let the people leave. There was one area along the elevator shaft where it was wider and when we didn't have any customers could stop and talk for a minute with the operator next to us and also look up and down the elevator shaft at the same time. It wasn't we were supposed to talk, but we did. We had one elevator of the four which ran express from the basement to the fifth floor and another elevator ran express from the fifth floor to the basement. Otherwise, we stopped on each floor. One day the girl next to me was in the express route, and no one had gotten on so she was dancing around and singing to herself. As she flipped her hand out and around, it touched someone! The person had ridden down a couple floors just to then express up to get there faster. They had been standing directly behind her, so when she let people out, all she saw in her main vision was an empty elevator. She wasn't aware that not everyone hadn't gotten off.

If for some reason an elevator stopped, we could call over to the other operator as they were going by, they immediately contacted maintenance so within a couple minutes we were on our way again. If it was something which stopped all elevators just with us looking over to the other elevator and joking around until the elevator started again, plus the fact people could also look up and down the shaft by stepping to the front wall if they needed, they didn't feel claustrophobic.

We had a very shapely young perfectly dressed and manicured woman who was a buyer for the company. The guys were always eyeballing her and following her around like puppy dogs. She had her bleached blonde hair done every week at our department stores beauty shop. One day I opened the door to see a very frustrated green haired buyer trying to get upstairs as fast as possible before anyone saw her. The beautician wasn't able to correct the green hair for four hours until the hair settled. That was really funny to see knowing she had always prided herself on being so perfect.

With driving the elevator I knew things the general public didn't know. For instance that the clothes on the second floor were the expensive clothes and where people with a lot of money went straight to, were the same clothes taken down to the street floor after a while to make room for new stock. The clothes on the main floor were then a little cheaper but the rich thought they weren't as good as the second floor. Then after a week, the stock people gathered those same clothes and brought them to the elevator where we transported them to the Bargain basement where the prices really got slashed. I could never convince my grandmother that she could get the same thing a lot cheaper in the basement. She lived across town where the rich people lived; not on our side where we less affluent were.

There was another woman who did personal shopping for the store. If someone needed a gift for someone and didn't know what to get or was unable to go shop for themselves they could call the personal shopper and give her sizes, color, likes and dislikes and the age of the person and she would buy and wrap the gift for them. Well, she became pregnant and was pretty far along but was still doing her job. One day I took her up to the fifth floor, but as she got off, the elevator lifted and kept going. We had had an elevator on other floors from time to time lift up a couple inches and then set back down, but this was the fifth floor. We only had five floors, and, it wasn't settling back down again but was going upward toward the roof. I grabbed her so she wouldn't lose her balance but pushed her at the same time to get her away from falling backward because she would have gone down the elevator shaft! Did I mention we were on the fifth floor?! She would have fallen down the shaft five floors! Then what about me? How can you go beyond the fifth floor of a five floor building? I had thoughts of my elevator going through the roof and me floating through the air among the clouds in my elevator! (There's a movie for you!) I needed the woman to stay by the elevator because I also was afraid a parent with her children might come toward the elevator and have one of them fall down the shaft. She was able to call out to someone to call maintenance for me and luckily the elevator did stop at five and a half floors, so I didn't become a flying missile!

The company was always putting on some big publicized product sale, and that meant we elevator operators were chosen to wear costumes to advertise it. One time we were in long dresses made of colored sheets for a Spring Maid sheet sale day and other time we were in kilts for savings day or something. They wanted us to wear them out of the building on our breaks or lunch hour to draw attention to pull people in to our store. We used to go to another store anyway where we knew the elevator operator, but I really didn't like riding on theirs. Theirs were open wire type walls on three sides where you saw the shaft going by on all four sides. You could look up and down the entire shaft. They also had the movable gate in the front. Anyone with motion sickness or fear of heights would have a problem there. I know, I was glad I worked where I did. I mentioned that from time to time the elevator would stop, and we were stuck between floors, but we were on our way within a couple minutes, and we didn't have the feelings of claustrophobia because we could see the shaft if we needed to see some open space. I didn't mind sitting between floors, so when they had to work on the elevators I volunteered to be the one inside, so I took a book to read. Remember, the front door of the elevator was a gate to open and close, so I sat with it open and spoke to the girl next to me from time to time as she went by empty. Today it is a total difference. The entire elevator is enclosed, and if it stopped with me in it, I would panic. There's something calming to be able to look up and down the shaft and not feel so entombed.

The operators took turns coming in before the store opened in order to take the person who put cash into the cash drawers from floor to floor. There usually were just three or four people in the store at that time. The two of us and a manager or two. One day I had just taken the manager to the fifth floor and returned to the first floor where the woman was putting cash in the registers. I opened the door to see this very shaken and white faced woman staring at me. She held out her hand, and there was a sliver similar to the huge size I'd had as a kid that went through my foot, but hers went in under her middle finger nail and came out two knuckles down. "Go get someone to take me to the hospital and to take over filling the cash drawers." She wouldn't go up with me because she needed to stay with the money. I never realized just how slow an elevator can go when you have an emergency.

Those slivers which are more like chunks of wood seemed to follow me through my life. That old farmhouse where we lived until our house was build, later became the house of a family with kids. The woman and I were friends and one day she called me on the telephone to talk. All of a sudden she gasped and said "Oh no, I just got a sliver of wood on my back. I have to come over to have you take it out." While she was coming, I got the tweezers out. She had been leaning against the casing of the old farmhouse door while we were talking and decided to sit on the floor while we talked. She slid down leaning on that casing as she did. When she arrived, I saw a piece of wood sticking out of her back about the size of your little finger nail. I grasped the end and pulled...and pulled...and pulled. That thing was about four inches long and the width of a finger nail! When people show me a teeny tiny sliver under the skin and complain of how bad it hurts and needs to have it taken out, I think to myself "You've got to be kidding. This is nothin'! You don't know what a sliver of wood can be!"

Even that piece of wood might have been nothing, compared to what almost happened to me at that house one day. I was getting ready to go to work at a job when working at a swimming pool in town and even though it was really raining hard I still had to show up. I was sitting at the kitchen table which was in direct line with the open doorway connecting to the utility room and back door. I still had ten minutes before I had to leave, when all of a sudden a lightning bolt hit the house and shook the house so hard it was like what you would imagine a bomb going off in a war zone would be. I watched as the lightning bolt, which had actually come into the house through the back door, zipped past me and followed the walls around the entire inside until it found its way out a bedrooms open window. The entire house had a cloudiness along with a sulfur smell. I thought that maybe the attic was on fire. I contacted the man next door who was on the volunteer fire department, and he came to check things out. Even though we had a flag pole in the front yard which you would think the lightning would have hit because it was the highest point but instead it came through the back door. Apparently the lightning hit a wooden power pole sitting on the property line down a slope by the farmer's field behind us and then bounced off it and came into the house. The neighbor had a name for it and said it was a "cold bolt." Well that cold bolt left a two inch deep hole about the size of a fifty cent piece in the cement block right next to the back door and the bolt apparently came in at an angle as it also hit a corner of the inside of the room and stripped a piece of wallpaper about an inch wide and a foot long, into tiny bits. It also pulled out the molding strip from around the door, nails and all. From there it traveled around the edges of the rooms going passed me and exited out an open window in the bedroom but as it went out left a souvenir of its visit by leaving a hole blown out of our alarm clock on the stand under the window. We soon found it also had also taken out both the front and back door bells.

Another close call with death came at the pool itself. (Let's see...a cat with nine lives? I think I mentioned that before and just within this book, I believe so far I've mentioned three and here is a fourth...I've got a lot of years ahead of me to go yet...I hope I make it!) This water incident actually hadn't gotten to the level I had had when a kid, but it had a potential threat and but for one thing, could have become worse than it was.

This pool was a new pool which was on the side of town I grew up on and had it been there then, would have taken me about ten minutes to ride my bike from my house to it, rather than having ride from the southwest to northwest side of town to the much larger pool where I had to go. Of course by now, I was living out in the country in a little town so to get to this pool I still had to travel. Now I was driving to the pool, but the pool was now a whole town away.

I was teaching swimming, and my class was ready to try going into the deep water. The deep water area was much narrower than that pool of my young years but was still wide enough to have one small and one high diving board. With nothing but classes going on we didn't need to worry about divers using the boards, so I had my class line up on one side of the deep end to jump in and swim to the other. I had them jump in one at a time and swim near the wall while I was on the other side of them. When that child got to the end and got out the next one would go. Everything was going fine until all of a sudden one girl got half way across and got scared. Even though she could have reached for the wall, she instead lunged for me getting me in a front head hold. Not only was I not ready for something like that, I had no time to get a large breath of air before she pushed me down under further and further while she was fighting to stay above the water. By then I thought I'd sort of like to have that vantage point myself! I'd taken senior life saving several times by then, and although I had had this hold done during practice, then I was ready for it and took a big breath. I also knew if I couldn't get out that we had a signal to our partner to let go and end the attack. Without any air, it is a totally different story.

All of a sudden I saw very large letters in front of my face. They were two foot high; three dimensional, bright red, block formed letters with black diagonal lines going from the one side edge to the other on each one. It looked like a cartoon strip and read, "P A N I C." Great, I was going to end up drowning, and I was going out with the funnies? What kind of sick guardian angel did I have? I'm getting a comic book sign?" Even then, though, it did sort of make me laugh inside. That brought my attention back to the situation at hand and I remembered that in just one of my many lifesaving classes one instructor said, "If you ever get caught in a front head hold, even though you are practicing this release, keep in mind, the best thing is to take the victim under water too. They don't want to be there so will release you to fight toward the top to get air." Those words came in loud and clear, so I did just that. I made myself go deeper under the water which caused her to come too, and she immediately let go. Then I just had to push her a couple feet to the wall to safety. Who knew a comic strip could help save your life!

I later got the job as the elevator operator at the department store and then later went to work as a file clerk at an insurance company where I could make more money.

It didn't seem to matter wherever I went because situations followed as if I were a magnet. We had some partially blind people come through our several story high office building with little signs that they couldn't speak or hear and needed financial help. We felt sorry for them and gave them some money, but our money must have been magic because when we looked outside and down to the alley below these people were talking up a storm and forgot to put their white walking stick in front of them when they walked. I was on the companies bowling team and one night we bowled against Merchants National Bank team. We laughed and joked with the other team and had a great time. The very next morning there were the newspaper headlines, "Merchant National Bank employee arrested for embezzlement!" We'd just bowled with her the night before! Geez, not again! That was the second person I knew who embezzled money. The other was from the court house when I was little.

I was a member of the American Red Cross and if there was a local emergency I could be taken from work and asked to help. One year we had another big flood but even worse than usual. They had to evacuate people, and I thought I was going to be used to do that, but instead I was sent to buy supplies at the grocery stores to fill the evacuation shelters. I then filled sandbags down by the river. As night fell, the Salvation Army was setting up food trucks to feed the workers, so I joined in to help them make and distribute sandwiches and drinks.

One of the girls I worked with had had a few people over to her apartment the evening before and when she left for work, the next morning emptied the cigarette butts into the waste basket before leaving. They had been sitting in an ashtray all night so figured they were safe to throw out. Well, guess what folks! That doesn't make any difference. They were still able to start a fire, and she got a call at work telling her that her apartment had burned down.

Another girlfriend I worked with got to be a close friend. I don't know if I can remember all the stuff that happen to her, but it was horrible. She was engaged to be married, and her fiancé died. (I can't remember if it was a car accident or what). She was devastated and then a few years later she was engaged again, and that guy also died in a car accident and I think was the only one in the accident to die. Something else happened, and she felt she was a jinx so she wouldn't date for a long time, but when she did and got engaged, she told no one until she actually got married. I think she ended up with several kids, and everything seemed to be going well for her at the last time I heard. We lost contact with each other when we both moved away, but I think of her a lot.

We had a girls club at work, and we had fun type meeting once a month. We did all kinds of things together but one night we went to a club for supper. (Here's another difference with either the time we lived in or the area of the country. We had breakfast, dinner and supper. Some places have dinner as the word for supper. I kept arguing we were right as what did Jesus had? Don't we call it "The Last Supper?"

Anyway, there was an obstetrician who did hypnosis at that time with women giving birth, and he was going to be the speaker that evening and talk about hypnosis. It was an interesting evening. His nurse had been born and raised until five years old in Germany so at that age could speak nothing but German. They'd come to the United States and over the years, she lost her fluent German speaking ability. He hypnotized her and regressed her to her fourth birthday when she was still living in Germany and asked her to tell him what was happening. She could speak only German.

He then made another hypnotic suggestion. After bringing her out from that one. He hypnotized her again and told her he was going to cut her finger, and she would not bleed. I sat there thinking to myself, "Ya, right. You think we're going to believe that one?"

Well, he cut her finger, and it did not bleed. It not only did not bleed then but even after she came out of hypnosis. He had me hooked. My thoughts then went to "If this is possible, then why couldn't they tell cancer cells not to grow and stop them?" Cancer, up to then, had been hidden in the closet, almost as a taboo subject. It was like you didn't tell anyone you or any family member had it. It was just beginning to be spoken about without that kind of taboo thought. We knew someone very close whose brother was only nine or ten and was dying of leukemia. (Here again was a repetition in my life. A kid in school with leukemia, then an algebra teacher and now this kid) That evening stuck in my mind forever. I wanted to know how to do hypnosis. I looked in the phone book yellow pages and found nothing. Over the years, I looked again, as well as if we were in any other area where I might be traveling in. The closest I ever came was every once in a while finding a hypnotist but never finding how to do it. This incident stayed with me and many many years later was to become a part of my life in a strange way. (Next book... spiritual? Paranormal?)

The insurance company started to be not the greatest place to work. It wasn't just me, but a lot of it eventually became me. Our boss use to sit at his desk laughing and giggling like a school girl and was actually talking to another boss but who was on the floor below us. He would soon laugh when the other guy would sneak upstairs and come from behind a set of files behind him. They were both married, but they were really weird dudes. Our boss decided he wanted to get rid of several of us who didn't seem to go along with his antics. He decided he'd use the excuse we weren't working hard enough or just not doing our job. To back him up he decided to set up a scoring system for points to everything we did. We got so many points for pieces of work filed, for a number of filing drawers cleaned out and looking for misfiles and points for finding misfiles they needed and couldn't find. That backfired because I had the top score. That upset him because now he didn't have a reason to fire me. He managed to get rid of a couple, but I became a thorn in his side. One poor older woman who was quiet and worked hard and whom you never heard much from but was friendly when you spoke to her, was to retire in a year. They fired her! There was no reason except apparently they wouldn't have to pay her retirement. That made me mad.

My boss supposedly gave me a raise by sending me down to underwriters department where I could find misplaced files and send things that took a lot of skill. I didn't even stay at that job for three days. That constant telling people I was allergic to cigarette smoke became true. Every underwriter smoked and no matter where I'd stand by their desk to retrieve things their cigarette smoke followed me. I threw up all day long for three days so got to keep the raise but ended back upstairs with the guy who didn't want me. Things continued on but when he tried confronting me, I didn't take his crap and stood up for myself. He then really wanted me gone in the worst way. By then it was just a battle of control.

It just happened his father in law was the vice president of the company. I volunteered to take employees down on the elevator after work each night to make a little bit more money. Well, one night the vice President got fresh with me when we were alone. I told some fellow employees and although it took a couple months for my boss to hear about it, when he did he point blank asked me. I verified it and within a week I was called down to the office where our personnel director was. I knew the handwriting was on the wall when I saw my boss sitting off to the side in an adjoining office. I walked into her office and said: "So, I'm fired!" She was surprised I knew. I told her everything that had been going on for months and the Vice President's actions, which she already knew about because that's why my boss finally got to fire me. She told me I should have come to her when it happened, and I said, "Why, so you could have fired me sooner?" She admitted that that probably would have happened. So I said, "So why then would I have come to report it? To get fired sooner?" Ya, the vice President is the jerk and wouldn't keep his hands to himself and yet the victim gets fired! Unfortunately, that's the same today! It's the only job I was ever fired from, but the way things were, a company that would fire a perfect employee after 19 years just so they wouldn't have to pay her retirement, isn't one I wanted to work for anyway.

It is time for the memories of my childhood years to come to a close and be tucked away within the pages of a book to hopefully be opened by people to both enjoy but also perhaps set a 'spark' to recall their own memories from back in time.

I end this book with the last memory of my childhood years which was also a tie to signs of the times. Carl and I got married and although we wanted to get married in the Little Brown church which is an Iowa famous place and which the song "The Little Brown Church in the Vale" was written, we had to get married in the Lutheran church.

Remember earlier when I mentioned my mother in law not wanting me to even go with Carl because I was a year older and I was also Methodist. Methodists were supposed to marry Methodists, and her Lutheran son was supposed to marry a Lutheran. Then again, she had also said no one should get married until they were 28 and then they were crazy if they did. Because Carl's mother wouldn't give her signature for Carl to get married, we couldn't plan a big wedding because if we couldn't get her to sign, we would be stuck. Boys at that time in Iowa had to be 21 in order to get married without parent consent even though the girls only had to be eighteen. (That was sort of dumb because the boys could go into the service to go to war before 21!) We planned a date but had no idea whether we would be getting married then or not. Carl's dad said he would sign, and we could go to another state to get married, but the other state needed both signatures because we were from Iowa. I had a wedding shower, but we had no idea as to whether it was really going to be a 'wedding shower' or a no wedding shower. Three days before the date we set, his mother said she would sign if we got married in their Lutheran church. We got to the courthouse to get the license, and when they asked if any of us were not of age, his mother said neither one of us were. I quickly said I was, and she said, "Well she is more than he is. Neither one should be getting married yet." Carl's sister who worked at the courthouse jumped in to get her mother on track to sign the darn thing.

So as I left my childhood memories behind and stepped into my new adult life, we had something to tie the two together as well as bring memories of the back in time era along. You see, we had an every Saturday occurrence which took place and no one had even thought about. As we walked out of the minister's office to go to the front of the church to get married in front of a couple friends and few relatives, the air raid siren went off. Yup! Another sign of the times because every Saturday morning at that time the air raid sirens were tested in case a real attack would ever occur. We returned to the office where the minister had a cigarette while waiting for the siren to go off. (You could have thought about the siren in two ways. It was either the normal Saturday siren test...or...was it sounding a warning about what we were about to do and what lies ahead?)

Little did I realize I was not only stepping into a new life as an adult, but one with would continue on toward to even more memories to be made to share, but the pendulum was about to swing to so many other topics of life. There again are the funny times, the sad or scary times, and a whole lot of animal stories concerning our family. (To become a book of its own but because of its size and so many expensive to print colored pictures, may be hard to find a publisher for.) Those stories aren't just typical stories but things like our goose trying to hatch a half deflated basketball, our squirrel monkey getting loose and being chased around the neighborhood, or getting a frog out of a snakes mouth. Life was to soon become far from dull! As the last part of my childhood stories had become more to do with personal experiences rather than tied to the period of time, so too did my future have a whole lot of those in store for me.

They started right after we got married. We left the church and went to my sister's house for a reception, and after an hour, my mother and step dad got into their already packed car and moved to Florida.

They had had the house for sale, and it hadn't sold yet so we were asked if we would want to buy it. Wow! A young couple to start out with a country house and acreage was great! Mom knew a friend who gave loans but not for kids as young as us but because they were friends he decided he would give it a chance.

They had to do a few things about the cost to be able for him to do it but everything was set to go! Well, almost! Carl's mom called him and said Carl wasn't old enough to sign a contract, and if he gave us the loan she would sue him! The guy could have just backed away but instead, just put the house in only my name. She also called our John Hancock Insurance man whom I think went to her church and told him to cancel our John Hancock Insurance because Carl had Lutheran insurance and we didn't need anything else. Luckily he called us, and we told him to keep our John Hancock insurance. (A week after we got married Carl turned Methodist! ... oh, and nine years later when Carl turned 28 his birthday card from his mother said: "Now is when you should have gotten married!")

So, life went on from incident to situations to experiences and from topic to subject to the category. There also was to become a spiritual/paranormal slant to our life which was a new adventure for us as a family. Such things in that category were things as our daughter who had leukemia (Here again, leukemia in our life) had her slides from blood work come back in the shape of a heart as if it were painted there, I caught orbs or strings of white mass showing up in pictures indicating spirits of some kind, or being directed by an audible voice but coming out of nowhere, to give instructions as to what to do for a first aid type situation.

The latest phenomena has been not only seeing but also photographing strange things in the sky, which are right now under investigation.

So while this book has been memories of an era called the "good ol' days" and mixes my personal adventures or stories with the images of what those times were all about, I've found the next part of my life will be of collecting stories of experiences and situations which on down the road might be something to look back on as memories, should I live so long. For the people now, though, they will be just stories to tell if anyone wants to listen.

Chapter 22

The candlestick telephone mentioned throughout the book was never described except for being a cowboy phone. Those from our days know what it was as it was seen in every old movie but especially in westerns. The mouth piece was at the top of a post and a receiver ear piece hung on a hook on the side. You had to put the ear piece to your ear but either pick up the candlestick to hold the mouthpiece close to speak into it or lean forward to talk into it.

There are a lot of things I missed mentioning, but you readers can probably even tell me a lot more I've missed. Using moth balls to keep the moths out of your woolen clothes when putting away for the summer, made sure when you retrieved them the next cold season they wouldn't be eaten away with holes. You could smell those mothballs in the clothes when you wore them.

I mentioned the pump in the back yards of many places. Again, for the younger folks who don't know. The metal pump was about five foot high and had a long handle which had to be manually pumped up and down vigorously to get the water to come up and go out the spigot where a bucket was hanging to be filled with the water.

Teens had typewriters, phonographs, and records. They lived within walking distance from the school. Catholic schools had uniforms and strict Nuns who smacked your hands with a ruler if you did something wrong. Boys had baseball teams, and girls did cheerleading with black and white kids going to the same schools. Girls dressed up with skirts and blouses or sweaters or wore dresses, and the boys were mostly clean cut and neatly dressed. Even guys with black leather jackets or known as greasers were still clean and decent type guys. Being gay was taboo as well was pornography which was merely magazines or written materials. The boys started using condoms, with the car the main culprit for secret sex. Getting pregnant before marriage was frowned upon by parents, relatives, friends, and the community. With not having a lot of homework, there was time for kids to get together to form friendships or get an odd job here or there. "Broken wires on the loose ...and dangerous!"

Compare those '50s with 2016, where kids have computers to do homework with and play fun games or to look up any kind of information, good or bad. They can also get pornography online, how to build bombs or join a radical militant group. Gay is normal, sex is open and as casual as kissing, teen pregnancies are accepted without any special views, ear and tongue piercings puncture the body, plus the skin is plastered with tattoos. Dress is unkempt and ratty looking, crime and dissension about everything are rampant. There are so many teens who are unhappy and fight their depression by using drugs, and have a uselessness feeling for life. Too many kids want everything given to them and don't want to work but just want to have fun. They want to change everything against the majority just to be in the atmosphere of negativity, without knowing the actual situation they march for, or against. Friends are through texting but not physical association.

So, for the last time of this book! Whose times are better? Who had the highest self-esteem and felt good about their world and themselves? Who are happier? Where have your memories led you? Sit back, relax, reflect, and enjoy their magic.

SPARKS

Use these pages to jot any 'sparks' that may come up of your own memories while reading my book. Put a word, topic, or sentence, so you can have your own memories to also view and have later to look back on.

_____

_____

_____

_____

_____

_____

_____

_____

_____

_____

_____

_____

_____

_____

About the Author

Pauline E. Petsel has written various articles over the years, which have included her photography. Her photos accompanied an All Children's Hospital quarterly *Tender Loving Care* in St. Petersburg Florida for the Leukemia patient's production of "Back to Normal Again." Petsel wrote an article with pictures for the premier issue of *Special Living Magazine* and had an article in *Hometown Memories* hardback book. She authored a book called *Teach Youur Tot to Swim* (Great Outdoors Publisher.) Following her swim book, the author had many articles over the years written about her in the St. Petersburg Times. She then moved to Tennessee and has had articles written about her, her photography and a one person display of 125 photos for six weeks in Morgan Inn Gallery. Other articles have appeared about Petsel's uncanny knack for picking up things on her camera which she didn't see when taking the picture, as well as some pretty weird things she has taken in the sky. Visit her online at paulinepetsel.com.

Coming Soon!

During her life, Pauline E. Petsel has had experiences of all kinds. These experiences will be the material for upcoming books. Her eventual book, which will go onward from the experiences she has had will be detailed in:

Will Be Stepping Out
Here I Come World!

Since her life has branched into different directions, one future book will be:

Silent World of the Animals

Then, there are the UFO pictures with the expected title of:

Night Skies Over Greeneville

The true paranormal experiences will be in
two different books; the first entitled:

Religious, Spiritual, Paranormal, and Ghosts!

The second one will be:

May Those With Eyes See and Ears Hear!

In 2016 she will release her first children's book:

Things That Go Bump in the Night

www.ingramcontent.com/pod-product-compliance
Lightning Source LLC
Chambersburg PA
CBHW031840090426
42741CB00005B/298